PATH OF THE PADDLE

BILL MASON

FIREFLY BOOKS

A FIREFLY BOOK

Published by Firefly Books Ltd. 1999

Cataloging in Publication Data

Mason, Bill, 1929–1988
    Path of the paddle : an illustrated guide to the art of canoeing

Rev. ed.
Includes bibliographical references and index.
ISBN 1-55209-328-X

1. Canoes and canoeing. 2. White-water canoeing. I. Title

GV783.M38 1999   797.1'22   C98-932809-0

Published in Canada by Key Porter Books

Published in the United States in 1999
by Firefly Books (U.S.) Inc.
P.O. Box 1338, Ellicott Station
Buffalo, New York, 14205

Printed and bound in Canada

Use of the information in this book is at the sole risk of the user.

99 00 01 02 03   6 5 4 3 2 1

CREDITS

The author wishes to thank Macmillan Publishing Company, Inc., New York, for permission to quote material from *The New Way of the Wilderness*, rev. ed., by Calvin Rutstrum. Copyright © 1958, 1973

Contents

To my Father
    whose tales of his journeys by canoe
fired the imagination of a small boy

To My Mother
    who watched with trepidation as I
launched my first canoe at the age of
twelve

Foreword

Introducing you, the reader, to this truly remarkable book on canoeing is both an exciting and a frustrating task. It is exciting because this is such a complete and absorbing book, with something of value for everyone from the beginner to the most highly skilled canoeist. It is frustrating because I am almost overcome by the strongest urge to grab my paddle and head for the nearest rapids.

I have known Bill Mason for many years. I have paddled with him, traded outrageous stories with him about past canoeing expeditions, and listened for hours as he shared his rich experience of nature, of wildlife, and of rushing waters. I have seen and greatly admired the many award-winning films on nature, conservation and canoeing which he has produced for the National Film Board of Canada.

This book is an extension of his film work into the print medium. It was written with the goal of sharing with others his expert knowledge and boundless enthusiasm for one of the most satisfying activities known to man.

The author of *Path Of The Paddle* is, as you will soon learn from the following pages, a genial fanatic on the subject of canoeing. He is a man so enthralled with the sheer joy of guiding a canoe through challenging rapids in the early spring, so awestruck by the beauty of nature as seen over the bow of a canoe silently traversing a mirror-smooth lake in the early morning, that he cannot understand why every man and woman on earth does not share his passion.

He is also a cautious fanatic; and in his caution lies one of the great values of this book. Alert to every sign of danger, skilled in reading the turbulent whitewater, he applies a lifetime of experience to teaching others how to reduce the risks and survive the mishaps of a wilderness adventure. Like a certain Newfoundland harbor pilot, he may not know where all the rocks are, but he "sure knows where they ain't."

This book is not just a how-to-do-it manual, however. It is a complete guide to rediscovering and enjoying the untamed natural world by canoe.

If this book should persuade you to abandon temporarily the sights and sounds of civilization, in order to experience from inside a canoe a natural world virtually untouched by man, then turning these pages will have brought you to a magnificent turning point in your life.

Read on, and learn from a master. And may every dip of your paddle lead you toward a rediscovery of yourself, of your canoeing companions, of the wonders of nature, and of the unmatched physical and spiritual rapture made possible by the humble canoe.

Pierre Elliott Trudeau

Acknowledgments

The production of this book can best be described as a cottage industry. It has involved my wife Joyce, daughter Becky, and son Paul, as well as a number of close friends over a period of many years. They not only assisted in the book's production but can also be found within the pages of the book in the anecdotal material. They have brought to the book a lot of fun and enjoyment, which I hope will be passed along to the reader.

My wife Joyce has been responsible for translating my scrawls into legible type. Her criticism, balanced with just the right amount of encouragement, was one of the things I appreciated most during the writing of the book. The partner I used most was my son Paul, but only because my daughter Becky volunteered to stay on shore to fulfill the role of photographer. As canoeists, there's little to choose between the two of them. This perhaps explains why Becky was able to capture the important aspects of the canoeing strokes so well. They both agree it was the nicest job they *never* had. (They worked for nothing.)

While Becky did most of the photography, there's scarcely a friend or member of the family who has canoed with me who did not get pressed into service as a second photographer. They are: Bruce Litteljohn, Paul Mason, Blake James, Ken Buck, Barry Bryant, Joyce Mason, Susan Buck, Terry Orlick, Allan Whatmough, Barrie Nelson, Peter Selwyn, Sally MacDonald, Mike Bedell, Derek Brown and probably a few others. The National Film Board of Canada was also a source for photographs. The printing of black-and-white photographs was done by Grant Crabtree with some additional printing by Howard Weingarden.

I would like to thank Chuck Tipp, my canoeing instructor at Manitoba Pioneer Camp, for showing me that a canoe is much more than a means of getting around on water. It was through him that I realized canoeing is an art. Thanks also go to Claude Cousineau who, many years later, gave me an invaluable critique on my flatwater paddling technique.

On the subject of hypothermia, I am indebted to doctors G. K. Bristow and Joseph MacInnis for their personal assistance. I also drew upon papers and material written by R. Smith, V. Lee, A. Auty, and W. A. Tweed; the editors of the Ceyana Canoe Club Newsletter; and, D. S. Smith, author of *The Cold Water Connection* published by The United States Coastguard.

Special thanks go to Wilber Sutherland, Brian Creer, Sally MacDonald, Terry Orlick, Moiya Wright, and other canoeing friends for reading the first draft of the manuscript and offering their constructive criticism and enthusiastic support. I would also like to thank the National Film Board of Canada for their co-operation and support. Many of the events I have described in this book were experienced while on assignment and many of the photographs were shot while on location.

And finally, I would like to thank my editor, Sara Jane Kennerley, for turning my final manuscript into this book without losing the language of the river. Watching the book take shape under the art direction of Brant Cowie was, for me, one of the most enjoyable experiences during the production of the book. Because of the large number of illustrations and the need to keep photographs, diagrams, and related text together on two-page spreads, it was a tremendous job. To Garry Lovatt, Laurie Coulter, and all the people I worked with at Van Nostrand Reinhold, I say thank you for your patience with an author who believes there is no such thing as the *last* word or the *last* photograph on the subject of canoeing.

— Bill Mason

Revised Edition

Dad called the original production of *Path of the Paddle* a cottage industry. I'm pleased to say that the revision took place under much the same circumstances and I hope it has retained the flavor of the original book.

My mom, Joyce, typed my scrawls (which may even be worse than my dad's) into a manuscript.

The photo shoots were a family affair involving my mom, my wife, Judy; and our daughter Jamie; my sister Becky; Reid McLachlan; and our good friend Ken Buck.

Thanks to Lloyd Seaman, Reid McLachlan, Becky Mason, Judy Mason and Mark Scriver for their comments and recommendations on the revised edition.

Special thanks to Bob Washer of Sirius Wilderness Medicine for reviewing the section on hypothermia and to Mark Scriver of Trailhead for his technical assistance with canoe designs and materials.

Thanks also to Key Porter and Renée Dykeman, my editor, who braved dealing with another Mason who also believes there's never a last word or photograph when it comes to canoeing.

— Paul Mason

Legend

Throughout the book you will find diagrams and photographs with the following symbols:

Canoe paddled solo — triangle represents canoeist and points toward direction of travel.	
Canoe paddled by two canoeists.	
Lines represent path of the paddle in water — triangles point toward direction of stroke.	
Single line represents paddle held stationary in water when canoe is underway.	
Direction of movement of canoe through water.	
Direction of movement of canoe in a turn.	
Direction of movement of canoe in a violent turn or pivot.	
Rocks at or near surface	R
Eddy	E
Downstream V, deep water channel	V
Ledge	L
Deepwater haystack	H
Direction of current	C

Dog River, Lake Superior, North Shore

1 INTRODUCTION

Lake Superior

The land

Canoeing in North America has expanded in recent years to include practically every part of the map. In the United States people of all ages are taking to the rivers in ever-increasing numbers. Rivers that once were considered too dangerous are now canoed regularly as whitewater skills grow. In each state—southern, prairie, mountain, or coastal—canoeing has become a means of journeying into wilderness areas and providing the adventure that people are seeking.

In Canada, you can put a canoe into the water at any major city and paddle to the Atlantic, the Pacific, the Arctic, or the Gulf of Mexico. The land is laced with a complex network of waterways; some are large, some are small, but most are navigable by canoe. When you look at the face of Canada and study the geography carefully, you come away with the feeling that God could have designed the canoe first and then set about to conceive a land in which it could flourish.

The waterways are navigable because the canoe can be portaged easily around the difficult stretches of water. Even the portages over the height of land between watersheds are no longer than those around most rapids and falls. In one place the waters flowing to the Atlantic and the waters flowing to the Arctic are separated by no more than a beaver dam.

It was the canoe that made it possible for the Indian to move around before and for several hundred years after the arrival of the white man. As the white man took over their land, the native people would regret the generosity with which they shared their amazing mode of travel. The more I study the birchbark canoe and what it can do, the greater is my admiration for these people who were here long before we arrived.

The birchbark canoe is made entirely from materials found in the forest: birch bark, cedar, spruce roots, ash, and pine gum. When it is damaged, it can be repaired easily from the materials at hand. When it has served its purpose, it returns to the land, part of a never-ending cycle. Once you understand this cycle of growth, manufacture, use, and return to the land you begin to understand why our modern culture is in such trouble. The noncycle of growth, manufacture, use, and garbage is a dead end. This is not to discredit the marvelous things that modern technology brings us; but we need to be more aware of where we are headed and from whence we came. An appreciation of the canoe and acquisition of the necessary skills to utilize it as a way to journey back to what's left of the natural world is a great way to begin this voyage of discovery.

The shrinking land

There was a time when traveling a distance of 5,000 miles (8000 km) in North America would have been regarded as a very long way. Before the railroad, covering that kind of distance meant extreme hardships any way you chose to make the trip. Improving methods of transportation has been a high priority of human beings as far back into recorded history as you care to go. With each improvement the world has grown smaller.

Today you can cover 5,000 miles in about eight hours. All you have to do is go to the airport (which is usually the hardest part), buy a ticket, and select a seat in the smoking or nonsmoking section of the aircraft. About the greatest discomfort you might expect to endure is to end up in the smoking section if you are a nonsmoker or vice versa.

When the choice of travel was limited to horse, canoe, wagon, ox cart, or on foot, this 5,000 miles could have taken a couple of years. Today, the earth is indeed getting very small. However, trying to convince the world of business and commerce that there are places on this earth where distances should remain undiminished is not an easy task.

Such an idea is very difficult to defend in monetary terms. Perhaps the best way to make a case for primitive methods of travel is in the form of a parable. Let's say you are hiking and come upon a beautiful, pristine lake nestled among high hills. You estimate the lake to be about ten miles (16 km) long and with great anticipation look forward to several days of a difficult but exciting journey of discovery around the shoreline. Before long a canoeist comes along and invites you to come aboard to make the journey easier. You gladly accept because the going is tough. Now you can get a better perspective on the shoreline and yet the pace is slow enough so that you do not miss anything. You are aware, however, that in accepting the ride the lake has diminished somewhat in size. You estimate that while hiking would have taken you at least four days, you will now be able to do it in an easy two. After a couple of miles, a motorboat comes alongside and you are offered a ride around the shoreline. The canoeist accepts, and while you are less than enthusiastic, you don't have much choice. As the 100 horsepower (74 600 W) engine roars into action, you slowly become aware that the lake is beginning to feel very small. As the trees and cliffs race by, you realize that what you had hoped to discover in four days is now going to be revealed in a couple of hours. The miles are eaten away as you speed through each bay and inlet and race by most of the islands. When the journey is over and you are dropped off at the point where you first came upon the lake, the mystery is gone. You've seen it all; yet,

you've seen nothing. The motorboat driver meant well, but he has only succeeded in diminishing the size of the lake.

You set up camp and watch the lengthening shadows. As you look far down the lake, you wish that you did not already know what lay around that point. You regret that your first view into the hidden bay will not be the reward of a difficult hike tomorrow.

For many people, the case I have just attempted to make would seem pointless. To them scenery is scenery, any way you get to see it. To others, it makes a lot of sense. It's all a matter of perspective. What encourages me to write about the concept of keeping things undiminished by means of primitive travel is the fact that people do change their minds. I enjoy writing for the already converted, but the possibility that other people might awaken to this subtle concept of keeping what's left of the natural world big is why I write this book. There is no shortage of road builders and people who make their living by shrinking distance. They will succeed too well if there are not enough of us around to present a case for the preservation of the natural environment. Some of it is already overcrowded to the detriment of the plants, animals and native people who lived there long before we arrived. They all have a right to exist because all, like us, were created. In our modern, man-made world we tend to forget this. A journey by canoe along ancient waterways is a good way to rediscover our lost relationship with the natural world and the Creator who put it all together so long ago.

The path of the paddle can be a means of getting things back into their original perspective.

The canoe

The canoe is the simplest, most functional, yet aesthetically pleasing object ever created. In my opinion, this is not a statement that is open to debate. It's a fact! It follows that if the canoe is the most beautiful work of human beings, then the art of paddling one must rank right up there along with painting, poetry, music, and ballet. In the ever-varying conditions of wind, waves, and rapids the possibilities for acquiring skill in the control of the canoe with poetry and grace are unlimited. I've been paddling canoes for over 40 years and rarely return from a journey by canoe without having discovered something new. No one will ever know all there is to know about the art of canoeing.

A team of kayakers once did just about everything possible to get themselves killed on the Dudkosi River that flows down Mount Everest. It was an insane venture that could best be described as free falling in a kayak. Despite all their efforts to wipe themselves out, they somehow survived. They pushed the possibilities of paddling far beyond what anyone could have contemplated in their wildest dreams.

However, closed canoes and kayaks, although closely related to open canoes, are not the subject of this book. They are too big a subject to contain in one volume. This book deals only with the traditional canoe-tripping style of the open canoe, the most attractive and practical means of travel in the North American wilderness today.

As you may have noticed, canoeists are a humble lot. We are the first to admit that the canoe is not the only way of getting around. We just think it's the best way. We are also the first to confess that the age of the canoe as the only vehicle of transport is long gone.

But the age of the canoe is not gone; it's just different. The canoe is no longer a vehicle of trade and commerce. Instead, it has become a means of venturing back into what is left of the natural world. It's true

there isn't much left to be discovered, but there is much to be rediscovered about the land, the creatures who live there, and about ourselves. Where do we come from and where are we going? There is no better place and no better way to follow this quest into the realm of the spirit than along the lakes and rivers of the North American wilderness in a canoe.

Canoeing, an addiction
There is one thing I should warn you about before you decide to get serious about canoeing. You must consider the possibility of becoming totally and incurably hooked on it. You must also face the fact that every fall about freeze-up time you go through a withdrawal period as you watch the lakes and rivers icing over one by one. Cross-

HEADING HOME – THE LAST CRACK FREEZES OVER

country skiing and snowshoeing can help a little to ease the pain, but they won't guarantee a complete cure. The canoeless season can be shortened somewhat by varnishing gunwales and sanding and painting canvas, unless you are the owner of a fiberglass or aluminum canoe. For you, it's cold turkey right through to break-up! The canoeists I really bleed for are the paddlers who don't even own a wooden paddle to sand and varnish. For those of you with aluminum or fiberglass canoes and paddles, you might try carrying your canoe around on the roof of your car anytime after New Year's Day.

Anytime before that looks pretty ridiculous. But after New Year's Day, you just never know. Spring could be early.

West coast and southern paddlers near the coast are in the enviable position of being able to canoe all year 'round. And don't think they'll let you forget it. They do confess to donning wet suits, neoprene gloves, and balaclava helmets though. Out west they know nothing about the dreaded winter withdrawal symptoms, just icy trickles down the back.

Probably the best remedy for the canoe freak is map watching. Poring over maps can often get you through the canoeless season when nothing else can. I recommend it highly. If you coat the maps with plastic you can even use them as tablecloths, curtains, and all sorts of things. However, no matter what you do, it isn't easy being a canoeist during the winter. But, oh what a feeling as the days get longer and you begin to hear the creeks running beneath the snow. Then open patches appear and soon they are big enough to accommodate your canoe. The patches lengthen and become a continuous flowing stream and it's canoe time once again.

FIRST OPEN WATER OF SPRING – OUR HOCKEY RINK

My addiction to the canoe began at a shockingly early age. I cannot remember a time when I was not fascinated by the canoe. My parents tell me that at the age of five or six my weakness for canoes began to show.

At Grand Beach on Lake Winnipeg, where we lived during the summer, I spent most of my time climbing around the canoes pulled up along the shore. My greatest thrill was to find one tied to the ladder on the pier. I would climb down into it and paddle it back and forth along the length of the rope. When you are only five or six years old and equipped with a vivid imagination, a three-foot rope is not a limitation to be taken too seriously. Along the length of that rope I paddled lakes, even oceans, and ran rapids that no one had ever run before. And then the man who owned the canoe would show up and kick me out.

The happiest time of my whole childhood was when my father rented a canoe for a week. He sometimes rented one for an hour or two, but only this once did he rent it for the week. It was just like owning it. We could go paddling whenever we wanted and stay out as long as we wanted. About the only thing that compared with that week was the day I bought my first canoe. Nothing I've ever owned compares with the thrill of that purchase. I parked it out in the yard under the kitchen window so I could see it while I ate. I moved it constantly so I could view it from different angles. I had discovered that a canoe's shape is beautiful from any angle, even lying overturned on the grass.

It was 1951 when I bought that first canoe, and I still spend a lot of time looking at them. My first canoe is long gone but it's been replaced. Replaced not by one canoe but about twenty-seven, most of which float. I could use a couple more but one has to make do.

GETTING THE FLEET INTO SHAPE

I find it hard to believe that not everybody is crazy about canoes. A canoe is the only thing I know that has no moving parts. There's nothing to break down and you don't have to feed a canoe. Take horses, for example: they've always got the heaves, or game legs, or they're off their feed. I must admit however, there is one advantage that horseowners have over canoeists. You put a bunch of horses together out on the back forty and pretty soon you've got more horses.

I understand that people can become addicted to horses, but I'm sure it's nothing like canoe addiction. Canoe addiction can affect your whole life. My first job after leaving art school was with a commercial art house. I liked my work and I liked the people, but every spring just before break-up time I would go into the boss's office and give two weeks notice so I could take off for the bush to go roaming by myself in my canoe from break-up to freeze-up. The boss always ended up firing me for letting him down in the busy spring season. I could never quite figure that one out. He wouldn't say much for the next two weeks, but on my last afternoon he would casually drop by to say goodbye. We would play a little game in which he would hint that he might be able to fit me in again at the end of the summer and I would allow that although I would prefer freelancing, it would be sort of nice to see

the boys again. This little ritual went on for about six years, until I found out that I could earn a living making films either about canoeing or with canoes in them.

The art of paddling

A long time ago, as I sat before my fire on the rocky shore of a northern lake, a canoe appeared out of the mist propelled by an Indian fisherman on his way to tend his nets. The poetry of motion was indescribable. He paddled effortlessly with his whole body, yet he went across that lake and disappeared into the mist faster than I would have thought possible. He looked as if he could keep up that pace forever without tiring. I leaped into my canoe and tried to emulate his technique. I've been trying ever since with less than perfect results. The reason is obvious. He had probably paddled every day of his life from break-up to freeze-up and I don't. It's as simple as that. Like riding a horse, you can learn to stay on the horse in a few hours, but it can take a lifetime to look like you belong there.

The first thing you must learn about canoeing is that the canoe is not a lifeless, inanimate object; it feels very much alive, alive with the life of the river. Life is transmitted to the canoe by currents of air and the water upon which it rides. The behavior and temperament of the canoe is dependent upon the elements: from the slightest breeze to a raging storm, from the smallest ripple to a towering wave, or from a meandering stream to a thundering rapid. Anyone can handle a canoe in a quiet millpond, but in rapids a canoe is like a wild stallion. It must be kept on a tight rein. The canoeist must take the canoe where he or she wants it to go, not where it wants to go. Given the chance, the canoe will dump you overboard and continue on down the river by itself.

The fastest way to learn to canoe is with personal instruction. Other ways are reading books, watching films and videos, or, in the near future, using interactive multimedia. Probably the best way is a combination of these. A film can transport you to remote, difficult places. It can quickly and vividly reveal the kinds of problems you will face and show you how to cope with them. A canoeing film can cover a lot of water quickly, but the difficulty of learning exclusively from a film lies in the need to store so much information in your head. After all, you can't take the film with you for constant reference. The value of a book is its portability. However, there is nothing that can replace a skilled instructor who is able to accompany you and help you acquire the skills of paddling a canoe in wind, waves, and rapids. If the instructor knows how to utilize books and films in the teaching process, so much the better.

Canoe instruction

It is no longer difficult to find and sign up with a canoeing school. Canoeing classes are becoming more and more common in schools, colleges, and universities. There are also commercial outfitters, sporting goods stores, and even canoe manufacturers who offer courses in flatwater and whitewater canoeing where you can attend weekend or week-long intensive whitewater courses in preparation for remote wilderness trips.

There is no question that running rapids is much safer if done in a group situation under the watchful eye of a skilled instructor. Many sporting goods stores across North America have recognized the need for providing an instruction service and now have expert canoe instructors on staff. Check around to see what's available in your area.

Canoeing has come a long way since I bought my first canoe in 1951. Early attempts by individuals and organizations to set up standards and tests for teaching canoeing left a lot to be desired. Now, at last, some order has been brought to the teaching of canoeing through the "Standard Tests of Achievement in Canoeing." Information can be obtained by contacting the head office of the American Canoe Association, 7432 Alban Station Blvd., Suite B 226, Springfield, Virginia 22150, or the Canadian Recreational Canoeing Association (CRCA) National Office, 1029 Hyde Park Road, Suite 5, Hyde Park, Ontario N0M 1Z0. The CRCA also publishes *Kanawa* magazine, organizes the biennial Waterwalker Film Festival, and sponsors the Bill Mason Memorial Scholarship. This scholarship is available to students who are studying outdoor recreation or environmental studies. In many states and provinces, a similar system of canoe instruction has been developed and implemented under the guidance of local sport-governing organizations.

Learning alone

Despite the emphasis on good instruction, it must be admitted that it is possible to learn to canoe by yourself. After receiving basic waterfront instruction at Manitoba Pioneer Camp, one of four camps for children run by Inter-Varsity Christian Fellowship, I never had the opportunity to go canoeing with anyone who knew much more than I did. I acquired my skill at running rapids by myself by trial and error. Unfortunately, I totalled two canoes in the process and was lucky to survive. I wiped out my first canoe before discovering the book that was to become a canoeing bible for me. It was Calvin Rutstrum's *Way of the Wilderness* now reprinted as the *New Way of the Wilderness*. My skills improved greatly after reading that book.

Since discovering this book so many years ago, the art of paddling has been growing constantly. It is alive and well thanks to the excellent canoeing programs offered at children's camps across North America. However, the possibilities for the further development of the art of canoeing have not been exhausted. It is for this reason that I dare to contribute what I have discovered about wilderness canoeing over the past 30 years. There are some very basic things about running rapids that to my knowledge have never been communicated or emphasized clearly in a book. I find it quite exciting to be able to add something to this beautiful art.

Wilderness cruising solo

Canoeing solo doesn't necessarily mean traveling alone. It simply means one paddler per canoe. There could be any number of canoes in the group. There are some people who do travel alone, though, but not as many as there used to be. The lone trapper, prospector, or Indian hunter has been replaced by the recreational paddler, paddling two to a canoe and in groups both for companionship and safety. Paddling alone or even double without another canoe on a wilderness trip is definitely discouraged by all the canoeing associations with which I am familiar. One writer has even gone so far as to say "The idea of a man paddling alone off into the sunset is Hollywood inspired nonsense and has no place in canoeing today." Well, I would just like to tell the author of that statement that I've been doing it all my life and I'm still here. However, I would be the first to admit it can be dangerous, almost as dangerous as driving your car down the highway at 50 mph (80 km/h) and passing within six feet (2 m) of another car going in the opposite direction at 50 mph. Every time you do this, you are six feet away from a 100 mph (160 km/h) impact. Driving a car is one of the most dangerous things we do, yet we drive every day without giving it a thought. I'll take my chances in a canoe anytime, solo or double.

Still, canoeing alone is very definitely a calculated risk. One mistake can mean a slow death in some remote place far from help. A slip of the axe, a fall on the portage with a ninety pound (40 kg) pack, an injury in rapids, appendicitis, heart attack, sickness — the list is endless. When one travels alone, the risks are many times greater than traveling in a group or even with one other person.

It's true that prospectors, trappers, and hunters, all solo paddlers, lived to a ripe old age, but they probably acquired their skill as children and grew up as accomplished wilderness travelers. As professional outdoorsmen, they traveled alone not necessarily by choice, but because their profit margin was so small and tenuous that they couldn't afford to hire someone to accompany them. The same is true today for writers, painters, or photographers, who are all engaged in solitary professions. With luck you might find that rare compatible individual to accompany you on such ventures, but it is rare indeed.

The greatest risk in traveling alone is, of course, for the novice canoeist. The second dangerous stage is when you think you know more than you really do. During my third year of canoeing solo, I left a very handsome canoe, or rather what was left of it, on the shore beside a turbulent rapid. By the time I walked out of the bush, I knew a lot more about canoeing than I did when I began the trip. I am now smart enough to portage all dangerous rapids when I'm traveling by myself. It is important to be willing to admit that those of us who are raised in cities and go to the wilderness for aesthetic reasons run a much greater risk than do old professionals. It's also a sobering experience to read about some of those old professionals who set out alone and never returned. We probably will never know what happened to Tom Thomson, the

gifted Canadian painter. His death was a tragedy that I shall never forget. Who can know what masterpieces he might have produced had he lived? But painting was something that he had to do in solitude. He took the risk and lost his life. Fortunately, most people prefer to paddle in groups. But for those adventurous few who long for that sense of freedom, that feeling of adventure that comes from roaming alone, I wish them *bon voyage*. I'll see you out there. Maybe we will sit down around a campfire and have a cup of tea. We will enjoy each other's company for a while; then we will push on in our separate directions.

I know of no greater thrill, of no greater feeling of carefree abandonment, than to load up a canoe in the spring as the ice goes out and roam at will with no other destination in mind than a different campsite on some remote shore each evening. The joy of these trips that I experienced as a young man is now only equaled by having my family who share my enthusiasm accompany me. On the joys of traveling alone, Calvin Rutstrum put it better than I ever could.

Man is a gregarious being, and he is constantly reminded of it. Yet his most profound moments generally occur when he is by himself.

Few of us have ventured very far into the wilderness alone, and we are not without loneliness when we do. Why, then, do we go alone? My experience has convinced me that, to feel profoundly the enchantment of the wilderness, we must go in complete solitude at one time or another. A journey with others has a separate set of values of unquestionable enjoyment, but it should never be categorically compared to travel alone. In the lone journey you live closer to the nerve ends of feeling, where subjective response to the world around you becomes complete–objective response having been lost in the very intimacy of your natural existence.

Alone at your very next camp, with a deep sense of escape and freedom, you prepare the foods you want in your own way, pitch your tent

on the site you choose. Alone you maintain a capricious schedule, traveling hard when you feel like it, quietly contemplating the scene when you are so inclined. As the solitary days draw on, much of the loneliness passes. Wildlife springs magically into view as you control every sound of your own movements and those connected with your craft, equipment, and its operation.

Senses actually seem to be made sharper by the concentration effected in solo travel. There is less diversion, less distraction–a clearing of the atmosphere for a sharper response. One develops a keener ear for sound, a more perceptive eye for movement.

Life of the solitary man by its very nature becomes subjective. You are not the intruder, you feel yourself an integral part of the composite natural scheme.

I agree with Calvin Rutstrum's philosophy about traveling alone. Most of my productive sketching and painting trips as well as some of my filming trips have been made alone. However, when I travel alone I am very aware that my first mistake could be my last. As a result, I can appreciate why all safety-conscious organizations are violently against traveling alone. I am as safety conscious as they are, yet I cannot bring myself to say that traveling alone is a thing of the past. I don't think anyone has the right to say that. But I would impress upon the reader that traveling alone in the bush on foot or by canoe is extremely dangerous, and if you do have a mishap you could be the cause of a very expensive search for you or your body. You must be careful not to overestimate your abilities. And then there is the element of chance or a freak accident over which you have no control. These are all things that must be taken into consideration if you ever choose to go alone.

Parts of the canoe

Cliffs on Old Woman Bay, Lake Superior

The canoe shown here, a cedar and canvas prospector, should be on the endangered species list. They are getting scarce. I've chosen this splendid canoe to illustrate the parts of a canoe because modern canoes don't have anything this one doesn't have. In fact, this one has a lot more than most modern canoes, including a beautiful shape. It's a joy to look at.

Stern deck   Triangular piece of wood or other material that provides strength to gunwales at stern.

Stern seat   Seat in the stern; it is narrower than the bow seat.

Stern thwart   Narrow spreader that strengthens and maintains the canoe's shape at the stern.

Center thwart   Narrow spreader that strengthens and maintains the canoe's shape. Often replaced by a yoke, which is more comfortable for portaging.

Ribs   Strips of wood that run across the canoe to form the frame of the hull.

Planking   Strips of wood that run longitudinally and are fastened to the ribs.

Bow seat   Seat in the bow; it is wider than the stern seat.

Gunwale   Strip of wood, aluminum, or reinforced vinyl that runs from end to end along the top of the hull.

Inwale   Inner gunwale.

Outwale   Outer gunwale.

Bow deck   Triangular piece of wood or other material that provides strength to the gunwales at the bow.

Stem band, bang plate, or skid plate   Strip of brass, aluminum, or, in the latter case, Kevlar impregnated with resin, which protects the bow and stern from damage.

Bow   Front of canoe.

Sheer   Shape of the canoe near the bow at the waterline.

Draft   The depth at which the canoe is riding on the water; measured from the waterline to the point at which the canoe is deepest in the water.

Waterline   Level of the water on the side of the canoe.

Freeboard   Distance from the waterline to the top of the gunwale.

Tumblehome   Inward sloping of the sides of the canoe near the gunwales. See page 184.

Skin   Usually made of canvas, although it can be made of fiberglass, the skin makes a cedar canoe waterproof.

Stern   Back of the canoe.

Hull   Basic canoe shell: birchbark, basswood, dug out, cedarstrip and canvas, aluminum, fiberglass, Kevlar, or ABS (Acrylonitrile Butadiene Styrene) foam.

Keel   Strip of wood or other material along the bottom of the canoe to prevent sideslipping in a wind or on a lake. It also affords some protection to the bottom of the canoe. Some canoes are equipped with two other keels called **bilge keels** for added protection.

Length   Distance between the two extremities from end to end.

Width or **beam**   Measured from the outer limits of the two gunwales or from the outer sides, whichever is widest.

Depth   Measured from the top of the gunwale amidships to the floor of the canoe; can also be measured from the top of the gunwale at the bow to the floor.

Trim   The variance of freeboard from one side to the other and from end to end. Trim is controlled by shifting the position of the paddlers or, if the canoe is loaded, by shifting the load.

Bilge   The inside of the canoe that is lying below the waterline. **Bilgewater** is the stuff that slops around in the bottom of the canoe.

Painter   A six-foot piece of floating rope tied onto the bow or stern of the canoe.

Layup   Manner in which the various materials are layered to create the shape and strength of the hull.

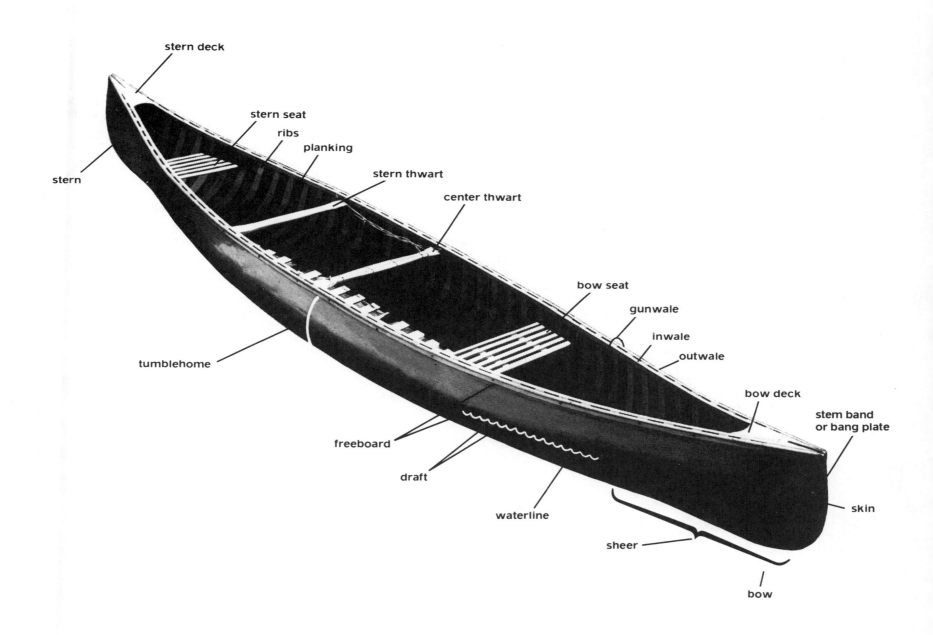

stern deck

stern seat

ribs

planking

stern thwart

center thwart

stern

bow seat

gunwale

inwale

outwale

tumblehome

bow deck

stem band
or bang plate

freeboard

draft

skin

waterline

sheer

bow

Paddles

In eight hours of paddling you will average around 14,400 strokes. Those are a lot of strokes, so what you use for a paddle is of considerable importance. What kind of paddle is most desirable and how long it should be are matters of opinion. If you want to look as if you paddle every day, all day, from break-up to freeze-up, you should use a short paddle with a narrow blade.

You rarely see authentic-looking paddling in historical films because the paddles are excessively long. The paddler dressed in the Indian suit or decked out in the trapper's outfit looks ridiculous because of his oversized paddle. The upper hand comes up much too high. There are other reasons why Hollywood paddling looks ludicrous, but the high hand position that goes with the long paddle is the give away.

For years I wondered why the old pros like the trapper, the prospector, the Indian and the Claude Cousineau crowd of the flatwater school in the east looked so good when they paddled. One of the main reasons is that with the shorter chest-high paddle the upper hand doesn't come up so high in the forward stroke. The upper hand drives out from the shoulder and rises no higher than the shoulder. There's no doubt about it! It looks and feels good.

If you want to burn off a lot of miles, a long paddle with a wide blade might be the paddle for you. Many seasoned canoeists insist that the short paddle with a narrow blade will get you there just as quickly and with less effort. And some of these experts really do push their canoes along at a very brisk rate with the small paddle.

I must confess to using both. I prefer the short narrow-bladed paddle when paddling solo in flatwater with the canoe in the leaned position. I use a longer paddle with a seven-inch (18 cm) wide square blade for whitewater. One method of sizing a paddle before buying it is this: kneel or sit on something that is the same height off the floor as your canoe seat is off the water. Place the grip on the floor so the paddle is vertical, upside down. The throat of the paddle (where the shaft meets the blade) should be level with your chin. A quick and less accurate method of sizing a whitewater paddle is to stand holding it in front of you with the blade on the ground. The grip should be somewhere between the pit of your neck and your chin. The square paddle blade allows you to utilize the full surface of the blade quicker and in shallower water compared with a long, narrow paddle. The narrow paddle takes longer to submerse, so there is no jolt at the start of each stroke — something your shoulders will appreciate on a long day of flatwater.

Kinds of paddles

The growth in recreational flatwater and whitewater canoeing has enabled manufacturers to produce a wide variety of paddles in wood and synthetics to suit your needs and budget.

Paddle A   Bent shaft paddle for flatwater racing and touring. Enables the paddler to apply maximum power throughout the stroke without lifting up on the water at the end of the stroke. Laminated wood with a urethane tip on the blade.

Paddle B   Voyageur-style flatwater paddle. Suitable for flatwater tripping. One piece of hardwood — or in this case laminated hardwoods — to create an attractive design.

Paddle C   Otter tail. A nice paddle for solo ballet or touring at a relaxed pace. Carved from solid hardwood. Needs to be handled and stored with care.

Paddle D   Beaver tail. A good multipurpose design and a real pleasure to use for flatwater tripping. All wooden paddles should be kept well varnished; watch for cracks and water seeping in the tip of the blade. Store your wood paddles in a cool dry place, preferably hung by the grip, off the ground.

Paddle E   Laminated wood flatwater or whitewater paddle. The short wide blade and square end allow maximum blade surface in shallow water. For whitewater use, the blade must have a reinforced tip.

Paddle F   Laminated wood whitewater paddle. A short wide blade for whitewater plus multidirectional veneers for strength make this a good choice for a high-performance wood paddle. The epoxy wrap protecting the oval shaft is a must for a serious whitewater paddle.

Paddle G   An injected plastic paddle with an aluminum shaft. It is the choice of many novice paddlers. Although well-suited to abuse and misuse, it lacks the aesthetic qualities of a wooden paddle and the performance of a quality synthetic paddle.

Paddle H   Fiberglass whitewater paddle. Tough, light, and stiff. It is the choice of many intermediate-to-expert whitewater paddlers. Plastic shrink wrap protects the shaft from wear.

Paddle I   Carbon curved-blade whitewater paddle. The choice of racers and expert whitewater paddlers. The curved blade lets less water slip past the blade, meaning more efficient and powerful strokes. The square aluminum reinforced tip is excellent for pushing off rocks because it won't slip. The price of a carbon paddle is almost double that of a fiberglass paddle; however, there is now a fiberglass curved paddle on the market.

Kinds of paddle grips

There are two main grip designs: the pear grip and the T-grip. The pear grip allows you to roll the paddle over smoothly and distributes the force evenly over the palm of your hand. The pear grip is an aesthetically pleasing shape to hold on to. The T-grip is a more functional shape and is usually associated with a whitewater paddle because your hand is less likely to slip off a T-grip in rapids. A T-grip can be wood or plastic.

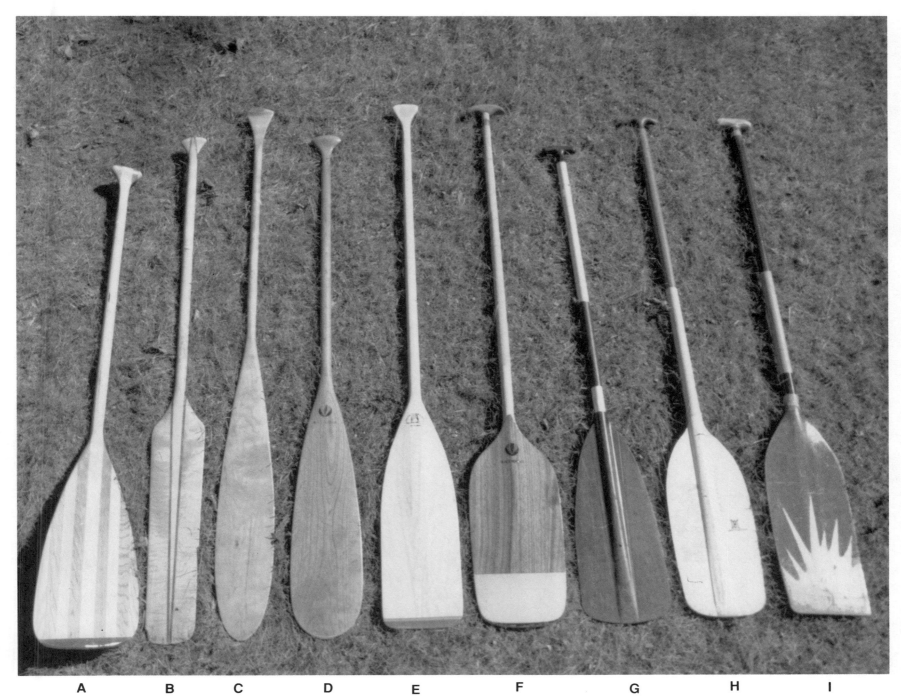

A   B   C   D   E   F   G   H   I

3 PADDLING SOLO

Canoe loaded for paddling solo

There is considerable controversy about whether or not one should begin by paddling solo or doubie. For practical reasons many camps teach paddling double first. In large classes where the number of canoes is limited, it is the logical approach. Another reason is the solo paddler's susceptibility to being blown out of control by the wind. Many times I've seen a whole class of solo students being blown down a lake with their instructors in hot pursuit.

On a one-to-one basis or in a small controlled class, I much prefer teaching solo first.

If you are learning to canoe without formal instruction, then it is wise to do so with another canoe and canoeist so you can help each other if necessary. Also, don't attempt to paddle solo for the first time in a wind.

Personal Floatation Devices (PFDs)

It is dangerous and, in most places, unlawful to step into a canoe without a PFD. Camps for both children and adults insist that they must be worn. This is a very logical practice when you are dealing with a number of people of unknown skill. No one can argue with the fact that there would be less drownings if everyone wore a PFD while in a canoe. A PFD, if it's a good one, has the added advantage of conserving body heat if you upset in cold water.

In view of these factors, I am sorely tempted to say that I always wear a PFD when I'm in my canoe. This would, however, be hypocritical as it is not the case. I always carry a PFD in the canoe and I always wear it in rapids, high winds, or when the water temperatures are cold. Unless you can swim a mile with your clothes on in wavy conditions, you would be wise to wear a PFD at all times in a canoe. When I am responsible for children and young people, I insist they wear PFDs. It takes the worry out of canoeing. Under these circumstances, I would wear one as well to set an example. On a fast river I always wear one because you really need it when making a landing above rapids. Many deaths have resulted from being swept into a rapid without a PFD.

When the water is warm, the surface is calm, and I am paddling along the shore in the hot sun, I might shed my PFD. But if I set out to cross a bay, or the wind picks up, or the current quickens, the PFD goes on.

PFDs must be comfortable and specially designed for paddling. They should fit well and snugly for ease of swimming and climbing back into a canoe from the water. If your PFD comes up around your ears when you are in the water, it does not fit properly. Not all PFDs are approved by the government, so keep in mind these guidelines. PFDs should be made of closed-cell foam with a nylon cover. Cinch straps that allow for some size adjustment are a real asset. A bright color is recommended for added visibility. Even high-quality PFDs will deteriorate if they are abused by using them as cushions around camp.

Footwear
Footwear is important. Shoes should be soft-soled. Hard-soled climbing boots can catch under the seats in an upset. It is also difficult to grip the bottom of the canoe with hard-soled boots. People who wear open-topped rubber boots in a canoe must have suicidal tendencies. They are impossible to swim in.

Ballast
Only resort to using ballast if you cannot trim your canoe by repositioning yourself. For example, if a small stern person cannot balance a heavy bow partner they can shift the packs toward the stern. Or if the canoe is empty of gear, try placing a plastic jug of water or a log in the stern. Never use material that is heavier than water — for example, rocks — to hold down the bow of your canoe. If you capsize, the rocks might lodge in the canoe and take it to the bottom of the lake.

Getting into the canoe

Confronting a canoe for the first time can be a bewildering experience for some people. I have a friend who is a professor of mathematics. Although he is an expert in his field, I'll never forget the day he stood on my dock staring at the canoe, wondering where to start. He had not asked for advice so I didn't offer any, but I watched as I pretended to be busy with something else. With his partner, who was also a mathematics professor, standing beside him he stared at the problem before him. At which end should he get in? Which way should he face? After a moment of hesitation, during which his computer-like mind took in the problem, sorted it out into the various possibilities, and speedily zeroed in on a solution, he proceeded to climb aboard. He went to the stern of the canoe and squeezed into the tiny space between the stern seat and the stern deck. He was facing the stern with his legs jammed between the seat and the stern. His partner then sat down on the bow seat facing the stern. I couldn't believe it! I thought to myself, he's got to be putting me on. Then he laid the clincher on me. He looked up at me and said, "Why don't they make the space here at the front (as he faced the stern) larger, so you have more room for your legs?" And his partner sitting on the bow seat, also facing the stern, turned around and looked behind her at all the space between the bow seat and the bow. She said nothing, but I knew exactly what she was thinking. She was thinking, "Yeah, just look at all the room back here." And with that they pushed off and proceeded to zigzag out into the lake.

To get into a canoe for the solo position, stand facing the canoe beside the bow seat. Then turn and face the stern. If the dock is lower or the same height as the gunwale you can kneel on the dock and place one knee in the canoe, then the other knee, while keeping your hand on the dock for balance. If the dock or shore is as high or

higher than the gunwale of the canoe; kneel down and place one foot right in the center of the canoe between the bow seat and the center thwart. Now lean forward and grasp the two gunwales putting your weight on the foot in the canoe. Bring your other foot in behind your first foot and sit down on the seat. Fold your legs back under the seat, spread your knees wide, pick up your paddle, and you're ready for anything. It's very difficult to fall out of a canoe in this position. There is only one problem. After a while you will get tired and will want to shift around a bit. Fortunately, there are lots of other positions that are almost as stable.

The procedure for doubles paddling is the same except that both paddlers face the bow of the canoe. The bow paddler gets in first while the stern paddler steadies the canoe by hanging onto the gunwale. Then as the stern paddler climbs into the stern, the bow paddler hangs onto the shore or dock. The bow paddler gets in first because the canoe is about two and one-half feet (75 cm) wide at the bow seat, and only one foot (30 cm) wide at the stern seat. If the stern paddler gets in first, the widest part of the canoe is raised right up out of the water, making the canoe very tippy. With only about one foot width of canoe in the water, it's like balancing on a log.

Conversely, when getting out of the canoe, the stern paddler gets out first leaving the bow again in the more stable position with a two and one-half foot width in contact with the water. If you ignore this basic principle, sooner or later you will be going for an inadvertent swim and it could just be above a dangerous rapid. This rule isn't quite as critical if you are carrying heavy packs in your canoe. When landing in a strong current, the rule has to be modified.

Paddling positions

Kneeling is without question the most stable position for paddling a canoe. The reason you seldom see canoeists in the kneeling position is because it hurts. The casual paddler doesn't spend enough time in the kneeling position to stretch the muscles and toughen up the pressure points, so invariably reverts back to the sitting position very quickly. Your legs can be conditioned to kneeling if the position is assumed every day for a short period of time.

Each position has its advantages and disadvantages. This kind of diversity is what makes solo canoeing the graceful and creative art it is. You'll find this same diversity in the many paddling strokes as well. When you're learning, it might seem as if many of the strokes are just other ways of doing the same thing. How and when to use the various positions and strokes comes with practice. I know of people who have paddled for years and never realized the joy of paddling solo. A well-co-ordinated team is a sight to behold, like a *pas de deux* in ballet, but paddling solo brings a special challenge and grace to the art. And the accomplished solo paddler invariably makes a better doubles paddler.

Kneeling braced against seat
The most common position for long-distance cruising is kneeling on the bottom of the canoe with your rump braced against the seat. This is a very stable position and should always be used when running rapids.

Kneeling with canoe leaned
Slide over nearer to the gunwale and put your knees together pointing towards the gunwale. You will find this is an extremely comfortable position for flatwater canoeing. The stroke can be made very close to your body. It is now much easier to reach the water for comfortable paddling, and the canoe becomes much more responsive.

Paddle-side leg extended
The paddle-side leg is extended so that your other leg can be brought back with the heel wedged under the seat. Your hip, thigh, and knee on the paddle side press against the gunwale. In this position you are literally wedged into your canoe. It is a position favored by many whitewater paddlers.

Kneeling and sitting on heels
The solo canoeist kneels with the buttocks resting on the heels. Because the canoe is heeled over and riding on its rounded side, the bow and stern are out of the water and the canoe turns, pivots, and sideslips with a minimum of effort. This is the fun position from which to savor the sheer beauty and poetry of paddling.

Racing position
The most powerful paddling position of all is to go up onto one knee in a high kneel. To maintain balance in the racing position, your forward foot is toed in while your back leg is positioned diagonally across the canoe with your toes gripping the bottom of the canoe for lateral balance.

Sitting position
There is nothing wrong with the sitting position for total relaxation of your legs in quiet water conditions. It does make sense, though, to spread your knees wide and press them against the sides of the canoe for balance. Your legs can be extended or folded back under the seat.

Kneeling with a saddlebag

The flatwater saddlebag helps the solo canoeist remain kneeling in a very low position without much of the agony associated with kneeling. You can easily make your own saddlebag. Fill a plastic bag with closed-cell foam chips and put it in a nylon stuff sack.

Knees spread wide

For difficult rapids or waves, position yourself in the center of the canoe for maximum stability, and spread your knees wide apart.

One leg extended

After a while your legs will begin to cramp. Extend your leg furthest from the gunwale almost straight out and turn in your foot. You will notice that you can put more power into your stroke because the body has less tendency to pivot. To rest your other leg, change paddling sides, extending your other leg out.

High kneel

The high kneel is a welcome opportunity to rest your legs and also to improve the view ahead. It enables you to see over your partner's head if you are in the stern.

Shortening the waterline

One of the most important accomplishments to be acquired in paddling a canoe solo with grace and style is the ability to lean the canoe. By leaning the canoe, the waterline can be drastically shortened thus making sharp pivot turns possible.

Jim Gear of the National Canoe School had a completely transparent canoe made in fiberglass. With it he can illustrate how the waterline changes as the canoe is leaned. We can see the waterline on the canoe in the level position (see photograph 11). By leaning the canoe, the length of the waterline shortens to about ten feet (3 m) (photograph 12). Gear also demonstrates how leaning the canoe that extra inch can shorten the waterline by as much as a foot (30 cm). This makes a big difference in making a flatwater pivot.

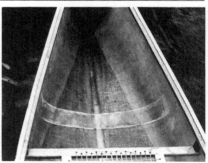

Standing

Standing in a canoe is a useful position for wilderness canoeing. Keep your legs spread wide with your foot on the nonpaddle side of the canoe slightly forward, toe in for balance. Press the back of your paddle-side leg against the seat. Keep the paddle in the water and scull back and forth for support.

Wind effect on the canoe

A canoeist seldom has the sheer joy of paddling a canoe on a completely windless day unless he or she is in the habit of getting up with the sun. At that time of day, when the forest edge is mirrored in the flatwater, you seem to float through space between heaven and earth. It's the closest thing possible to effortless motion, for the canoe responds to the slightest pressure from the paddle. It would be great if everybody could begin to learn in such conditions, but this seldom happens. So let's begin with an understanding of how the wind affects the canoe and what to do to counteract it.

An empty symmetrical canoe will be blown broadside down the lake (*see* photograph 1). The force of the wind on both ends is identical so the canoe drifts sideways. Now get into the canoe and position yourself in the middle of it (photograph 2). Be sure to tuck your knees right up under the center thwart or the experiment won't work. You will find that the canoe continues to drift broadside down the lake. Why? Because with you sitting in the center, the canoe is still symmetrical. Now, to appreciate the effect of the wind on the canoe, move back and kneel in the stern (photograph 3). You must kneel because you are now in a very precarious position. You are positioned where the canoe is only about a foot (30 cm) wide as compared with three feet (90 cm) in the middle. If you watch someone else do this, you will notice that only about a third of the canoe is in the water, the narrowest third, right under you. It's like riding a log. A very dangerous position as we will see in a moment.

From your position in the stern, you will notice that the canoe is blowing around (photograph 4) so the high end is pointing downwind (photograph 5). This is because the canoe is like a weather vane. The canoeist is the pivotal point. Kneeling close to the stern pushes it deep into the water where the wind can't affect it much. With the bow riding high and exposed, the canoe

will blow around until it is pointing downwind. Now pick up the paddle and try to paddle the canoe around into the wind. If the wind is brisk, it can't be done, no matter how strong you are. Anyway, it's hard work. It makes a lot more sense to slide forward into the center of the canoe (photograph 6) and turn around (photograph 7) to face into the wind (photograph 8). In a strong wind you will have no difficulty controlling the canoe from this position. Be sure your knees are tucked right up under the center thwart. In a light wind you can move back and lean against the bow seat (photograph 9). This is a very stable and comfortable position from which to paddle. You would have to be pretty uncoordinated to fall out of the canoe from this position, especially if you're kneeling.

Now let's assume that a gale begins to blow. This is the time to make the wind work for you instead of against you. Move up just ahead of center (photograph 10). The stern, which is now riding slightly higher in the water, will blow downwind. You are now pointing into the wind, the direction you presumably want to be in, and you haven't even started paddling yet. Most of your effort can be used to propel the canoe forward against the wind. If the wind lets up a little, you can move back to just behind the center thwart (photograph 11), lean the canoe away from the wind so the wind glances off the bottom and turn the canoe a few degrees off the wind. In this way the wind will assist in steering, making it unnecessary to apply a steering component to your forward stroke. This is called tacking into the wind. It's all a matter of using your skill and knowledge to utilize the force of the wind rather than fighting it.

Another reason for paddling amidships rather than in the stern (photograph 12) is the narrowness of the waterline near the ends of a canoe. Twenty inches (50 cm) rather than thirty-six inches (1 m) in the middle of the canoe. Most people who fall

out of canoes do so from the stern (photographs 13, 14, and 15). Some of them drown, because if the canoe doesn't capsize, which it often doesn't (photograph 16), it will quickly be blown out of reach. If you're not a strong swimmer and are not wearing a life jacket, this would be a very dangerous situation.

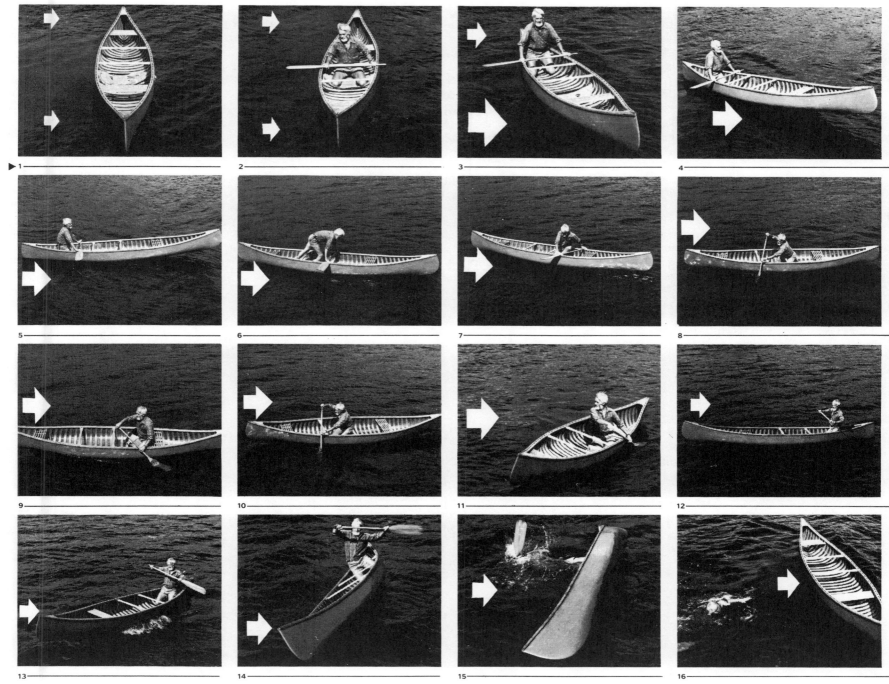

You just pick up the paddle and go where you want to go, right? Well, not quite. Each time you take a stroke the canoe veers away from the paddling side. To compensate for this problem, most beginners change the paddle from one side to the other every few strokes. You get where you want to go, but you cover a lot of extra miles because of the zig zag course. You also waste a lot of energy in the constant changing of paddling sides.

Stern pry
A much better way to travel a straight line is to pry away from the canoe at the end of each stroke. The canoe still zigzags because, without instruction, you almost certainly will pry away with the wrong side of the paddle blade. This is called a stern pry and is not the best way to steer a straight course. It's been nicknamed the "goon stroke" because of its inefficiency. This is rather unfortunate, however, because it does have its uses in whitewater canoeing. This will be covered later, so for now let's just say the goon stroke is to be avoided like the plague.

J stroke
There are four correction strokes that make the canoe go in a straight line. The first is the J stroke. Near the end of the power stroke, the power face of the paddle, which is the side that pulls against the water, turns out and is pried away from the canoe bringing the canoe back on course with a minimum of zigzagging. The path of the paddle describes a "J". Use your upper grip hand to control the angle of the paddle blade, while letting the shaft rotate freely in your lower hand during the steering component of the stroke. Steering is accomplished at the end of the stroke. The clue to whether you are doing the J stroke correctly is to freeze at the end of the stroke and look at your upper grip hand. If the thumb is pointing down, you're doing it right. If it's pointing up, you're doing the goon stroke. Another

common problem when learning is not rolling the paddle over far enough. The blade should be parallel to the side of the canoe. If necessary, pry the paddle off the gunwale for maximum leverage.

Inside turn with the C stroke
To turn toward the paddle side, you can modify the basic J stroke into a C stroke. The C stroke is particularly helpful in getting the canoe moving from a stationary position. Start the C stroke by reaching out from the canoe at the beginning of your stroke; pull in toward the bow, then take a forward stroke, scooping slightly underneath the hull and finishing with a strong J stroke. If the canoe veers away from the paddle side, you are probably not rolling the paddle over early enough during the J portion of the stroke. The blade should be perpendicular. Or, you are not reaching far enough back toward the stern for the steering action. Prying away beside the body will only sideslip

the canoe. If the canoe persists in veering away from the paddle side, push or pry away harder at the end of the stroke. Also keep the paddle in the water longer. Don't take it out of the water until the canoe is on course. Don't forget to draw in toward the canoe at the beginning of each stroke, especially when beginning to move forward. It is quite common to teach a person the J stroke one day, only to find that the next day the paddler has reverted back to the natural inclination to turn the power face of the paddle in toward the canoe with the thumb on the upper hand pointing up.

Constantly check at the end of the stroke to see if your thumb is pointing down. It is unlikely that any person has picked up a paddle and done the J stroke naturally. It must be learned.

Kneeling in center with load forward gives control in any wind

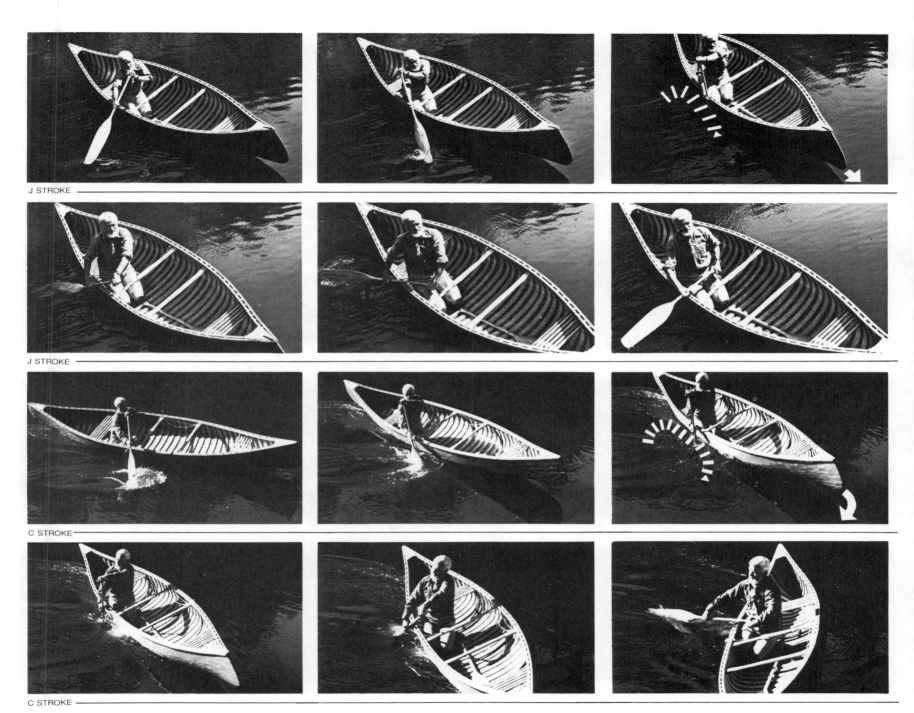

J STROKE

J STROKE

C STROKE

C STROKE

19

Steering strokes...

Canadian stroke

Now that you are able to travel in a straight line using the J stroke as well as doing inside turns with a C stroke that emphasizes the draw in at the bow and a strong J at the stern, it's time to move on to the Canadian stroke, a variation of the J. It used to be called the knifing J but American canoeists began referring to it as the Canadian stroke.

At the end of the J stroke, the paddle is knifed forward underwater with the power face of the paddle almost flat and facing up. Steering is accomplished by pulling up on the blade as it is arced forward. About halfway through the recovery the paddle is allowed to slip out of the water in readiness for the next power stroke. The trick is getting a very slight angle on the blade as it arcs forward. If the angle is wrong the paddle will plane out of the water or dive too deep. The angle is controlled by the upper grip hand.

Most people require personal instruction to master this stroke but carefully studying the diagrams should help. You might be one of those natural paddlers capable of mastering this stroke on your own. Just remember most of the steering action comes from pulling up hard with your lower hand as the paddle is knifed forward. How hard you pull up on the blade and how long you knife the paddle in the water during recovery determine how much the canoe turns toward the paddling side. It's a very efficient stroke since you have to bring the paddle forward to begin the next power stroke, so why not do your steering along the way. The J stroke works fine but with the steering done at the end of the stroke, time and effort are wasted. A well-done Canadian stroke is the pinnacle of perfection in motion; however, it can take years to master.

Offside forward stroke

The offside forward stroke is a way to keep maximum forward power while turning toward your paddling side. Reach as far forward as you can on your offside while keeping the paddle vertical. Using your body, thrust the canoe past your planted paddle. As soon as the paddle reaches your knees begin the recovery by turning the paddle blade parallel to the canoe with your upper grip thumb pointing forward and slicing your paddle forward before you get all tangled up. Admittedly this stroke is extremely difficult to do well in a wide tripping canoe. It is used primarily to start the canoe moving from a standstill.

A very stable, rough water position

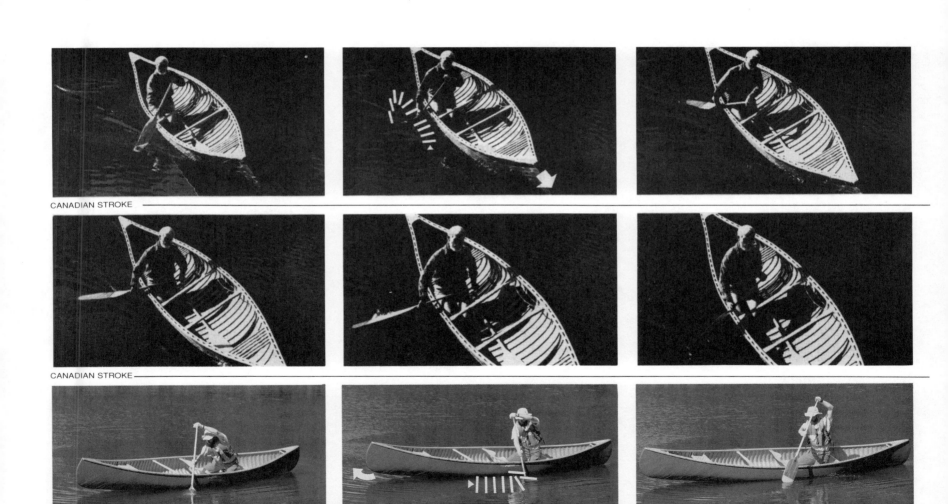

CANADIAN STROKE

CANADIAN STROKE

OFFSIDE FORWARD STROKE

Steering strokes...

Pitch stroke

Another stroke for paddling a straight course is known as the pitch stroke. This is the most powerful and strenuous stroke of all. Calvin Rustrum was the original proponent of this stroke. Not everyone agrees with him that it is the best stroke, but when it comes to getting somewhere in a hurry I sure would agree. With the pitch stroke, the steering action takes place during the last half of the power stroke. Toward the end of the stroke, the paddle is brought forward without delay to begin the next power stroke. Very little time is wasted in steering. The steering is accomplished during the power stroke by rolling the paddle very early in the stroke. This is why it is called the pitch stroke. The paddle is pitched at an angle to the water like an airplane propeller. It is the pitch on the paddle that steers the canoe during the power stroke. Some paddlers claim that there is a loss of forward power as the pitch increases because of slippage of the pitched blade. This is true, but it can be compensated for partly by bringing the paddle in under the canoe during the stroke. Otherwise the prying action at the end of the stroke does tend to slow up the canoe.

Whether you use the J stroke, Canadian stroke, or pitch stroke, bring the paddle back feathered (flat) to cut wind resistance. It's amazing the difference this can make during a day's paddling against the wind.

Sweep stroke outside turn

One of the first things you learned about paddling was that the canoe always veers away from the paddle side if you don't put enough steering action into your stroke. If you want to turn away from your paddle side, just do a forward stroke. Don't put any steering action into your stroke. To turn more sharply sweep your paddle wide in an arc. This is where the name sweep stroke comes from. For maximum turning effect, begin the stroke as far forward as you can reach and end it as far back as is comfortable for you.

Efficient paddling techniques

A good paddling technique requires the use of the whole body. Your back, shoulder, and stomach muscles are a lot bigger than your arm muscles so why not use them.

The secret to tireless paddling lies in complete relaxation during the recovery. Your upper hand drops very low and the paddle is brought forward in the feathered position (flat) to cut wind resistance on the blade. Just remember that if you are going to average 14,400 strokes a day on a wilderness journey, good form makes for efficient use of your available energy.

To assist you in following instructions for the various strokes, it helps if you can identify which side of your paddle blade is the power face. The power face is the side of the blade that pulls against the water in a forward stroke. Mark one side of your paddle in some way and then always use that side as your power face. This will avoid confusion when following instructions for all the strokes except the Indian stroke. In the Indian stroke, the paddle is rotated.

Forward stroke

There are several kinds of forward strokes. Here are two extreme examples. One is a traditional effortless forward stroke suitable for a long day of flatwater. The other is a strenuous maximum-power stroke for quick acceleration, as is often required for whitewater.

First, the traditional forward stroke. Knife your paddle in at your knee. Your upper grip hand then drives out straight from your shoulder like a boxer, punching forward and down toward the gunwale. Bending slightly at the waist and rolling your shoulders brings the larger muscles of your upper body into use. Your lower hand acts mainly as a fulcrum. Your upper grip hand delivers the power through a lever action. This is a very efficient use of the body's energy. During the recovery keep your arms slightly bent.

The maximum-power forward stroke applies the same principles, using the larger torso muscles rather than your arms, but the emphasis is on torso rotation. Plant your paddle as far forward as you can reach by twisting at the waist so that your inside shoulder is toward the front. Do not lean too far forward! It will cause the canoe to bounce, which will slow you down. Your body should be wound up like a spring. Now unwind as you take your forward stroke, keeping your paddle vertical and using your stomach muscles to pull the canoe forward past your paddle. Initially your lower arm should be straight as your body unwinds. When the paddle reaches your knee, your lower arm will bend as your upper hand punches forward. If you are doing the stroke correctly your stomach muscles should feel sore afterward.

The length of the stroke in these photos has been exaggerated slightly for demonstration purposes.

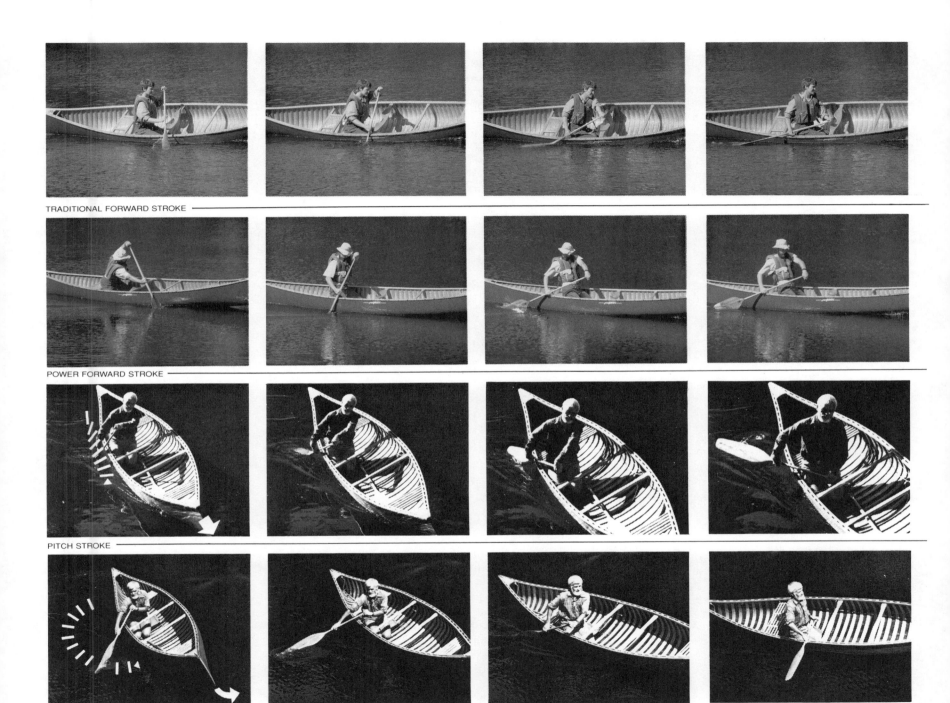

TRADITIONAL FORWARD STROKE

POWER FORWARD STROKE

PITCH STROKE

SWEEP STROKE OUTSIDE TURN

23

Steering strokes...

Indian stroke

There is one other stroke for paddling a straight course that should be covered here. It is a very useful stroke for paddling in a strong wind, running rapids, and paddling silently to sneak up on animals. It is called the Indian stroke or underwater stroke and is an extension of the Canadian stroke. As the paddle knifes forward, the grip of the paddle is rotated in the palm of your upper hand. The rotation makes it possible to bring the paddle around, ready for the next power stroke without taking the blade out of the water. Keep the throat of the paddle above the waterline so that the shaft does not create noisy splashes. It's a very nice stroke to know because with the paddle remaining in the water, the canoeist is in control throughout the entire stroke.

If done slowly and carefully, there is no sound from the paddle. It's a fun stroke for sneaking up on turtles, beaver, muskrat, and even deer or moose. I often use the Indian stroke when rounding a point, in the hope of catching deer or waterfowl by surprise, and I have paddled right up to deer and moose along the shore. Animals are frightened by smell, sound, or movement, but by paddling slowly, and with the wind in the right direction, they express only concerned interest until you are very close. They will sometimes explode into flight only to stop and turn around to look again at the intruder. If you don't react, they seem unwilling to leave without satisfying their curiosity.

On one occasion a large buck even returned to the water's edge, snorting and stamping his feet as though frustrated in his desire to know what I was. On another occasion, paddling on a small, mirror-smooth stream, I saw a muskrat sunning himself on a small log with his back to me. I pointed my canoe in his direction to see how close I could get to him. Using the Indian stroke, I came right up behind him. Just as the bow would have touched him on the back, I veered slightly to the left. As the bow slid by, half an inch from his left eyeball, he shot straight into the air and hit the water swimming. He soon broke the surface a couple of feet from the canoe, unable to resist the temptation to see what it was that had startled him. Within a split second, with his curiosity satisfied, he disappeared for good.

The Indian stroke is a stroke that no canoeist should be without.

Inside turn with Indian stroke

The Indian stroke is a powerful stroke for making an inside turn into the wind, or for controlling the canoe in gusty wind conditions or nasty crosscurrents. At the end of the forward stroke, do a very heavy J. Then, as you knife the paddle forward underwater, open the face of the paddle toward the bow and reach out from the canoe. At the same time rotate the grip in the upper hand so you can begin a strong draw in at the bow. Be sure to begin the draw very far out from the canoe to increase the strength of the draw. As you approach the side of the canoe, round out into a strong power stroke and go into your heavy J again. Repeat this as long as desired. The Indian stroke with strong emphasis in the right places makes it possible to overcome the strongest winds and currents.

I wouldn't be surprised if by now you are saying to yourself. "Who needs all these steering strokes? It just seems like a lot of ways of doing the same thing."

There is no such thing as the perfect stroke. The diversity of opinion about which is the most effective stroke is part of what makes canoeing fascinating. I look back with fond memories to many hot and heavy arguments around a campfire, their amiable hubbub competing with the roar of the rapids far into the night. Fortunately, even the computer cannot supply definitive answers, because canoeing conditions and the purpose of each paddler are so varied that there is no one, perfect canoe, paddle or paddling technique for all times and seasons. Any paddlers disagreeing with what is written here would not upset me greatly if they tore out the offending page and used it to kindle a fire, so long as the site was well chosen and the fire well laid.

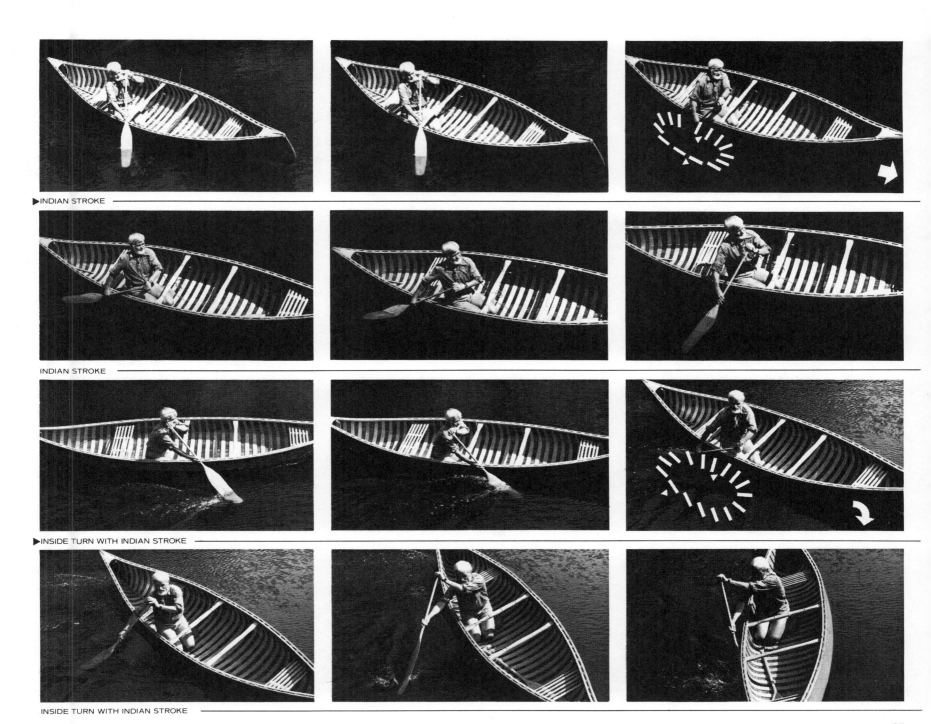

▶INDIAN STROKE

INDIAN STROKE

▶INSIDE TURN WITH INDIAN STROKE

INSIDE TURN WITH INDIAN STROKE

25

Pivot strokes (stationary)

Pivot point

Now that you've got the canoe going in a straight line and turning left and right with ease, you will find that there are times when you need to turn much more sharply than is possible with a stern steering stroke. Using bow strokes, you will discover that even under full power it is possible to do a 360-degree turn within the length of the canoe. First let's try it from the stationary position (stationary in relation to the water).

It helps if you think of the canoe as having a pivot point. In any empty canoe this pivot point is located in the center of the canoe. For maximum maneuverability and control, the canoeist should kneel amidships. This puts the canoeist at the pivot point.

Stationary stern draw

To pivot the canoe away from the paddle side, reach back and out from the canoe at about a 45-degree angle and draw the paddle to the stern of the canoe, using the power face. Remember that the power face is the side of the blade that pulls against the water in a power stroke, and you must use it to do the stern draw effectively. Grasp the paddle as though you were going to do a power stroke, but instead reach back and out from the canoe and draw the paddle toward the stern. In fact, to get the idea, slap the paddle against the stern of the canoe. The bow swings away from the paddle side.

Stationary stern pry

To pivot the canoe toward the paddle side, reach back and sweep or pry the paddle away from the canoe. The further back toward the stern that you do the pry, the more effective the stroke is. It's like increasing the radius from the pivot point.

Stationary bow draw

The canoe can also be pivoted toward the paddle side by reaching forward and out at a 45-degree angle and drawing with the power face toward the canoe. If the power face is pulling against the water, you are doing it right. Nine times out of ten the student will use the nonpower face, or back of the paddle. To increase the distance of the blade from the pivot point, which makes the stroke more effective, slide your lower hand up the shaft until your upper hand can cross under your chin without socking you in the jaw.

Stationary bow pry

To do a bow pry reach forward as though you were going to begin a power stroke. Instead, slip the paddle into the water as far forward as comfortable and well under the canoe. Slide your lower hand up the shaft until your upper hand fits under the chin. Now pry away from the canoe, using the gunwale as a fulcrum. The nonpower face of the blade pries against the water. Feather the blade (slice the paddle through the water sideways) into an underwater position close to the canoe in order to begin the next pry. You will find that this is one of the most effective strokes because of the levering action. The most difficult thing about the stroke is getting the angle of the blade just right. To make sure you're learning it correctly assume the power stroke beginning position with the paddle in the water, turn the inside edge toward the bow, and pry away. Now check to see if the nonpower face is prying against the water. The bow pry turns the bow away from the paddling side. Applying a bow-turning stroke to supplement the stern-turning stroke more than doubles the turning effect. With the bow riding slightly higher than the stern, the bow strokes are more effective. If the stern is riding deeper in the water, it's more difficult to push or pull the stern sideways to execute a pivot turn.

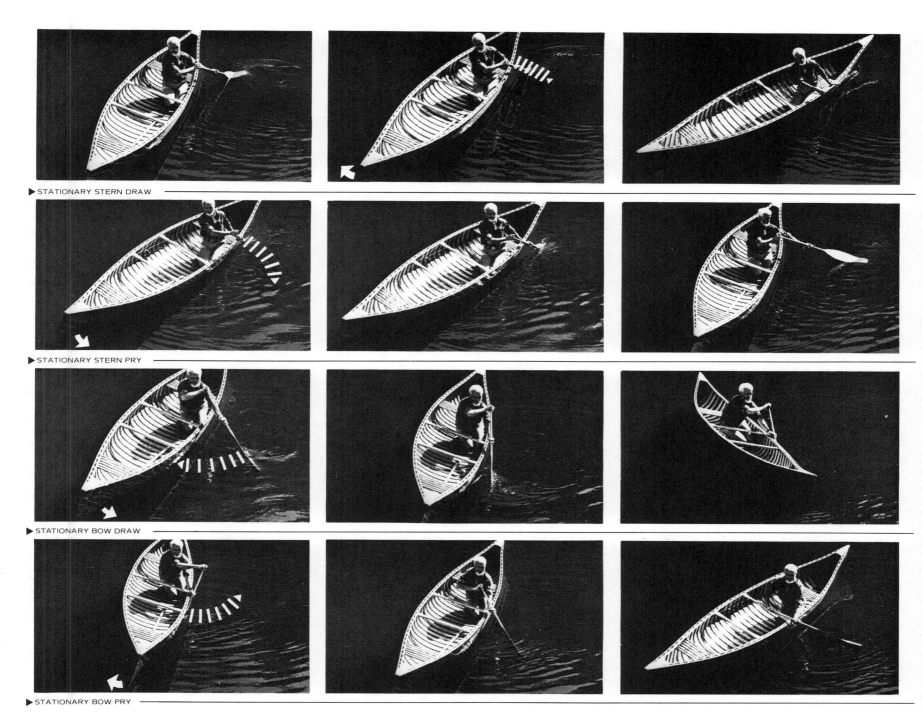

▶ STATIONARY STERN DRAW

▶ STATIONARY STERN PRY

▶ STATIONARY BOW DRAW

▶ STATIONARY BOW PRY

27

Pivot strokes...

Box-stroke pivot away from paddle side

If you follow a stern draw with a bow pry, you'll be surprised how drastic the turning action is. To get from the stern draw to a bow pry, knife the paddle through the water on edge (in the feathered position) to the bow. After you do the bow pry, knife the paddle back to the stern, reaching as far out from the canoe as is comfortable for an effective stern draw. Repeat this series of strokes as often as desired; the canoe will pivot on the pivot point.

Box-stroke pivot toward paddle side

To pivot the bow toward the paddle side, do a bow draw. Then knife the paddle to the stern for a stern pry. Knife the paddle back to the bow for a bow draw and repeat as often as desired. When you master the box stroke, you can start smoothing it out into one graceful continuous motion with the canoe leaned right to the gunwale for ease of pivoting. The stroke will then resemble more of a circle than a rectangle.

BOX-STROKE PIVOT AWAY FROM PADDLE SIDE ————————————

BOX-STROKE PIVOT AWAY FROM PADDLE SIDE ————————————

Circle stroke

There is a stroke called the circle stroke, which is another way of doing the same thing. The paddle is swept in one, continuous 360 degree circle. Half the circle must be done under the canoe. The paddle is rotated in the hands to complete the 360 degrees. The canoe must be leaned right to the gunwale for the stroke to be effective. It is a graceful stroke when done well and fun to do.

Lake Superior, north shore

▶CIRCLE STROKE

CIRCLE STROKE

Pivot turns when under way (running pivots)

The bow pry and bow draw are used for violent turns when underway, but they are preceded by a bow jam and a bow cut.

Running bow cut followed by bow draw
To make a sharp pivot turn toward the paddle side, the canoe should be moving briskly. Reach out from the canoe and plant the paddle in the water. The power face of the blade is angled at about 45 degrees and toward the direction of travel (forward). The force of the water on the angled blade will pull the canoe around into the turn. This is called a cut. As the speed of the canoe slows down, the turning effect decreases proportionately. To continue the turn, draw in hard toward the bow. Do a power stroke with strong emphasis on the J, pitch, or Canadian at the end. You often will hear this stroke referred to as a C stroke because the path of the paddle describes a C. One word of caution:

almost all canoeing books show the cut done very close to the bow with the shaft in contact with the gunwale. This is not a good way to do a cut because you can't go from the cut to a bow draw without taking the paddle out of the water. You also can't lean your weight on the blade and put some muscle into it if you don't reach well out from the canoe.

▶RUNNING BOW CUT FOLLOWED BY BOW DRAW

RUNNING BOW CUT FOLLOWED BY BOW DRAW

Running bow jam followed by a bow pry

To make a sharp pivot turn away from the paddle side, the canoe again should be moving briskly. Slip the paddle into the water parallel to the canoe (feathered). As you quickly slide the paddle forward smoothly increase the angle of the blade so that the nonpower face is toward the direction of travel (forward). When the angle is about 45 degrees, brace the shaft against the gunwale and hold. You must lean your weight *away* from the paddle side. If you don't anticipate a violent grabbing effect from the water hitting the angled paddle, it will yank the grip out of your upper hand or fire you over the gunwale and into the water.

For maximum effectiveness, you must reach well forward to increase the distance of the paddle from the pivot point of the canoe. As the momentum of the canoe decreases the turning effect falls off, so you must complete the turn with a pry off the gunwale, a series of many pries, or a sweep stroke. There is one other very essential part of this stroke, which I've left to last. It's called the set-up. The last power stroke before the pry is changed to a wide sweep stroke to begin the turn. If you neglect to do the sweep, the canoe just won't make the turn properly.

The bow jam is the only stroke that's ever caused me to fall out of a canoe. And it happened at the worst conceivable time—soon after I had arrived at a well-known canoe school for instructors. I was billed as the guy who was turning out these expert films on how to canoe. That night I was due to screen the films to test them for clarity of presentation before completion. Anyway, I was executing some turns through the gates of their slalom course earlier that afternoon when I caught the wrong angle of the blade on a bow pry and catapulted myself unceremoniously into the water. I came up and launched myself back into the canoe (which hadn't capsized) as quickly as I could in the hope that no one had seen me take a swim. But just in case, I maintained an air of nonchalance throughout to suggest that I do this all the time just for fun or to cool off. However, the fact that I was fully dressed and it was a cold spring day didn't do much for my credibility.

►RUNNING BOW JAM FOLLOWED BY A BOW PRY

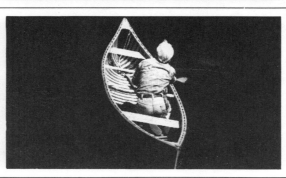

RUNNING BOW JAM FOLLOWED BY A BOW PRY

Pivot turns...

One-hand pry pivot turn

To add a little class to the maneuver, try it with one hand. Do your set-up sweep stroke. Let go of the paddle with your upper hand and slide your lower hand up to the neck. Plane the blade toward the bow, angle the paddle as you bring the shaft into contact with the gunwale, and hold. As momentum slows, follow with a series of one-handed prys. If you like, you can hang onto the center thwart with your free hand. This is a very difficult stroke to describe. The hardest part is slipping the paddle in at the bow at the proper angle and keeping it from sliding back along the gunwale.

All these pivot strokes work best when you are kneeling amidships just behind the center thwart so that the bow is riding slightly high. You also should be positioned very close to the gunwale in order to heel the canoe over so that the water is about an inch from the gunwale. The canoe is very responsive to the turning strokes at this angle because the shortened keel line lessens the drag in the water when executing a pivot.

▶ONE-HAND PRY PIVOT TURN

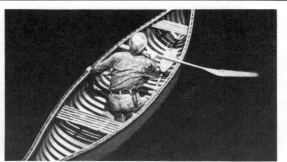

ONE-HAND PRY PIVOT TURN

Running crossdraw

To do the crossdraw make a sweep stroke set-up. Bring the paddle across in front of you to the other side without changing hands. Reach out at a 45-degree angle from the canoe and draw the paddle toward the canoe with the power face. If you're not using the power face to pull against the water, you're doing it wrong. Slide your knee across to increase the reach on the other side. One of the advantages of the crossdraw is that the paddle can be kept near the surface to avoid catching a rock in shallow water. This is a distinct advantage over the pry in shallow, rock-studded rapids. The advantage of the pry is that you can go instantly from a draw to a pry without taking the paddle out of the water.

There are many highly skilled canoeists who have very little interest in solo flatwater canoeing with the canoe in the leaned position. This is true of some of the whitewater fanatics who canoe the mountain rivers out West and believe that flatwater canoeing is only a prelude to running rapids. They feel that because the knees are always spread wide when running rapids, leaning the canoe to the gunwale is of no practical value. Some even feel that this form of canoeing was invented to keep children attending summer camps from getting bored with flatwater canoeing, since running rapids was looked upon for years as much too dangerous for children. Rapids were avoided because of the responsibility placed upon the camp operators.

This could be true, but paddling a canoe in the leaned position is a beautiful and graceful art. It is also sound basic training prior to whitewater.

►RUNNING CROSSDRAW

RUNNING CROSSDRAW

Sideslip toward paddle side

In rapids, it's often more desirable to change the course of the canoe by slipping sideways across the current than by turning. The sideslipping maneuver avoids the danger of broadsiding onto a rock. A three-foot (1 m) wide, sixteen-foot (5 m) long canoe has five times the chance of hitting a rock if it's traveling down a rapid broadside. By keeping the canoe aligned with the current and moving back and forth across the current in a sideslipping motion, only a three-foot wide target is offered to the rocks. In the photographs the action has been exaggerated, and the paddle is kept near the surface for clarity. In reality the paddle would be kept vertical and deep in the water for maximum efficiency.

Draw sideslip
The draw is used to sideslip toward the paddle side. Instead of reaching forward and drawing in at the bow or reaching back and drawing in at the stern, which would pivot the canoe, you reach out at a 90-degree angle and draw straight toward the body. Repeat the stroke as often as desired, using an above-the-water or under-the-water recovery.

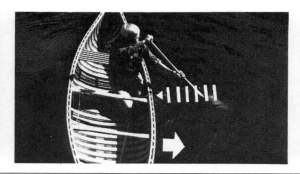

▶DRAW SIDESLIP

DRAW SIDESLIP

Sculling draw

The sculling draw has an advantage over the draw sideslip. With the paddle remaining in the water, there is a continuous bracing effect. It's a lot more difficult to learn, but worth the effort. Reach back and sweep the paddle toward the bow, holding the blade at a 45-degree angle. In other words, put a pitch on the blade like the pitch on an airplane propeller. At the end of the stroke, change to the opposite pitch, sweep the paddle to the stern and repeat. If you put the same amount of pitch and power into each sweep, the canoe will sideslip without turning. For maximum efficiency keep the paddle vertical by pushing out with your upper grip hand and pulling in with your lower hand.

The sculling draw sometimes is referred to as feathering. This is not technically correct. When you feather a paddle, you turn it on its edge toward the direction of travel so

it doesn't do any work. Therefore, sculling is a more valid term.

Figure eight

The figure-eight stroke is a modification of the sculling draw. At the end of each stroke, draw in toward the canoe to enhance the sideslipping. The path of the paddle describes a figure eight.

▶SCULLING DRAW

▶FIGURE EIGHT

Sideslip away from paddle side

Sideslip pry

The pry is used to sideslip away from the paddle side. To avoid turning the canoe, the pry must be done right beside the body. At the end of the pry, feather the blade to recover the paddle underwater and begin the next pry. Make sure that your thumb on the upper grip hand turns away from the canoe on the recovery. This ensures that the blade will slice back in smoothly for the next stroke. The pry is a very effective and powerful means of moving the canoe sideways because of the leverage on the gunwale.

Sideslip pry, Magnetawan River Canyon, Georgian Bay, east shore

▶SIDESLIP PRY

SIDESLIP PRY

Sculling pry

The sculling pry accomplishes the same thing. Instead of the power face of the paddle doing the work as in sculling, the non-power face is pried away, against the water. It is a matter of opinion whether or not it is as effective as the pry. In any case, it is a very beautiful and graceful stroke and part of the art of paddling. If the canoe turns when doing a sculling draw or pry, you can compensate by doing the stroke a little toward the bow or stern as the need arises. You can do this stroke with a moving fulcrum, as illustrated, or by keeping the heel of your hand resting on the gunwale as a stationary fulcrum.

First Canyon below Virginia Falls, Nahanni River, Northwest Territories

▶SCULLING PRY

·SCULLING PRY

Running sideslip

Once you've mastered sideslipping toward and away from the paddle side, the maneuver can be attempted when moving. This is the way it will usually be done. Because of the movement of the canoe through the water, the cut and jam can be used to initiate the sideslip.

Running draw sideslip

To sideslip the canoe to the paddle side when underway, reach out at a 90-degree angle and do a cut (power face toward the bow). As the paddle moves through the water the pitch on the blade will draw the canoe sideways toward the paddle side. As movement slows, begin the sculling draw to continue the sideslip.

Running pry sideslip

To sideslip away from the paddle side while moving, do a jam right beside the body (nonpower face toward the bow), brace against the gunwale, and hold. To avoid being catapulted into the water, don't forget to lean away from the paddle side. It also helps to slip the paddle into the water parallel to the canoe and increase the angle of the paddle to 45 degrees. To continue the sideslipping, begin the pry strokes as momentum slows. If you position the paddle too far forward or too far back, the canoe will turn. Adjust the position forward or back as necessary.

Running crossdraw sideslip

The crossdraw can be used for a running sideslip if it is done as far back toward the stern as you can reach. You really have to twist your body around. The advantage of the crossdraw is that the paddle is less likely to catch a rock in shallow water. It also has a tendency to slow the canoe down long enough to get it into the desired position in the current. The crossdraw stroke is a very essential stroke for running rapids solo.

▶RUNNING DRAW SIDESLIP

▶RUNNING PRY SIDESLIP

▶RUNNING CROSSBOW DRAW SIDESLIP

Cascade Falls, Lake Superior

The braces

In violent cross-currents and the foaming waves of rapids, the canoe can be stabilized to an amazing degree with braces. You can keep yourself from tipping toward your offside with a high brace. You are not likely to upset to your paddle side because of your lean and the bracing effect of the flat of your paddle blade pressing on the water. The paddle becomes an outrigger. If you are extending your paddle out three feet (1 m) to the side, the canoe becomes six feet (2 m) wide instead of three feet (1 m) wide. However, in trusting your weight out on the paddle, you must learn to keep it (the paddle) at just the right angle. If you allow the blade to turn and dive deep, there is a good chance you will too.

High Brace
The high brace is done by assuming a chin-up position — that is, with your elbows bent and under the paddle shaft. Place your upper grip hand under your chin and hold it

there! This will keep the elbow of that arm against your chest and will bend the elbow of your lower arm, avoiding the possibility of a painful shoulder dislocation. Place your paddle 90 degrees to the canoe and apply some weight to it. To extend your brace, lean out with your body, keeping your upper grip hand at your chin. If you have forward momentum before doing a high brace, the paddle will plane on the water until you lose your momentum, at which point you will have to scull your paddle to keep it on the surface. The high brace is a good ready-for-anything brace. You can quickly revert to a stroke from it because it uses the power face of the paddle. Or if you tip to your offside you can change to a drawing motion to pull yourself back upright.

Low Brace
With the low brace your paddle is parallel to the water and is very effective if the canoe begins to tip to your onside. To do a low

brace, assume a push-up position with the knuckles of your grip hand down. Your lower arm should be bent and positioned over the paddle. Place your upper grip hand at your belly button and keep it there. As you lean out to put weight on your paddle keep your elbows bent. Bracing with straight arms is an invitation to a dislocated shoulder. If you have no forward momentum you will need to scull your paddle to keep it at the surface.

HIGH BRACE

LOW BRACE

Bracing strokes

During a maneuver, particularly in white-water, strokes often have a bracing component to them. Many strokes utilize the water going past the canoe, allowing you to put a lot of weight on the paddle without it sinking. The best examples of this are the draw and backsweep eddy turns.

The draw eddy turn uses a combination draw stroke and high brace. The idea is to transfer weight to your paddle, but keep the paddle more vertical than in a high brace. This ensures that the canoe will pivot around your paddle once it is planted in the eddy.

The backsweep very closely resembles a low brace. The big difference is that your paddle will be moving in an arc, starting against the stern and sweeping out to be perpendicular to the canoe. It is important to start the backsweep with a pry to initiate the turn. As the paddle moves out to the side flatten the angle of the blade for maximum bracing. In this position you can really tilt the canoe into the turn. As with the low brace, keep your upper grip hand near your belly button and your lower arm bent.

An aggressive approach ensures that you will cross the eddy line quickly and have enough forward momentum to keep your paddle planing on the surface, providing a solid brace.

The tilt of the canoe is a key factor in creating graceful and effective eddy turns. Tilt enough that the gunwale is no more than an inch or two (2-5 cm) from the water. If you are doing the proper strokes that incorporate some bracing the canoe will still feel stable.

This covers some basic ways of using strokes with bracing action, but there are other variations that you will discover for yourself. In fact, all the strokes can be used in a variety of ways and in endless combinations with other strokes.

DRAW EDDY TURN

BACKSWEEP EDDY TURN

Backpaddling

When running rapids with a loaded canoe in wilderness situations, you will spend more time paddling backward than forward. Anything you can do when paddling forward you should be able to do paddling backward.

To make the canoe go backward under control, you must be able to go backward in a straight line, turn toward or away from the paddle side, and sideslip toward or away from the paddle side. You simply apply all the same principles involved in moving forward to moving backward. Keep in mind that you are moving backward in relation to the water, but that in relation to the rocks and shore you are descending the rapids slowly. It's not very often that you can backpaddle faster than the rate of flow of the current. When the canoe is sideslipped right or left while backpaddling in rapids, the maneuver is called setting because the canoe is set over.

Major correction strokes control the angle of our canoe. Minor correction strokes combine backpaddling and steering in one stroke with the emphasis on moving backward in a straight line.

Major correction strokes

Backdraw (remember the canoe is moving backward)
To turn the stern away from your paddling side, do a backdraw. Place your paddle at 90 degrees to your canoe with the power face of your paddle toward the bow. Now pull the paddle in an arc toward the bow, lifting it out of the water just before it hits the canoe. To be efficient, push your top grip hand out past the gunwale.

Crossdraw
To turn the stern toward your paddling side use a crossdraw. Emphasize the rotational twist of your torso to maximize each stroke.

Both these strokes pivot the canoe powerfully, but supply little backward motion. Alternate these with the minor correction strokes, which feature more power on the backpaddling phase of the stroke and only minor turning motion.

Minor correction strokes

Backsweep
To turn the stern away from your paddling side, use a backsweep. Start the backsweep against the hull of the canoe as far toward the stern as you can comfortably reach. Push the paddle blade out in an arc away from the stern, lifting it out of the water as it reaches the gunwale.

Reverse J stroke
To travel in a straight line or to turn the stern toward your paddling side while maintaining reverse power, use the reverse J stroke. Begin the stroke slightly behind you, with your lower arm bent and your upper grip hand held high and about one foot (30 cm) out from the canoe. Using the nonpower face, push the paddle toward the bow, keeping it vertical and against the hull. Complete the stroke by pausing at the end as you pry off the gunwale using the same blade face.

Compound backstroke
You begin this stroke by rotating your torso to face 45 degrees behind you. Then use the power face of your paddle to draw the paddle to your hips. Flip it to the nonpower face and continue with the reverse J. These strokes are used to maneuver the canoe backward, but nothing moves you backward more quickly than a backpaddle stroke. For maximum efficiency, keep your stroke vertical and close to the canoe.

COMPOUND BACKSTROKE

Major correction strokes

BACKDRAW

CROSSDRAW

Minor correction strokes

BACKSWEEP

REVERSE J

Crystal clear water, Lake Superior

5 PADDLING DOUBLE

The paddler who has mastered the canoe alone is well on the way to becoming a good doubles paddler. Paddling solo gives a special feel for the canoe and how it reacts to wind, waves, and current. Paddling double is also a beautiful and challenging art. A well-co-ordinated team working together in either flatwater or difficult rapids is a sight to behold. Most canoeists prefer to travel in pairs on wilderness trips because two people can propel a canoe easier and faster than one.

There are both advantages and disadvantages to paddling double in rapids. With two paddlers you have two people who can make a mistake and cause the canoe to upset. On the other hand, with two paddlers you can execute a brace on both sides of the canoe, making it extremely stable. However, in large waves, on lakes, or in rapids, the extra weight and positioning of the paddler's weight in the ends of the canoe cause it to plunge deep into the waves. Shipping water over the bow is a real problem unless you have a spray cover. Nevertheless two canoeists do have twice the power to control the canoe and so the argument goes. It's a trade-off. I like to canoe both ways as long as my partner and I are working smoothly as a team.

Paddling a straight course

When paddling a straight course with only relatively minor turns, such as you would do following a curve in a river, the stern paddler does the steering with a J, Canadian, or pitch stroke. It's his job to keep the canoe on course, without losing power in his stroke and without slowing down or altering the rhythm of the stroke. The bow paddler mainly supplies power when paddling flatwater except when making tight turns, a pivot, or a sideslipping maneuver. It's in rapids that the bow paddler finds himself with a lot to do. In fact, a safe passage depends just as much on the bow paddler as on the stern paddler, and in some situations even more.

Dog River

Wide power turns

The secret to easy, relaxed, long-distance paddling is to keep the canoe going with a constant rhythmical stroke. When a turn is needed it is done without either paddler changing pace or missing a stroke. A good bow paddler can assist in making the turn by means of three strokes.

Bow J

To turn away from the bow paddler's side without sacrificing forward speed, the stern paddler does a heavy J, Canadian, or pitch and the bow assists by shortening his stroke, putting a J on the end of the power stroke and prying hard off the gunwale. The bow J shortens the radius of the turn without slowing down. The efficiency of the stroke depends on shortening the power stroke and prying the J off the gunwale beside the body, not behind it. If you do the J too close to the center of the canoe, the turning effect is reduced.

Bow sweep

To do a bow sweep, begin your forward stroke close in beside the bow and sweep the paddle wide. For maximum turning effect keep the stroke short. The bow sweep is not as effective as the bow J.

Diagonal bow draw

To turn toward the bow paddler's side, the stern paddler does a sweep while the bow paddler does a diagonal draw. Reaching out at a 45-degree angle toward the bow, the bow paddler draws the paddle directly toward his body. The bow paddler is in effect pulling the canoe around into the turn without slowing down. To turn even more sharply, the bow paddler reaches out at a 90-degree angle and pulls straight toward the body. These are called power turns.

Keep in mind that the job of the bow paddler is to assist the stern in making the turn without sacrificing momentum.

Pivot-point doubles

The main difference between canoeing solo and double is the alteration of the pivot point. Obviously the pivot point can't be under both paddlers. It is located instead about halfway between the two. A clear understanding of this is most important when doing pivots, power turns, and side-slipping. The canoe will pivot if both paddlers do the *same* strokes (the bow prys, the stern prys) on their respective sides.

▶BOW J

▶DIAGONAL BOW DRAW

Pry pivot

To pivot away from the bow paddler's side, the stern and bow paddlers both do a pry. The stroke is most effective if the bow paddler does the stroke as close to the bow and the stern paddler as close to the stern as possible. By increasing the distance of the paddle from the pivot point, the turning effect is enhanced considerably.

Draw pivot

To turn toward the bow paddler's side, both paddlers do a draw or sculling draw. The advantage of the sculling draw is that with the paddle remaining in the water and the weight leaning on it, the paddlers are in a constant brace.

Crossdraw pivot

Another method of pivoting away from the bow paddler is for the bow paddler to do a crossdraw instead of the pry. The advantage of the crossdraw is that the paddle can be kept close to the surface to avoid catching a rock in rapids or shallow water. Keep the blade well toward the bow by moving your lower hand up the shaft and keeping your upper grip hand low. The pry is more effective and the results more dramatic, but it requires a higher level of skill.

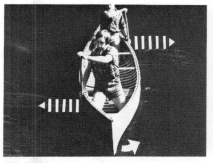

▶ PRY PIVOT

▶ DRAW PIVOT

▶ CROSSBOW DRAW PIVOT

47

Running pivots

Just as in solo canoeing, pivot strokes applied when the canoe is moving are very effective because of the force of the water against the blade of the paddle.

Running pry pivot
Do the running pivots slowly at first, then increase the speed as you improve. To turn away from the bow paddler's side both the stern and bow paddlers do a jam. The non-power face of the paddle is forward. In doubles, it is particularly important that the bow paddler does the jam correctly. With practice it becomes one quick, continuous motion. As momentum slows, begin a series of prys and continue until the desired turn is completed. If you lose control, release the paddle in the upper hand or you may fall overboard. The same procedure applies if you catch an unseen rock in rapids.

In rapids, the pry pivot turn is stabilized by the stern paddler, who goes from the forward stroke into a wide backsweep with the paddle planing on the water. The sweep provides a solid bracing effect.

Running draw pivot
To make a sharp turn toward the bow paddler's side when underway, the bow paddler does a cut. With the power face of the paddle open to the direction of travel, you can really lean your weight out on the paddle. The force of the water on the blade will pull the bow around into the turn. As momentum slows begin a series of draw strokes or go into a sculling draw and continue until the turn is completed. The stern paddler also does a cut and completes the turn with a sweep or sculling draw.

Running crossbow draw pivot
As in solo paddling, the bow paddler can do a crossbow instead of the jam and pry. It's not as effective but it's a lot easier. The paddle can be kept near the surface to avoid hitting rocks in shallow rapids.

Some canoeists regard the crossbow in doubles with scorn. They see no merit in the stroke, pointing out that time is wasted in crossing over. They also claim that with both paddles on the same side of the canoe, you forsake the brace on each side. They are right about this, but occasionally the crossbow does come in handy in those shallow, rock-studded rapids. However, I would agree with the critics that the crossbow is often used to excess. The pry is a better stroke if you can do it well. And you will never learn to do it well if you always play safe with the crossdraw.

▶RUNNING PRY PIVOT

▶RUNNING DRAW PIVOT

▶RUNNING CROSSBOW DRAW PIVOT

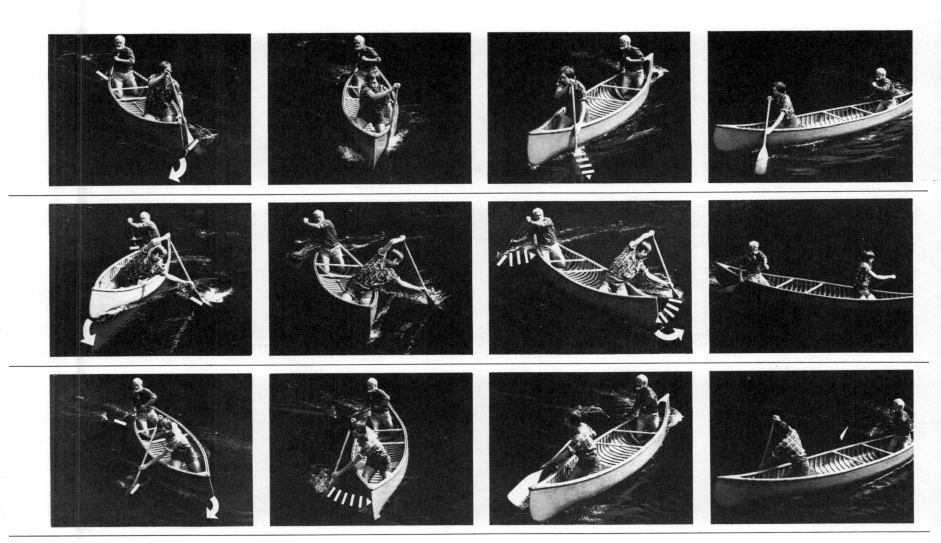

Sideslip

The sideslip is more often used to change course in rapids rather than to steer the canoe in the desired direction. This is also true when paddling solo. Sideslipping and keeping the canoe aligned parallel with the current avoids the danger of broadsiding into a rock. To sideslip the canoe, both paddlers do *opposite* strokes.

When sideslipping, the two paddlers must work as a team, being careful not to outpull each other. If one paddler works too hard, the canoe will turn. Sometimes this might be desirable, but the paddlers should be able to sideslip the canoe parallel with the direction of travel. The stronger paddler must not outpull his partner.

Sideslip away from bow paddler's side
To sideslip away from the bow paddler's side, the stern paddler does a draw or sculling draw; the bow paddler does a pry or sculling pry.

Sideslip with crossdraw
If preferred, the bow paddler can use the crossdraw. Although the canoeists have not changed sides, the crossdraw puts both paddles on the same side of the canoe. The stern is doing a draw, the bow is doing a crossdraw, and both strokes require reaching out. You shouldn't both lean out aggressively to take your strokes, or you will be wishing this book were waterproof.

Sideslip with a stern pry
If preferred, the stern paddler can do a modified pry. By keeping the stroke behind you, and therefore shallow, you won't catch any rocks in a rapid. Because the pry is now farther away from the pivot point, it is even more powerful than the regular pry.

Sideslip toward bow paddler's side
To sideslip toward the bow paddler's side, the stern does a pry or sculling pry; the bow paddler does a draw or sculling draw.

SIDESLIP AWAY FROM BOW PADDLER'S SIDE

SIDESLIP WITH CROSSBOW DRAW

SIDESLIP TOWARD BOW PADDLER'S SIDE

SHALLOW WATER STERN PRY

Running sideslip

When sideslipping under power, the paddlers hold the paddle in the jam or cut position to take advantage of the force of the water against the paddle. When doing a sideslip with forward momentum it helps to let the bow lead a bit. As the momentum slows, they follow with a series of prys, draws, or crossdraws.

Running sideslip away from bow paddler's side
To slideslip away from the bow paddler's side, the bow paddler does a jam while the stern paddler does a cut. As the momentum of the canoe decreases, the bow paddler goes from the jam to a series of prys and the stern paddler goes from the cut to a series of draws or a sculling draw.

Running sideslip with crossbow draw
Some bow paddlers opt for the crossdraw in place of the jam and pry, especially in dangerous situations. They hold the crossdraw cut until the canoe slows down and then do a series of crossbow draws. The crossbow draw is an effective stroke but puts you in a vulnerable situation while the paddle is in the air on the crossover.

Running sideslip toward bow paddler's side
To sideslip toward the bow paddler's side when underway, the bow paddler does a cut (power face toward bow). The paddle shaft should be vertical in the water for maximum efficiency. As momentum slows follow the cut with diagonal draws or a sculling draw. The stern paddler goes from the jam to a series of prys.

► RUNNING SIDESLIP AWAY FROM BOW PADDLER'S SIDE

► RUNNING SIDESLIP WITH CROSSBOW DRAW

► RUNNING SIDESLIP TOWARD BOW PADDLER'S SIDE

Braces

In paddling double the braces are performed exactly the same as in solo paddling. With a paddle on each side of the canoe, it is extremely stable. This is an advantage of paddling double.

High brace

In paddling double the high brace has a tendency to pivot the canoe toward the bow paddler's side. If you find that your high brace is pivoting the canoe, try taking some weight off your paddle. The paddle can remain in the position, but only push down on it when you need to.

Low brace

In the low brace position, the canoe is not only very stable but has less tendency to pivot. There is less drawing effect toward the paddle side, but you must anticipate any difficulties ahead of time and assume the brace position before you get into rough water. Otherwise you will be in the water before you have a chance to get into the brace position.

The success of your brace depends on leaning your weight out on your paddle blade. When the canoe is not moving in relation to the water, your paddle will sink if you hold the brace for more than a few seconds. You must scull or do forward or back sweeps. High and low braces stabilize the canoe in rough water.

Bracing position, with paddle-side leg extended

Some west coast paddlers use a rather unique paddling position that I discovered recently. With this position, they seem able to perform very stable braces for violent maneuvers in turbulent rapids. At first I was skeptical about this position, but after some

bow pry eddy turns into some very difficult eddies with my stern paddler bracing in this position, I came away convinced of the solidity of it. The paddler was Brian Creer of Sport Canoe, British Columbia. As soon as he climbed into my stern, I could tell right away that this paddler probably spends more time in a canoe than anywhere else.

You can imagine my surprise when he extended his leg on the paddle side, and brought the other leg back, and hooked his heel under the seat. I ventured a tentative "Are you sure that's the way you want to do it?" He smiled and said "Watch." We then bore down on what I can best describe as the wildest looking eddy I've ever encountered, with an ugly looking rock garden right below it. He insisted I enter the eddy with a bow pry rather than the more cautious crossbow. With a feeling of impending doom, I jammed the paddle in as we crossed the eddy line and heaved. To my surprise, that canoe pivoted right around on my paddle with all the feeling of stability I could wish for.

Brian claims that with his foot wedged under the seat he can't possibly fall out and the canoe can't upset to his paddle side because of his brace. The way he was leaning parallel to the water, there is no way that canoe could have tipped to my paddle side. I would have gone overboard before that could have happened. One other neat maneuver that he does is to position the load so he can brace his extended foot against it.

I observed that his seats are lower than mine so that the foot really is wedged under the seat. The toe touches the floor of the canoe and the heel is wedged up against the seat. The great advantage of this position is the extreme lean to the paddle side that can be accomplished. I came away convinced of the merit of this position.

HIGH BRACE

LOW BRACE

COMBINED STERN LOW BRACE AND BOW DRAW

Backpaddling

Controlling the direction and position of the canoe while backpaddling is one of the least understood skills in running rapids. Just paddling backward won't do it because it doesn't control your direction. Both paddlers are responsible for positioning the canoe and holding the right angle. However, the bow paddler has more steering control when the canoe is being back-paddled upstream against the current. The bow paddler assumes the role of the stern paddler when moving backward. In theory, because the canoe is moving backward, one might assume that the bow paddler would do all the steering. This rarely works in practice because the canoe is nearly always riding lower in the stern, making the canoe very sloppy when moving backward. To compensate for this, the stern paddler can slide forward to the stern thwart or shift a pack to lighten the stern so it won't be digging into the current. The strokes required for backpaddling on flatwater or whitewater can be separated into two groups: major correction strokes, which have a strong steering component but do not add much backward motion; and minor correction strokes, which emphasize strong backpaddling with subtle directional control.

MAJOR CORRECTIONS

Backdraw
To turn the stern of the canoe away from the bow paddler's side, the bow paddler does a backdraw with the power face of the paddle, which starts at 90 degrees to the canoe (photograph 1A) and travels in an arc (photograph 1B) to the bow (photograph 1C), where it is lifted out of the water for the recovery (photograph 1D). The secret to a strong backdraw stroke is to push out with your upper grip hand as you pull in with your lower hand. Because this is a major correction stroke, the stern paddler should help out by doing a modified backdraw. The stern paddler reaches out and back at a 45-degree angle and, keeping the paddle vertical, draws it toward their hips.

Crossdraw
To turn the canoe toward the bow paddler's side, the bow paddler does a crossdraw. Rotate your torso around to face the stroke (photograph 2A) and plant the paddle well toward the bow (photograph 2B) so that it is far away from the pivot point at the center of the canoe. Then pull in with your lower hand and push out with your upper grip hand, keeping it low (photograph 2C). Lift the paddle out before it makes contact with the bow (photograph 2D). Again, because this is a major correction stroke the stern paddler can help out by doing a stern pry, making sure to start with the paddle blade right against the stern (photograph 2A) for maximum turning effect.

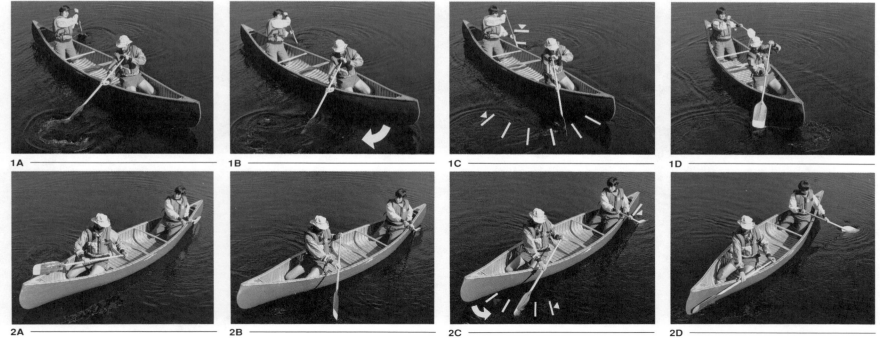

1A   1B   1C   1D

2A   2B   2C   2D

MINOR CORRECTIONS

The minor correction strokes are used to keep the canoe traveling in a desired direction that has been obtained with the major correction strokes.

Backsweep

To turn the stern away from the bow paddler's side, the bow paddler uses a backsweep. Caution — this stroke is fun and feels good, but don't use it to the exclusion of the backdraw. The paddler uses the non-power face of the paddle (photograph 3A) and starts the stroke at approximately 120 degrees to the canoe (photograph 3B), then pushes the blade in an arc toward the bow (photograph 3C). Note that the paddle shaft will hit the gunwale before the blade reaches the bow (photograph 3D). This is why the backsweep is a powerful backpaddling stroke, but not an efficient turning

stroke. The stern paddler supplies reverse power with a backpaddle stroke.

Reverse J

To turn the stern toward the bow paddler's side, the bow paddler does a reverse J stroke. Take a regular backpaddle stroke (photograph 4A) and as your paddle reaches the bow (photograph 4B), or as far as you can reach without lifting your bum off the seat, throw in a reverse J (photograph 4C) by prying off the gunwale. Using the same paddle face, hold this position until the water has a chance to "catch" the blade, creating the turning effect (photograph 4D). Once again, as this is a minor correction the stern paddler supplies reverse power with a backpaddle stroke.

Backpaddle

When no directional corrections are required both paddlers should do a backpaddle stroke. The key to obtaining maximum power is to keep your paddle as vertical as possible so you aren't just pushing down on the water. As well, try to keep the blade close to the side, and therefore the center line of the canoe, to minimize any turning effect.

3A 3B 3C 3D

4A 4B 4C 4D

Trimming the canoe

The most important thing about back-paddling is that the stern must not ride lower than the bow. If it does, the stern digs in, causing all sorts of problems. It stands to reason that if a canoe steers more easily if it rides slightly higher in the bow when traveling forward, the canoe should steer better if it is riding slightly higher in the stern when traveling backward. In reality, trimming the canoe heavily in the bow would cause other problems. You would have to shift your weight back toward the stern when you paddle forward. The constant shifting of weight is impractical. Just settle for level trim or very near level trim.

The point I am trying to make is that if your stern is riding much deeper than your bow, you've got three strikes against you and you haven't even come up to bat. When you have trouble doing back ferries, the first thing to do is ask someone if you are riding level. There are two reasons why almost everyone rides stern heavy. First, canoes were never designed with back ferrying in mind. With the stern seat closer to the stern than the bow seat is to the bow, the canoe will ride stern heavy even if the paddlers are of equal weight. Second, the heaviest person often sits in the stern.

The solution is for the stern paddler to slide forward, right up against the stern thwart, before beginning the backwater or to trim the canoe with the weight forward when paddling with a load. Even when backpaddling on flatwater you will find the canoe slews around out of control if the stern is riding deeper than the bow. In a strong river current, the problem is compounded many times because of the force of the river on the stern. Once the stern starts to swing, it is difficult or even impossible for the stern paddler to do much about it. The bow paddler must correct the angle by swinging the bow downstream. With the canoe trimmed level both paddlers can work together to change the angle at will.

It is not possible to overemphasize the importance of keeping the canoe trimmed properly. It will be a recurring theme throughout the book. If there is one single reason that I could use to rationalize adding to the proliferation of "how to canoe" books, it is the fact that, to my knowledge, the other writers of canoeing books have neglected the unweighting of the upstream end. And yet the principle applies to ferrying, poling, lining, tracking, wading and, most important of all, to landing above a dangerous rapids or falls.

Standing

Many years ago—no one knows when—someone said "You should never stand in a canoe." If there is one single thing that everyone *thinks* they know about canoeing, it's that! Never stand in a canoe! It's the one apparently intelligent thing that people can utter about canoeing without fear of being wrong. And yet, nothing could be further from the truth.

Standing is one of the main advantages that the canoeist has over the kayaker or canoeist in the specialized covered whitewater canoe. In the standing position the increased visibility over the brink of a rapid is considerable, and the position is also advantageous in cutting the reflection from the surface of the water when paddling through shallows. In low water conditions, it is possible to run small rapids to find the best and deepest channels, and by using a pole while standing, it is even possible to navigate otherwise impossibly shallow rapids. In fact, in some areas of North America, canoeists do much more poling than paddling.

Added to these advantages, standing makes it possible to rest and stretch your legs without going ashore — an accomplished canoeist can even walk around in a canoe with no danger of falling overboard! It's all a matter of practice, of course, and I hasten to add that common sense must prevail while acquiring the skill. You don't practice in deep water or above a dangerous set of rapids. Above rapids is a very dangerous place to be, and standing should only be attempted after you are thoroughly familiar with the position. Your partner should be in the low brace position for stability.

STANDING

VIEW OF RAPIDS KNEELING

VIEW OF RAPIDS STANDING

MAGNETAWAN RIVER CANYON

Riding haystacks, Petawawa River, Ontario

You've probably heard the old saying "only fools run rapids." I don't know who said it; probably the saying originated with the same guy who said you should never stand in a canoe. Whoever it was, I feel sorry for him. He never knew what he was missing.

The rapids and falls that break up the free flow of most of Canada's rivers can be regarded in two ways. You either love them or you hate them. Most of the earlier travelers along North America's inland waterways hated them because they were a barrier. A falls meant transporting tons of furs and other goods around them by means of an excruciatingly difficult portage. More often, rapids were feared because of the high risk to the heavily laden, fragile canoes in the seething whitewater. The bounty of ancient trade goods divers dredge up at the base of many rapids along the old routes is evidence of many disasters. And an upset in those days really was a disaster, since it could mean losing a year of many men's labor, not to mention losing lives.

As we cavort in these same rapids in our small, tough, lightly loaded canoes, it is well to remember those travelers of long ago. Today the risks we take are by choice, not of necessity. Improved equipment and paddling techniques have enabled modern canoeists to attempt rapids that never would have been run when life on the river was a serious business. In spite of these improvements the risks, though they are different, have not diminished. The almost indestructible canoes of today can cover a multitude of sins, all of them perpetrated in the name of whitewater canoeing, but it is well to remember that the dangers to a canoeist who wipes out are just as great now as they ever were.

Rapids are much more than a place to play. It is because of these rapids and waterfalls that great islands of wilderness exist today. These barriers to navigation have cut off all the modern forms of transportation and with them, development along large stretches of rivers and lakes. It is true that here and there a road or railroad intrudes to follow the river, but as soon as the river curves away from the desired direction, the river is once again left to go its own way. One portage in these areas puts the traveler beyond the reach of motorized transport.

The rapids and falls always have been the lock and bar to this secret world — a world beyond the whitewater and portages, to be enjoyed only by those who acquire the skills and are willing to expend the effort to get there. It can be strenuous work, even arduous, but the wilderness traveler knows that the greater the difficulty, the greater the sense of stepping back into a time when life was simpler and basic. Not easier, just simpler. Out there it is possible to rediscover the joy to be derived from just looking, listening, and thinking.

In those times, professional canoeists, such as trappers or prospectors, would have run rapids of moderate difficulty, but there was too much at stake to fool around in rapids just for the fun of it. They could not go off to the store to purchase another canoe and outfit. Nor could they return home and save up enough money to start over, since the lost outfit was the means by which their livings were earned.

Today recreational paddlers, with not so much at stake, have developed the skills of whitewater paddling to an amazing degree. People run rapids that a few years ago would have been considered suicidal. Several factors have contributed to this high level of whitewater skill. The most dramatic change has been in canoe material and design. The use of various plastic laminates means that beginners can afford to make mistakes and the experts can push the limits of the sport, while not having to worry as much about damaging their canoes. This results in a sharper learning curve and a sport that's more accessible to the general public.

Then consider the crossover of skills from slalom racing, which emphasizes precision and speed; rodeo paddling, which focuses on control and stunts in holes; and hair boating, which pushes the limit of what rapids an open canoe can run. All these create a perfect forum for an increase in overall paddling skills. But regardless of skill level, when it comes to wilderness travel the recreational canoeist must always keep in mind the price of failure in a remote area.

What is a rapid?

To understand rapids and really get to know what they are and how they work, it helps to think of them as a living, breathing organism, like a wild animal. A stretch of rapids can be as gentle as a lamb or as wild as a rampaging rhinoceros, as playful as a kitten one moment and as deadly as a man-eating tiger the next.

Many times I have eddied out of a gentle current above a tight corner to check out what's ahead to find that certain death was waiting around that bend. I've seen rapids that, given the choice between the rapids and a cage of Bengal tigers, I think I would take my chances with the tigers.

Most of the recent books on whitewater canoeing talk about vectors, kinetic energy, hydraulics, current differentials, and so on. I have avoided the use of such scientific terminology for the sake of simplicity. However, the science of flowing water is a fascinating study if you want to get into it. I have rendered the illustrations in a very realistic technique so you can more easily associate the diagrams on these pages with the rapids you will confront out there.

It's easy to talk about upstream and downstream Vs, but when you actually get out there and attempt to read a rapid; they are not always as clearly defined as they are in a simple diagram. One V merges into another, creating a very complex conglomeration of whitewater patterns.

I have attempted here to give you all the information you need to fully understand what happens under the water's surface, how to avoid the dangerous elements that make up a rapid, and how to take advantage of its weaknesses to get through it safely. The most important aspect of running rapids is to be able to predict the degree of difficulty from shore instead of finding out from an overturned or swamped canoe.

River morphology

I must confess that the first time I heard the word *morphology* it sounded pretty awful, but it simply means the workings of a river. How water flows downhill on its journey to the sea is a very important subject for the whitewater canoeist.

Study these photographs carefully and see if you can figure out where all the rocks are, how close they are to the water's surface, and where the deep water channels are.

An experienced canoeist knows exactly what's under the surface and how the surging currents will affect the canoe, even before the run begins. This is possible because every wave, every disturbance is caused by the bed of the river. By learning what it is that causes haystacks, downstream Vs, upstream Vs, eddies, rollers and souse holes, you can formulate a mental picture of the riverbed. You will know exactly where the rocks lay, how far beneath the surface they are, and whether or not they will present a problem. But what is even more important, you can tell with reasonable certainty where the rocks aren't. Now you are probably saying to yourself, "That's what I want to know. Who cares where they are as long as I don't hit them."

The canoeist must learn to read the rapids from shore to appraise the degree of difficulty and choose a course if the rapid is to be run. Once you've chosen the course you are going to run you need to convey your plan to your partner. It can be confusing if looking upstream you refer to "that rock on the right," because when you start paddling downstream that rock will now be on the left. To avoid confusion remember that left and right are always referred to as if you were looking downstream. Most canoeists call this *river left* and *river right* when describing a rapid. Rapids also must be read from the canoe during the descent, far enough ahead to give time to make all the right moves to avoid the problem areas. It is quite possible to run easy rapids without knowing much about what's going on by allowing the current to carry you along. If you keep the canoe aligned with the current, the canoe will tend to follow the deep-water channel.

But in a rapid of even moderate difficulty, canoeists must choose the course and position their canoes where they want them to go. Anything less is not running rapids under control. It is not only dangerous but much of the fun of running rapids cannot be fully experienced. There is very little merit in getting through a rapid on a hope and prayer. It's a lot safer and much more enjoyable to put some effort into acquiring the knowledge and skill to do it under complete control.

Madawaska River, Ontario

Picanoc River, Quebec

Nahanni River, Northwest Territories

61

Varying water-flow rates

The rate at which water flows down a river varies across the width and depth. It is very important for the canoeist to understand how these variations in current affect the behavior of the canoe. The canoeist not only must learn how to cope with these differentials, but also how to use them to advantage. For example, if you are drifting downstream, the canoe can spin right around at the most inopportune moment, perhaps above a dangerous rapid or falls. On the other hand, an understanding of flow rates can enable you to exit from the main stream quickly under complete control.

Let us assume you are canoeing a straight stretch of river with a straight shoreline and a relatively smooth riverbed. The slowest water flow is along the banks and bottom of the river because of friction. The water flows progressively faster toward the middle of the river (see diagram 1), with the fastest current right in the center (diagram 2). To understand how these current differentials can affect the canoe, let's imagine you are paddling downstream close to shore for reasons of safety. Assume your bow paddler allows the bow to get into the slower water by the shore. Your stern, which is in the swifter water further from shore, starts to move faster until it swings around, putting you broadside to the current. If a rock happens to come along at this moment, it's wipeout time. Otherwise the stern will keep moving downstream until you end up facing upstream by shore.

Varying flow rate around a bend

Now let's imagine we come to a bend in our river. Because of centrifugal forces, the deep water channel moves to the outside of the bend as it sweeps around the corner (diagram 3). The water on the inside of the turn moves very slowly, like the hub of a wheel. Another current develops as the water on the surface is carried toward the outside of the turn and downward like an undertow (diagram 4). This undertow can be dangerous in a large river. The outside of the turn is always deep, while the inside corner is always shallow.

Helical currents along the shore

Have you ever wondered why a stick or floating object is always held out in the mainstream, away from shore? I recently discovered an excellent explanation by Norman Strung in the book titled *Whitewater*. As the water near shore grows gradually shallower toward the bank, the friction causes a helical current to form. Imagine a corkscrew-like current flowing up near the shore, spiraling away from shore near the surface, and diving downward, out near the edge of the mainstream, to return to shore once again along the bottom of the river (diagrams 5 and 6). This current can present a problem when, after a swim, you are attempting to get yourself and your canoe to shore if you are unaware that the current exists.

This current spiraling out from shore will tend to hold you, along with your swamped canoe, out in the mainstream. However if you know the current is there, it isn't all that difficult to overcome. You just have to work at it a little.

Helical currents around a right angle corner

A situation where these helical currents can present a real problem is to be found on a right-angle corner. As the water flows toward the corner, the helical currents along the shore on the outside of the corner are smothered by the power of the main current (diagram 7). Conversely the helical flow on the inside of the corner is greatly increased as the water corkscrews out from shore and dives for the river's depths on the edge of the mainstream. As you attempt to hug the inside of the corner you have to overcome the tendency of the helical current to push you out into the mainstream. Failure to stay inside will allow the mainstream to carry you into the rock face, where you will be swamped and maybe pinned. In extremely swift, deep water, the helical current could be strong enough to pull you under. The trick is knowing how strong a current you can contend with. The currents coming out of the corner are very confused and disoriented. Not far downstream, however, the river gets itself back together, and the currents become predictable once again.

In low water conditions, there is one other problem you can always count on below fast turbulent rapids. In high water conditions, boulders are rolled along the bottom and dumped at the base of the rapids, where the river usually widens out, forming an apron of rubble stretching from shore-to-shore and curving downstream. It's called a rock garden and it creates a riffle that is difficult to get through in low water without hitting rocks. The deepwater channel, if there is one, is usually very hard to find. In low water, rock gardens usually make it necessary to get out and wade.

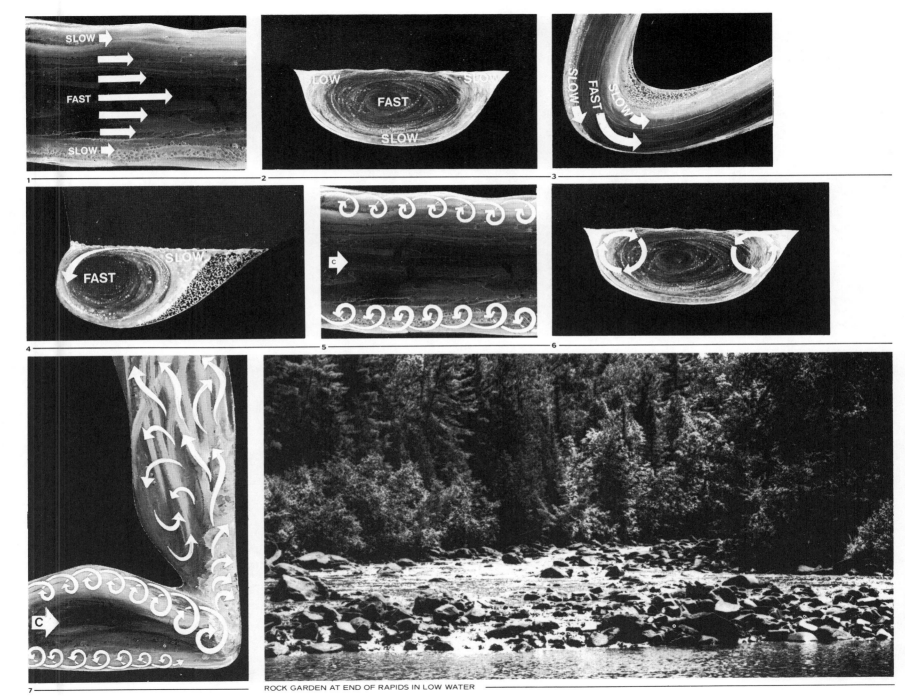

ROCK GARDEN AT END OF RAPIDS IN LOW WATER

Backwater brace, Magnetawan River Canyon

Reading rapids

Rocks in current cause turbulence

The next thing one must know about rapids is how a rock located in swiftly flowing water can affect the surface. While the canoeist is concerned only with the surface of the water, it is important to understand what's going on along the bottom. Knowing where the rocks are, recognizing the deepwater channel, and putting your canoe exactly where you want it is what running rapids is all about.

Rock in still water

In deep, quiet, or slow-moving water, the surface tells you nothing about the bottom of the river. Even a rock that is only a couple of inches under the surface gives no sign of its presence unless the water is clear. But river water is often dark or reflections make it difficult to see beneath the surface. As a result, it's quite common to run aground in the slow water above and below a rapids.

Rock in slow current

As the speed of the river increases, the rocks near the surface cause disturbances just downstream, usually in the form of a wave curling upstream. The wave isn't much of a problem, but the rock in front of it sure is.

Rock in deeper, faster current

An increase in the depth of the water and the speed of the current causes a corresponding increase in the size of the wave. If the rock is deep enough and the wave isn't too large, you can run right over the rock without hitting it.

Rock in deep, very fast current

With a further increase in water depth and velocity of current, the curling wave builds to the point where it can swamp the canoe. This wave must be avoided or taken off to the side.

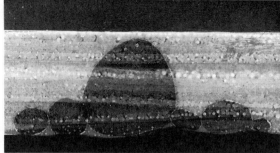
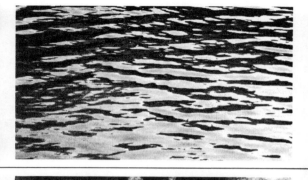

▶ROCK IN STILL WATER

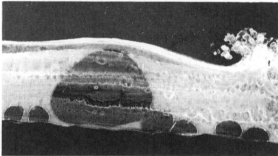

▶ROCK IN SLOW CURRENT

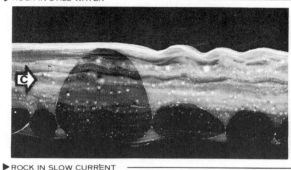

▶ROCK IN DEEPER, FASTER CURRENT

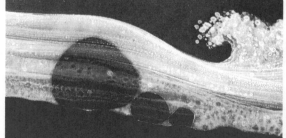

▶ROCK IN DEEP, VERY FAST CURRENT

Reading rapids...

Large rock in very fast, deep current causes a roller wave

In a rapid with a large volume of water and a sufficiently steep gradient, a big wide rock can cause a very large, wide-curling wave that falls back on itself. This wave is known as a roller. A canoe that turns and hits the wave sideways will roll for sure. If the drop-off over the rock is not too abrupt, the current will carry you downstream under the wave and free of it.

Hole (keeper)

One dangerous obstacle to watch out for is a hole. It can be caused by a large volume of water pouring abruptly or vertically over a large rock or ledge. The fast-moving water seems to scoop out a deep hole filled with foaming, aerated water that rolls back upstream. There is a tendency for the canoe or swimmer to be held in the hole. The foaming, aerated water has little buoyancy and will swamp the canoe or cause it to upset in the turbulence. The canoe must be powered out of the hole quickly. Large holes will engulf the canoe and must be avoided . If the boil line is any distance downstream from the face of the hole, the hole may be a keeper. It is known as a keeper because it will push a swamped canoe or swimmer back into the hole again and again. The swimmer can try to swim out the sides of the hole into the current or dive deep, catching a bottom current to escape the hole, but it's easier said than done. This is not a pleasant prospect for your average canoeist. Extraordinary presence of mind and training is required for self-rescue. It is also very difficult for anyone to render assistance to a canoeist caught in a hole or

keeper. Any rapids that have keepers that are difficult to avoid can be considered unsuitable for the traditional open canoe.

Diagonal curling wave

Another nasty thing that sometimes accompanies a hole is a diagonal curling wave which is often hard to avoid. In fact, in spring flood many rapids offer you the choice between a diagonal curling wave and a hole. In an open canoe it's often necessary to forego them both and take to the portage trail. A diagonal curling wave is created when a constriction in the river accompanies a sharp drop or ledge. The whole river funnels into one large V terminating in a hole. The sides of the V, which extend all the way from the shore to the hole, consist of a wave curling diagonally. Only a very strong brace into the wave as you shoot through it can keep you upright.

Eddies

In a rapid it's the rocks that cause all the problems and obviously are to be avoided. However, they aren't all bad. Hiding just downstream of the bigger rocks and rocks that protrude above the surface, you will find eddies of flatwater. Water can't flow through the rock, so it is forced to go around or over it. If the rock is sufficiently near the surface, very little water is going over it and a pool of relatively still water is created behind the rock. These areas of flatwater provide a haven in the midst of the worst of rapids — if you can get into them without hitting the rock or upsetting. The eddies are an escape route that can be used to avoid a dangerous area downstream or to rest and plan your next move.

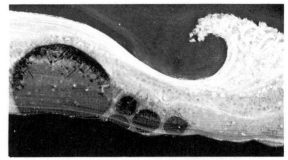

▶ LARGE ROCK IN VERY FAST, DEEP CURRENT CAUSES A ROLLER WAVE

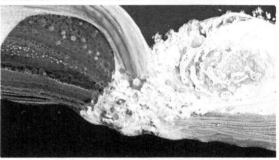

▶ SOUSE HOLE (KEEPER)

▶ DIAGONAL CURLING WAVE

▶ EDDIES

Reading rapids...

Downstream and upstream Vs
You want to look for the deep-water channel between the rocks. The water flowing between the rocks forms a dark V pointing downstream. If these dark Vs are clearly defined and aligned in such a way that you can follow them throughout the entire length of the rapid, the rapid can be considered easily runnable. A V that is pointing upstream is pointing directly at a rock. Whether or not you can see the rock beneath the surface, you can be sure it's there.

Haystacks or standing waves
Haystacks are usually found at the apex of the downstream Vs. They are a friendly deepwater wave caused by the fast water racing down the V and hitting the deep, slower-moving water. There is usually a series of these waves aligned downstream like a roller coaster. Haystacks are what make a rapid fun, but the larger ones have to be taken off to the side to avoid swamping. The canoeist must learn to tell the difference between a deepwater haystack and an upstream curling wave caused by a rock.

Haystack with rock in it
Although haystacks are a deepwater wave, they are not always to be trusted. A rock could be hiding there. If this is the case, it is very difficult to tell. It's one of the hardest things to read in a rapid. Sometimes you can actually catch a glimpse of the rock if you study the wave closely. Watch to see if there is any upstream curl to the haystack downstream of the suspicious wave. If the haystack is curling there is probably a rock hidden just upstream.

Rock in the path of a downstream V
If the rock is located right in the main path of a fast V after a sharp drop, the water can spray in all directions. You also will see a hump of water upstream of the turbulence. Remember that when water flows over a rock, the curling wave is located downstream of the rock. You will want to stay clear of this area. Hitting the rock will cause severe damage because of the speed of the current.

Undercut rocks
An undercut is narrower at the bottom than at the top, so water flows under its edges. The danger for a paddler who runs up against an undercut rock is that he can be flipped and pushed under the rock. The water will try to push the paddler out the other side and may succeed, unless debris trapped underneath the rock has formed a strainer that traps the swimmer. An undercut rock can be recognized by the lack of an upstream pillow, and sometimes water will be visible boiling up downstream of it.

Potholes
A pothole is an eroded depression in the rock. Sometimes the rock can be worn right through to create a tunnel. Even though the water flows through the tunnel the danger is that debris or a constriction in the tunnel can block a swimmer.

Boils
A boil is an upheaval of water, usually after the river has passed through a constriction. The water wells up in the center, then flows off the edge of the boil. Cross a boil line aggressively perpendicular to its near side and maintain momentum as you do so. If your canoe turns sideways on the edge of the boil, you will be side surfing the opposing currents — a very tippy situation indeed.

Whirlpools
Most small whirlpools form and then die out. If the whirlpool is constant, stay away!

When approaching the smaller variety of whirlpool, slow the canoe down and brace until the whirlpool dies out. If one forms behind you, pour on the power and paddle away from it.

▶DOWNSTREAM AND UPSTREAM VS

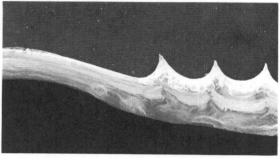
▶HAYSTACKS

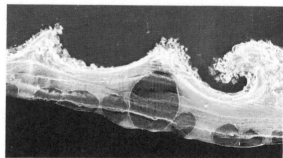
▶HAYSTACK WITH ROCK IN IT

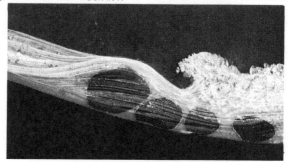
▶ROCK IN THE PATH OF A DOWNSTREAM V

Reading rapids...

Fast-water narrows, haystacks

The easiest form of rapids is found where a narrowing in the river causes an increase in the speed of the current. Haystacks usually result as the water surges through the gap.

Fast water with a few rocks

In a rapid with a few rocks, the upstream Vs indicate the presence of the rocks, making them easy to see and to avoid.

Fast water with many rocks but clearly defined downstream Vs

Despite the presence of many upstream Vs, the downstream Vs are clearly discernable and are aligned in such a way that they can be easily followed. The haystacks at the end of each downstream V are of moderate size and will not swamp the canoe.

Fast water with unaligned Vs

In a rapid where the downstream Vs are unaligned, it becomes necessary to employ the back ferrying and eddy turn maneuvers in order to follow the Vs. Without holes and drop-offs, the price of error is not too great. A mistake can usually be rectified by jumping out of the canoe onto the rock or into the shallow water to get the canoe off the rock.

Man-made obstructions

Be very suspicious of any man-made obstructions or alterations in the riverbed. Blasting fragments the rocks into dangerous sharp-edged angular chunks. The rocks in a normal riverbed tend to be somewhat rounded. Old log chutes and dams often have spikes sticking out. Artificial abutments and drop-offs can create recirculating hydraulics. I find it hard to accurately appraise the dangers of such places with any degree of confidence.

As a general rule, if it's a man-made obstruction portage around it.

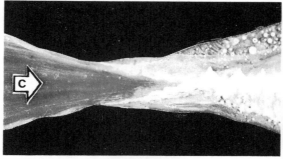

▶FAST-WATER NARROWS, HAYSTACKS

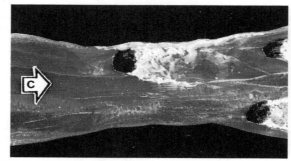

▶FAST WATER WITH A FEW ROCKS

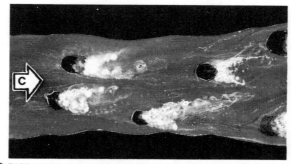

▶FAST WATER WITH MANY ROCKS BUT CLEARLY DEFINED DOWNSTREAM VS

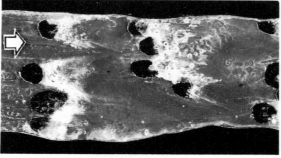

▶FAST WATER WITH UNALIGNED VS

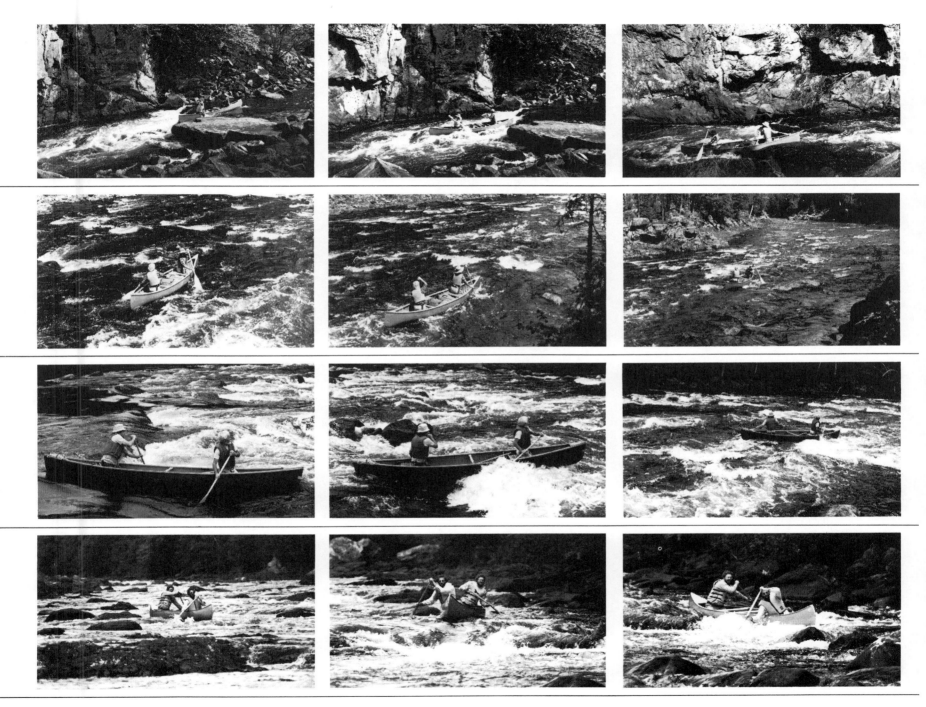

Reading rapids . . .

Rapids with unaligned Vs, ledges, and holes

Holes and ledges render rapids a lot more difficult because failure to avoid them can send you swimming. Whether or not the rapid should be attempted depends on many factors. Can the obstacles be avoided with your present skill level? Do the ledges have a clearly defined V? The most important factor is the length of the rapids. What would be the price of an upset? Would an upset mean a long, dangerous swim through holes and over ledges? A long rapid with the difficult stuff at the top is much more dangerous than a long rapid with the difficult stuff at the end. If you wipe out in the dangerous stuff at the end of a rapid, you would very quickly be carried into the deep quiet water to safety.

Another factor that determines the danger factor of rapids is the distance between rapids. Is there sufficient distance between rapids to recover the canoe before being swept into the next rapids? You just can't appraise the difficulty of a rapid by looking at it. What lies downstream should have a lot to do with your decision.

A ledge in low water

Ledges sometimes extend all the way across a river. They can be a dangerous hazard if the drop is abrupt because of the roller or hole at the base. The hazards are similar to those encountered in a narrow hole but worse because of the width, making it difficult or impossible to avoid them. If there is no break in the ledge, which would be indicated by a downstream V, it is not runnable. Even a drop of only one or two feet (30 to 60 cm) can cause enough of a backwash to entrap the canoe. Throw a log into the water parallel with the ledge and watch it roll over and over in the backwash.

A ledge in high water

In high water the ledge can become drowned out, but the huge curling wave downstream of the ledge becomes a menace. If the open canoe is powered through the wave, it will dive deep and swamp. If the ledge is taken slowly, the canoe will back surf on the wave and swamp.

The secret to getting through a manageable roller or keeper wave in an open canoe is to drift with the current into the abyss in front of the roller. Then just as your bow enters the wave, pour on the coal and get the canoe up and over that wave as fast as you can. As you penetrate the wave, water pours in over your bow and all along the length of your canoe. If you sit there in the wave too long, you will sink for sure. The current tries to push you through the wave, but remember you are climbing uphill out of the hole in front of the wave. If current equals gravity, then you will just sit there until the canoe sinks. On the other hand, if you attempt to power through it, you will submarine into the wave. You must learn to estimate just how big a wave you can or cannot break through.

Ledge with a V

A ledge becomes easily runnable if there is a clearly defined V anywhere along its length. The main problem is locating the V as you approach from upstream. You must trust your weight out on the paddle in a high brace for stability as you go off the lip and drop into the haystack.

If you look at the photographs in this book, you will notice that when running rapids the paddle is always in the water in a brace position or ready to go into a brace. You won't find any shots of the paddle waving uselessly around in the air.

▶RAPIDS WITH UNALIGNED VS, DROP-OFFS, AND SOUSE HOLES

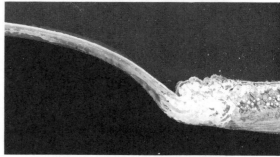

▶A LEDGE IN LOW WATER

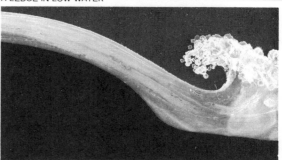

▶A LEDGE IN HIGH WATER

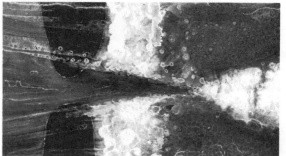

▶LEDGE WITH A V

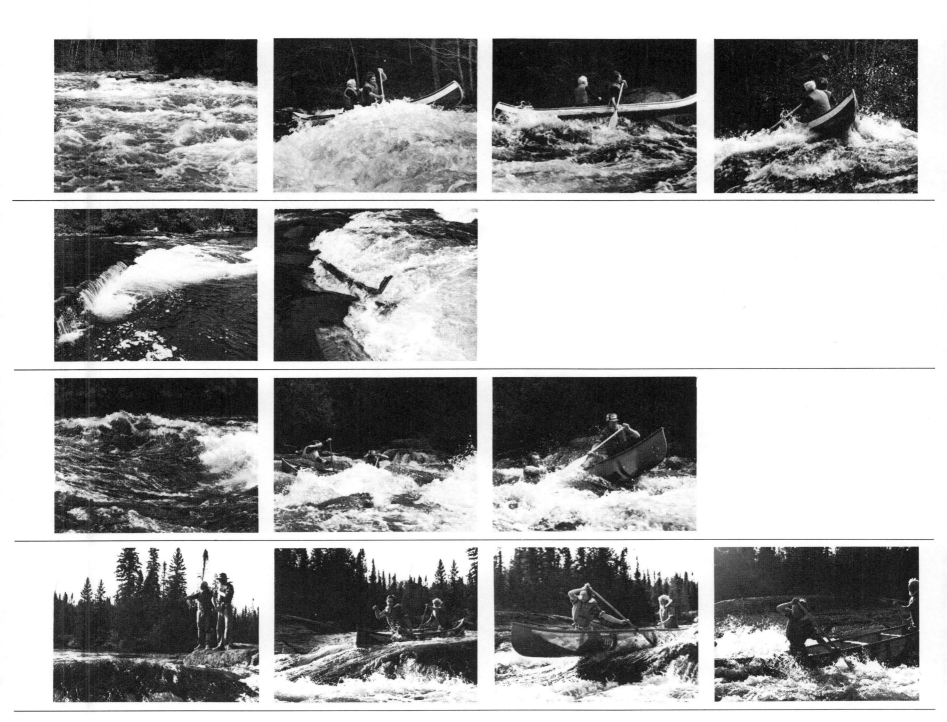

Petawawa River

Dangers of running rapids under power

Years ago, when I first began to run rapids, I had no one to teach me how, and I was not aware of any good books on the subject apart from references to running rapids in books about the voyageurs. I instinctively developed a technique of backpaddling down the rapids to give me time to make the necessary corrections in course. I was doing quite well when I discovered that any references to running rapids talked about running rapids under power to maintain steerage. If you didn't paddle faster than the current, you wouldn't be able to steer around the rocks. In my desire to run rapids correctly, like the voyageurs and Indians, I decided to give it a try.

I chose a particularly tricky rapid, half way down the Whiteshell River in Manitoba, that I had run successfully on four occasions. It had one particularly nasty rock right smack in the middle of the main surge of the current. It was necessary to bear left soon after entering the rapid to avoid the rock. I lined up well above the rapid and poured on the coal. I hit the brink at about 5 mph (8 km/h), shot through the V and accelerated to about 10 mph (16 km/h) on the 5 mph current. The rock came at me out of nowhere, and before I could even begin my sweep stroke to power around it, I smashed into it head on. The canoe swung broadside to the rock and caved in. I rolled out of the canoe and was swept downstream. The canoe didn't fold around the rock but swung free and drifted down after me. I was downstream from the canoe and it looked very much like it was coming after me. Drifting broadside to the current with 16 feet (5 m) of length, it managed to hit most of the rocks near the surface that were in its path. Much to my surprise, I didn't hit anything. I flowed around and over the rocks with the water. I kept looking back and could see pieces of the canoe breaking loose. A gunwale rolled up above me, revealing that there was little of it left. I could hear the crunching of the splintering

wood against the rocks. Each time the canoe came in contact with a rock it was slowed down a little, so it never did catch up to me. When I recovered it at the foot of the rapid, I pushed it ashore and found that it was torn three-quarters of the way around in two places: the thwarts were gone and the gunwales were pulverized. It was then that I gained some idea of the power of flowing water.

In retrospect, I realize that this was the closest I ever came to getting killed. I gave what was left of the canoe a decent burial and walked the ten miles (16 km) out to the road. So much for steerage or powering

through rapids! I went back to descending rapids slowly and developing skills in side-slipping back and forth across the current with a strong backwater or backpaddling. It wasn't until many years later that books appearing on the market began describing the art of running rapids with a heavy backwater. I realized then that what they referred to as back ferrying was what I was doing. Running rapids under power can be a lot of fun but it is more suited to playboating and whitewater racing. Back ferrying is an essential maneuver for a heavily loaded canoe in wilderness rapid running.

Swim time on the Gatineau River, Quebec ————————————————

A deceased laminated wood canoe ————————————————

International Scale of River Difficulty (from The American Whitewater Affiliation)

In order to provide some kind of guideline for canoeists using the well-traveled canoe routes, a grading system has been worked out and accepted by all accredited and reputable canoeing organizations. However, everyone using the system agrees that, at best, it is only a guideline. The most reliable method of assessing a river's difficulty beforehand is to compare it with a river that both you and the person supplying the description have paddled at similar water levels. This sets a benchmark from which you can tell whether that person generally rates rapids easier or harder than you do. Rapids vary in degree of difficulty with changes in water levels. Some rapids that are very difficult in medium water conditions disappear altogether in high water. In other cases, rapids that are very easy in low water can become very dangerous in high water. On the Petawawa River in Algonquin Park, Ontario, a man drowned in a rapid in high water conditions that is nothing but a mere ripple in low and medium water conditions.

The grading guide is nevertheless a great help when planning a trip on an unfamiliar river. Keep in mind that the classifying of a rapid is usually done in average flow conditions, so you must learn to compensate for high or low water levels when making your own judgment. The ideal guide would include classification of rapids in low and high water conditions as well as average flow conditions.

Class 1: Easy
- Few or no obstructions — all obvious and easily missed.
- Fast-moving water with riffles and small waves.
- Risk to swimmers is slight.
- Self-rescue is easy.

Class 2: Novice
- Straightforward rapids with wide, clear channels that are obvious without scouting.
- Occasional maneuvering may be required, but rocks and medium-sized waves are missed easily by trained paddlers.
- Swimmers are seldom injured and group assistance, while helpful, is seldom needed.

Class 3: Intermediate
- Rapids with moderate, irregular waves that may be difficult to avoid and are capable of swamping an open canoe.
- Complex maneuvers in fast current and narrow passages requiring good boat control frequently exist.
- Large waves, holes, and strainers may be present, but are easily avoided.
- Strong eddies and powerful current effects can be found, particularly on large-volume rivers.
- Scouting is advisable for inexperienced parties.
- Chances of injury while swimming are low, but group assistance may be required to avoid long swims.

Class 4: Advanced
- Intense, powerful rapids requiring precise boat handling in turbulent water.
- Depending upon the character of the river, there may be long unavoidable waves and holes or constricted passages demanding fast maneuvers under pressure.
- A fast, reliable eddy turn may be needed to negotiate the drop, scout rapids, or rest.
- Rapids may require "must" moves above dangerous hazards.
- Scouting is necessary the first time.
- Risk of injury to swimmers is moderate to high, and water conditions may make rescue difficult.
- Group assistance is often essential, but requires practiced skills.
- A strong Eskimo roll is highly recommended.

Class 5: Expert
- Extremely long, obstructed, or violent rapids that expose the paddler to above-average risk of injury.
- Drops may contain very large, unavoidable waves and holes or steep, congested chutes with complex, demanding routes.
- Rapids often continue for long distances between pools or eddies, demanding a high level of fitness.
- What eddies exist may be small, turbulent, or difficult to reach.
- Several of these factors may be combined at the high end of this class.
- Scouting is mandatory.
- Rescue is extremely difficult, even for experts.
- A very reliable Eskimo roll and above-average rescue skill are essential.

Class 6: Almost impossible
- Difficulties of Class 5 are carried to the limits of navigability.
- Nearly impossible and very dangerous.
- Risks are high and rescue may be impossible.
- For teams of experts only, at favorable water levels, after close study, and with all precautions.
- The frequency with which a rapid is run should have no effect on this rating, as there are a number of Class 6 rapids that are regularly attempted.

CLASS 1: EASY

CLASS 2: MEDIUM TO DIFFICULT

CLASS 3: DIFFICULT

CLASS 4: VERY DIFFICULT

CLASS 5: EXCEEDINGLY DIFFICULT

CLASS 6: DIFFICULTY EXTREME

7 WHITEWATER MANEUVERS

Up to now, everything in this book can be self-taught. However, a good instructor or learning in a group could speed things up considerably and make the learning process more fun. The price of error at this point should cost you only a dunking or two, if you are learning under the proper conditions.

As you begin to apply your skills in rapids, the price of error is much greater. It is possible to learn on your own as I did, but it's a lot safer and the learning process is much more enjoyable when you learn as a group with a competent instructor. When you begin to run rapids you will certainly make mistakes. Having help on hand will assure that you survive to try again.

Most whitewater courses don't cover the many subtleties and details that you will find in this book. You will begin to appreciate many of these subtleties only after you have taken a basic canoeing course.

When you find things going wrong, a closer study of the various chapters might help you to correct the problems. Personal instruction and this book are meant to complement each other.

For those of you who have read the book so far but have no interest in running rapids, your efforts have not been wasted. Improving your basic skills can greatly enhance your canoeing enjoyment. I know many people who have enjoyed canoeing for

Wide kneel with solid brace

High brace

Low brace

many years and do not run rapids. There are many wilderness rivers that still can be enjoyed.

For those of you who do choose to tangle with whitewater, these maneuvers are your arsenal of tricks. They will enable you to run rapids under complete control. These maneuvers remove the element of luck and replace it with skill, which is not only safer but much more fun.

Bow pry, eddy turn

Powering through haystacks, paddling amidships

Back ferry

Eddy turns

An eddy is something you start looking for when you are firing down a rapid and see trouble ahead. The eddy turn is one of the most essential maneuvers in running rapids. In fact, even if you have no intention of running rapids and portage instead, the eddy turn is a must for escaping from the current and pulling into shore safely. There are probably more people killed by being swept into rapids unintentionally than by running rapids by choice.

A protusion sticking out from shore will always have an eddy of still water behind it. If you are in the middle of a river, watch for a medium-to-large rock protruding above the surface, or very near the surface, with no more than a thin layer of water washing over it. Behind the rock (downstream) you'll find that eddy, a haven in time of need. From upstream a covered rock will appear as a hard, straight line with swirling eddies beyond. If the hard line is followed by a large curling wave, forget it. Pass that one by and keep looking.

Because the river current is going downstream and the eddy is flowing in the opposite direction, the canoe will abruptly turn when the bow enters the eddy and the stern is still in the fast-flowing mainstream. The currents will pivot the canoe without any help from you. Your job is to stay upright and assist with appropriate strokes. It is this basic principle that makes eddy turns so exciting and useful.

Components of an eddy turn
The three main ingredients for a successful eddy turn are angle, motion, and tilt. Angle refers to the direction the canoe is pointing relative to the eddy line that is being approached. A general rule of thumb is the smaller the eddy being approached, the wider the angle. Once the angle has been set with pivot strokes, motion is applied with efficient forward strokes. This motion will carry the canoe across the eddy line. As the

bow crosses the eddy line the canoe is tilted into the turn as if you were riding a bicycle. This tilt will thwart the attempts of the upstream eddy current to grab the side of the canoe and tip you. How you vary the quantities of angle, motion, and tilt will dictate the speed of your eddy turn.

Eddy turn to bow paddler's side
Both paddlers set the angle of the canoe and paddle forward toward the top of the eddy (photograph 1). As the bow crosses the eddy line tilt the canoe so its bottom is presented to the oncoming current of the eddy (photograph 2). The bow paddler does a draw as the bow crosses the eddy line. The stern paddler keeps the forward momentum going while assisting the turning action with several sweep strokes. Because the bow paddler has planted his paddle securely in the eddy, he will only have to hold it there throughout the turn (photograph 3). You both finish the turn off with forward strokes in order to keep the canoe high in the eddy (photograph 4). If you fail to get the canoe into the eddy, you will end up running the rapids backward.

Eddy exit to bow paddler's side
Having determined your next move from the safety of the eddy, you now are ready to re-enter the current. To do an eddy exit, the same three components are needed: angle, motion, and tilt. Both paddlers do a draw stroke (photograph 5) to set the angle of the canoe to the eddy line, approximately 45 degrees. Both paddlers then take a couple of powerful forward strokes to drive the canoe across the eddy line (photograph 6). As the bow crosses the eddy line, the bow paddler reaches out to plant a solid draw stroke, 90 degrees to the downstream current, while the stern paddler does a sweep stroke; remember, the emphasis is on helping the boat to tilt downstream (photograph 7). By changing the pitch of the pad-

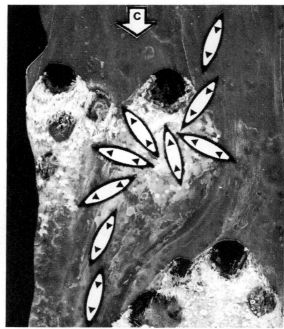

EDDY TURN INTO AND OUT OF EDDY

dle blade, the bow paddler keeps his blade 90 degrees to the current and uses its force to pull the bow around. This means he can keep a stable tilt on the canoe throughout the turn and finish off with a forward stroke (photograph 8). The stern paddler's sweep stroke helps maintain the tilt until the canoe is facing completely downstream.

▶EDDY TURN TO BOW PADDLER'S SIDE

EDDY TURN TO BOW PADDLER'S SIDE

▶EDDY EXIT TO BOW PADDLER'S SIDE

EDDY EXIT TO BOW PADDLER'S SIDE

Eddy turns...

Crossdraw eddy turn (turning to the bow paddler's offside)

The crossdraw eddy turn allows you to do a reasonably stable turn to the bow person's offside without changing paddling sides. The same components of an eddy turn apply: angle, motion, and tilt. Both of you set the angle of the canoe to the eddy line, well upstream of the eddy. Because you have set the angle well ahead of time, forward motion can be applied as soon as it is needed. This makes it easier to hit the eddy line right behind the rock, where the difference in the opposing currents is the strongest. The bow paddler does a crossdraw, reaching into the eddy and placing the paddle blade 90 degrees to the current of the eddy for maximum effect. In the stern you lean out on a backsweep, which will help to pivot the canoe while allowing you to tilt the canoe with a solid brace (photograph 1A). Notice how the bow paddler rotates his upper torso to face the stroke for maximum power (photograph 1B). Stern paddlers should be aware that it is possible to tilt too far, causing your bow paddler to fall out. As you finish your backsweep and the bow paddler finishes his crossdraw you will both be ready to do a forward stroke. Your bow paddler can finish with a couple of offside foward strokes or go back to his paddling side and do regular forward strokes to keep the canoe high in the eddy (photograph 1C).

Pry eddy turn (turning to the bow paddler's offside)

The pry eddy turn is a very effective way to make an eddy turn. However, it is more difficult than using a crossdraw, and riskier, because of the chance of catching the paddle on a rock while prying. The same components are required as in any eddy turn: angle, motion, and tilt. Set your angle of approach to the eddy. In this case, given the speed of the current and the size of the eddy the angle is approximately 45 degrees to the eddy line; a smaller eddy would require a greater angle. Both paddlers apply forward motion. In the stern a pry stroke will turn into a backsweep as the bow crosses the eddy line (photograph 2A). It is very important that you initiate the tilt before the bow paddler does the pry (photograph 2B). As you finish your backsweep your paddle is in position to do a hard forward stroke. Your bow paddler also finishes off with a forward stroke to keep the canoe high in the eddy (photograph 2C). A pry eddy turn is a difficult maneuver to accomplish in whitewater and must be done well. You can't pussyfoot around or you will miss the eddy. You have to go for it with full power and jam that paddle in at the bow. Although a crossdraw eddy turn is the more cautious method, you won't know what you are missing until you try the pry eddy turn.

Pry eddy exit (to the bow paddler's offside)

The pry eddy exit requires the same components and strokes of an eddy entry: angle, motion, tilt. Set your angle, approximately 45 degrees to the eddy line. Paddling forward toward the eddy line, tilt downstream as you do a backsweep and your bow paddler does a pry as the bow enters the downstream current. The bow pry eddy turn or exit has a very quick turning action, so get into your backsweep before the bow paddler begins his pry stroke. If you don't, it's swim time for sure. Be certain to practice where the price of an error isn't too high.

What can go wrong in an eddy exit

If you are the stern and you paddle too hard, you can drive the canoe out into the current before the turn is completed. You will then be traveling down the river broadside, a very precarious position to be in, even for an instant. If on the other hand, no effort is made to get the canoe out into the current, the bow will swing around and you'll end up still sitting in the eddy, facing downstream.

How not to do an eddy turn and exit

To illustrate the importance of timing when entering or leaving an eddy, I would like to refer to a situation where a sense of timing — as well as an understanding of how to utilize the force of the currents — was completely lacking. The instructors, who were a little heavy on enthusiasm and a bit light on technique, were demonstrating how to exit from an eddy from the facing upstream position. They paddled hard out into the current and left the eddy completely before beginning the turn around. Because of the speed of the canoe, the sidewash on the angled canoe drove them very quickly across the river while they were attempting to swing the canoe around to face downstream. The sheer brute strength of the bow paddler's draw brought the canoe around just before they were about to hit the far shore. The second canoe, following the example of the instructors, powered out into the current at an angle. The sidewash of the current on the side of the angled canoe drove them all the way across the river and straight into the rock face on the far shore. They stopped dead, of course, and the current swung the stern downstream so they were facing upstream. Now they were in the same position as when they started, but on the opposite shore. They had executed an upstream ferry. The instructors berated the bow paddler for not drawing hard enough. The rest of the canoeists fared little better. The harder they worked at it, the harder they hit the far shore. Their mistake was leaving the eddy before the current had swung the bow around downstream.

CROSSDRAW EDDY TURN TO THE BOW'S OFFSIDE

PRY EDDY TURN TO THE BOW'S OFFSIDE

PRY EDDY EXIT TO THE BOW'S OFFSIDE

PRY EDDY EXIT TO THE BOW'S OFFSIDE

Ferrying across the current

The back ferry enables you to move back and forth across the current without exposing the side of your canoe to the rocks or waves.

Trimming your canoe level (bow and stern riding at the same depth) is absolutely basic for doing a controlled ferry. If you have trouble doing a ferry, chances are your upstream end is riding too deep.

Failure to understand this basic principle can cause a lot of problems, especially among students. This was very evident recently as I stood on a bridge above a nice little set of rapids, watching the same instructors I mentioned earlier attempt to teach ferrying. Because the strongest and heaviest paddlers, usually males, seem to gravitate to the stern end, the front ferries were working okay, but the back ferrying was a disaster. As each canoe left the eddy to begin the back ferry, the stern swung around despite the efforts of the stern paddler to hold it upstream. A few canoes managed to blunder across the river broadside to the current. The instructors were yelling instructions to paddle harder and to hold the angle, but all to no avail. They had no idea what was going wrong. When they demonstrated the back ferry, they managed to blunder across half broadside but with no control whatsoever. In a controlled ferry the canoeists should be able to enter the current and make the ferry as fast or as slowly as desired. They should be able to stop and hold halfway and come back again. The instructors were swept across the current to the other side and would have been powerless to change the angle on the canoe to come back. In most of the whitewater maneuvers, if brute strength is required, then you are probably doing something wrong. It's all a matter of understanding the river and how to work with it, thus utilizing its power.

To pull this back ferry maneuver off properly, the canoe must be moving much slower than the current to buy time to get the canoe over. Vigorous backpaddling must be combined with the correction strokes as required. When done properly the canoe can be held stationary relative to the shore while the ferry is being made, if the current isn't too strong. Some people refer to back ferrying as setting because the canoe is set over, across the current.

To appreciate the use of the ferry, let's assume that we've just completed an eddy turn (eddied out) by the river-right shore. We've landed, looked the rapid over from the bank, and have found that the deep water is way over along the river-left shore.

Back ferry

To get across the river to eddy A, on river left (illustration 1A), we need a ferry. Since it's a long way across and we have to cross without being carried downstream, we have decided to go for a front ferry. The same three components that we learned for an eddy turn also apply to a front ferry: angle, motion, and tilt. How much of each we use will determine whether we do an eddy exit or a successful front ferry. To front ferry we first sideslip over to the eddy line. Then we set a narrow angle relative to the downstream current (photograph 1B). With our angle set we paddle forward to obtain motion (photograph 1C). As the bow crosses the eddy line we tilt downstream. The tilt accomplishes three things. It places the canoe on its rounded side, which makes it easier to pivot, and therefore it will be easier to control the angle of the canoe. It also keeps the bow from catching the current and turning downstream. Third, the tilt presents the bottom of the canoe to the current, so we won't be tipped upstream. Note — we could be more generous with our tilt in these photos. It is easier to control the angle of a ferry from the downstream end of the canoe rather than trying to pull the upstream end against the current. So with this in mind, the bow paddler supplies the forward power while I control the angle with a stern pry or a draw. When the whole canoe is in the downstream current we can open the angle for a faster crossing (photograph 1D). The current pushing on the side of the canoe will propel us across the river. But with a wider angle we will also be pushed downstream faster and risk hitting rocks. A narrow angle means that our ferry across the river will be slower and more controlled, but we will be paddling against the current for a longer time, so it will also be more tiring. The bow paddler could do a diagonal draw to add a little sideslipping motion to the front ferry.

If the bow paddler were on the left side of the canoe and I were on the right, then I could use a draw or high brace to control the angle and the tilt of the canoe, making it a very stable side for me to be on. To increase the angle or make the canoe sideslip while ferrying, the bow paddler — if he were on the left — could do a bow J stroke. If we lost the angle we would both do a pair of pivot strokes to regain our ferry angle. If we have too much angle leaving the eddy the downstream current will force the canoe to turn downstream.

This time we have the right amount of angle, motion, and tilt, so we successfully front ferry out to the rock in midstream (illustration 1A). After having another look at the rapids from this midstream eddy, we agree that the river-left channel doesn't look all that great, so we decide to run it down the center. We can either eddy exit, turning into the current and ending up facing downstream, or we can turn around in the eddy and back ferry out to the center channel. We agree on the latter.

Turn around in eddy

To turn the canoe around in the eddy without leaving it, you stick the bow out into the current with a crossdraw. You also could have used a pry on your paddle side. I hold the stern in the eddy with a backsweep. The current swings the bow around downstream, and we end up still in the eddy facing downstream.

Back ferry (setting)

Before we enter the current and perform a back ferry into the center of the river, let's check our trim. Trim is the depth of the stern in relation to the bow. If we both weigh exactly the same, the stern will ride lower because, as I mentioned earlier, the stern seat is positioned closer to the stern than the bow seat is to the bow. This causes the stern to act like a rudder which the current will grab and swing downstream as soon as we attempt to backpaddle against the current. To prevent the canoe from swinging around when backpaddling, the canoeists must be extremely skilled in keeping the canoe perfectly aligned with the current, or the upstream end (the stern) must be lightened by sliding forward up against the stern thwart. If you are running loaded, you can move a pack forward. Even if the canoeists are very skilled, it still makes sense to level the canoe for ferrying.

I slide forward and kneel behind the stern thwart to lighten the stern. We will use the now familiar components angle, motion, and tilt as we did in the front ferry. First we sideslip the canoe until it is on the eddy line. Next we pivot the canoe so that we have a very narrow angle (photograph 2A). Then I backpaddle to create backward motion while the bow paddler does a draw as he tilts the canoe downstream. It is easier to pull an end of the canoe downstream with the current rather than push it back upstream, so the bow paddler is primarily responsible for the angle of the canoe during a back ferry. The bow paddler should start off with a draw stroke to make sure that the canoe does not get swept sideways (photograph 2B). Then, as soon as the canoe is in the current, the bow paddler uses a backdraw or crossdraw for major angle corrections and a backsweep or reverse J to help supply backward motion and correct minor angle problems. If the canoe turns completely broadside we will both do pivot strokes to re-align it with the current. Once we have recovered control, we will re-establish the correct angle so that the water pushing on the angled side of the canoe will move the canoe across the river as we backpaddle (photograph 2C). When the canoe reaches the clear channel we align it with the current, stop backpaddling, and head downstream (photograph 2D).

Varying your speed

When in the back ferry position, you are backpaddling, so you are descending at a rate slower than the current. If you decide to go for an eddy turn, you must suddenly accelerate toward the eddy and get your canoe traveling faster than the current in order to drive the bow into the eddy behind the rock. Otherwise, you will probably go right by it or catch the eddy too far downstream. Your accelerated speed also enables you to go into the low brace or high brace to stabilize the canoe. With your paddle planing on the water, your brace is very secure.

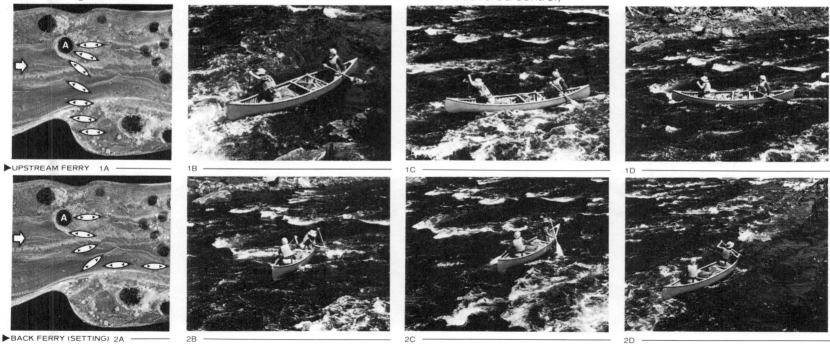

▶UPSTREAM FERRY 1A ————— 1B ——————————————————————————————— 1C ——————————————— 1D

▶BACK FERRY (SETTING) 2A ———— 2B ——————————————————————————————— 2C ——————————————— 2D

Use of the back ferry on the Dog River

The rapid illustrated here is on the Dog River, which flows from the north into Lake Superior. It's a typical example of a rapid that would be difficult, if not impossible, to run without the use of the back ferry. The rapid begins with a narrow constriction on the right side of the rapids (*see* position A). Assume you are facing downstream. Below the constriction there are some large haystacks (position B), followed by large rollers on the right, caused by large deep rocks (position C). Still on the right, the river breaks into many curling waves (position D). At the end of the rapids a rock garden extends from the right shore, well past the middle of the rapid (position E). The deep-water channel is on the extreme left (position F).

The canoe enters the constriction and easily makes it through the haystacks. By backpaddling vigorously and going into a back ferry to the left, the canoe doesn't quite miss the rollers but avoids being carried through the big waves. Continuing the back ferry, the sidewash assists in working the canoe over to the left, easily missing the really big stuff. Continuing the ferry, we easily line up with the deep water at the left of the rock garden and make it through with no problem.

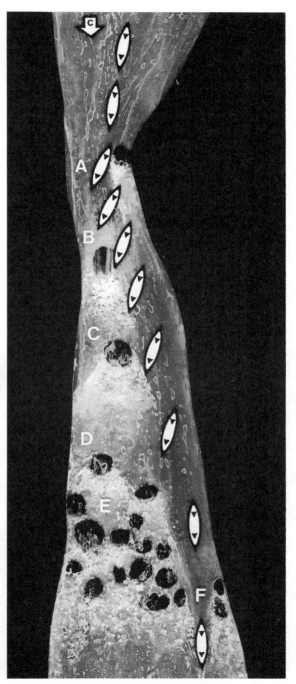

▶ BACK FERRY

BACK FERRY

86

Use of the back ferry to set into or out of an eddy

In shallow, rock-studded rapids, it is sometimes desirable to set into or out of an eddy by using the back ferry. It's called setting because the canoe is set over into the eddy. The advantage of setting compared to the eddy turn is that the canoe is always facing downstream in the desired direction of travel and is never turned broadside to the rocks. In fast, deep rapids however, setting is usually not effective enough to catch a difficult eddy.

Setting into the eddy
Let's say you are paddling bow on the left side and we decide to go for an eddy on the river right (photograph 1A). We agree that we should set over into the eddy rather than do the eddy turn. Despite the fact that we want to go right, you do a backdraw to put your bow to the left. This enables me to get my stern over toward the rock with a backdraw. Now, with the stern angled toward the rock and both of us vigorously backpaddling, our descent is slowed and the sidewash on the canoe pushes us across the current to the right. We time it so that the stern barely clears the rock, and as it does, we really pour the coal to the backpaddling. The stern enters the eddy first (photograph 1B), followed by the bow (photograph 1C). It's more difficult than it sounds. The tendency is to not backpaddle hard enough to catch the eddy. You then end up too far downstream.

Setting out of the eddy
To set the canoe over and out of the eddy, I ease my stern out into the current with a pry while you make sure to time your entry immediately after mine (photograph 2A). Otherwise there is a danger that my end will be grabbed by the current and swung around. If the bow enters the mainstream first, it will be pushed back into the eddy by the main current. The stern must enter first and be followed quickly by the bow (photograph 2B). The canoe is ferried out as far as desired before the downstream run begins (photograph 2C).

▶SETTING INTO THE EDDY   1A   1B   1C

▶SETTING OUT OF THE EDDY   2A   2B   2C

Running rapids at an angle

Now that you have a pretty good idea what rapid running is all about, it is time to modify the statement that the canoe should always be aligned with the current, except when ferrying or doing an eddy turn, to avoid broadsiding onto a rock.

I believed this implicitly until a few years ago when I noticed that Wally Schaber always angles his canoe when he is drifting at the speed of the current, anticipating his next move. This enables him to see past his bow paddler and plan his route well ahead. I believe he developed this technique because, being a commercial guide and outfitter, he almost always puts the least experienced paddler in his bow. He is also the lead canoe to show the route, so he has to see where he is going. By angling the canoe, he can see clearly what's coming up and go into a ferry to the left or right. I tried it and found it is a marvelous way to view the water ahead and plan the next move when I knew that my bow paddler was inexperienced at choosing the course. In fact I like it so much, I now use it at all times, even with a good bow paddler.

It works something like this. You are descending a rapid that requires a lot of maneuvering to follow the deep water channel. You are paddling on the right in the stern with a bow paddler who knows nothing about choosing the course. It is very difficult to see the water ahead. At best you catch glimpses of what's coming up. Your maneuvers are all last minute attempts at dodging the rocks and following the deep water channel. You decide to try letting the canoe drift at an angle.

You pry your stern to the left. Your bow paddler draws to straighten out the canoe, but you ask him or her to allow the canoe to drift at an angle. Now you can see right by the bow paddler for a full view of the rapids ahead.

Rocks are coming up fast and it doesn't look very good on the river right, but over on the river left there seems to be black water. You backpaddle and, because the canoe is already in the back ferry position, you glide across the current until you are above the black water. You stop backpaddling and drift downstream still at an angle. The way is clear of rocks for a while. Then you see rocks ahead again. It looks even worse on the left, but the right looks encouraging. However, you can't see way over on the right because the bow paddler is obstructing the view. You draw your stern over to the right and the bow paddler prys left.

The stern of the canoe is now angled to the right. Now you can see not only dead ahead but way over to the right as well. You see what looks like deep water and you backpaddle. So does your bow paddler. You are already in ferry position to the right. The canoe glides across the current to the right until you are above the deep-water channel.

It is a marvelous way to run rapids regardless of whether your bow is experienced or inexperienced at picking the route. If you see an eddy that you want to catch, you set your angle, accelerate to a speed faster than the current, drive the bow into the eddy, and execute the turn. By picking up speed, you are able to perform a stable brace with the paddle planing on the water. So it goes all the way down the rapids.

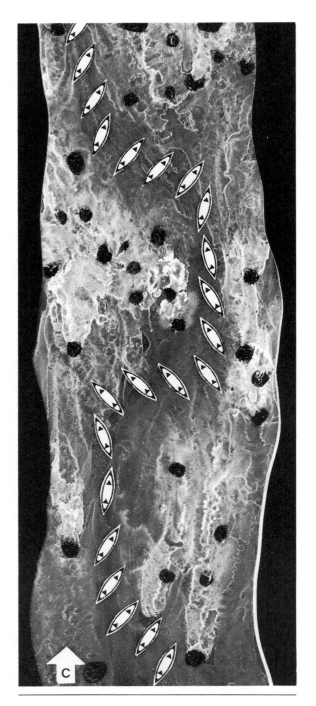

The S ferry

There is one other method of ferrying the canoe across the current. It's called the S ferry. It's a maneuver that is more commonly used in whitewater racing, but in certain situations it can be used with the open canoe.

Let's assume you are sitting in eddy A, facing upstream. You want to reach eddy B across a stretch of very fast water that is free of rocks. As you power out of eddy A (see photograph 1) with aggressive pad-

dling, the bow is pushed downstream slightly because it enters the current before the stern (photograph 2). You continue the fast pace broadside to the current (photograph 3) until you reach eddy B. As the bow of the canoe enters the still water of the eddy the stern, which is still in the current, is shoved downstream (photograph 4) until it too enters the eddy (photograph 5). If you look at the path of the canoe from eddy to eddy it would describe an S.

The danger of the S ferry is that while crossing the current you are broadside and therefore exposed to the rocks. For this reason, it is important to read the water carefully before attempting an S ferry. You must be confident that you will not be carried downstream onto rocks before completing the crossing. An upstream ferry is safer because you are not carried downstream and the canoe is not broadside.

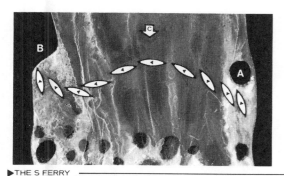

▶THE S FERRY

THE S FERRY

THE S FERRY

Whitewater maneuvers solo

Before dealing with some of the problems you may encounter when executing a back ferry, I would like to make a few comments about running rapids solo.

In some ways, paddling solo is easier than paddling double because you only have yourself to worry about. If there are any mistakes, you are the one who is going to make them. Another advantage of paddling solo is buoyancy; the lighter load takes in less water. Given the choice, I would rather run a dangerous rapid solo than with an unfamiliar partner. On the other hand, if I have complete confidence in the skill of my partner, then I *would* prefer to paddle double. Two paddlers have twice the power and control as well as the capacity of a simultaneous brace on both sides of the canoe.

When paddling solo you can only brace on one side at a time, so it's no sin to change sides before a difficult maneuver or to favor the high and low braces and draws over the prys and crossdraws. There is also no substitute for a powerful sweep stroke to power the canoe across the current into an eddy.

Back ferrying solo

Executing a back ferry solo is more difficult than doubles. Sitting in the shore eddy on river right, facing downstream (photograph 1), you find your way blocked by a rock garden. Over on river left a deep downstream V is clearly visible. Choosing a back ferry maneuver will allow you to cross the current while facing downstream, ready to continue downriver. Let's say you are paddling on the left, as in the photograph. First slide forward to unweight the stern so that it won't catch the current and spin your around. Sideslip over to the eddy line, then set a narrow angle and start to develop momentum with several strong reverse J strokes. As your stern crosses the eddy line tilt downstream and be prepared to throw in a backdraw, with the emphasis on the draw into the bow to correct too much angle (photograph 2). Now reapply reverse power with reverse J strokes as the current, pushing on the side and bottom of your canoe, helps you cross the river (photograph 3). If your angle is a little too wide, but not wide enough to warrant a backdraw, correct it with a backsweep. On the other hand, if your reverse J is not giving you enough angle you might need a crossdraw to perform the major correction. When the canoe is in the desired position (photograph 4) let up on your back ferry and head for the V. By utilizing the back ferry, you were able to get the canoe out into the middle of the current to avoid being carried into the rock garden just off the right shore. Broadside in the rock garden is where you would end up if you forgot to lighten the upstream end and were unable to hold the proper angle for the ferry. Be sure to perfect your maneuvers in rapids where there is nothing dangerous downstream, just in case you make a mistake.

1

2

3

4

▶BACK FERRYING SOLO

Eddy turns solo

Let's say you are descending a rapid while paddling on the left side. You see a rock coming up on river left and decide to go for the eddy behind it. Remember the three components of an eddy turn? Angle, motion, and tilt. Use a stern pry and bow draw to angle your canoe toward the eddy. Second, apply motion by paddling aggressively toward the eddy (photograph 1A). Passing the rock as closely as you dare, use a bow draw or a backsweep to tilt the canoe into the turn so that the upstream current of the eddy does not catch the side of the canoe and flip you. Create this tilt by pushing down on your inside knee. If your canoe is loaded with gear you will need to cheat by sliding your body over to help the tilt. Your paddle is there to help you maintain your balance as the eddy current completes the turn for you (photograph 1C). Ensure that you don't slide out of the eddy by finishing with a couple of powerful for-

ward strokes, then plan your next move (photograph 1D) from the safety of the eddy.

Eddy exit solo

To leave the eddy, use the three same components: angle, motion, and tilt. First do a pivot stroke to angle your canoe toward the current. Either a stern pry or bow draw would work in this case. Then paddle forward to apply motion (photograph 2A). Just as your bow crosses the eddy line, tilt downstream and do a backsweep, which will help to turn the canoe as well as provide a bracing action (photograph 2B). Once the canoe has turned downstream, finish your backsweep, which will lead nicely into a forward stroke to ensure that you do leave the eddy. Eddy turns are essential if you are

going to run rapids above Class 1. When making an eddy turn toward the offside, many canoeists prefer not to change paddle sides. If you choose to paddle on the right throughout this maneuver, power toward the eddy with a sweep and complete the turn with a crossdraw, finishing off with a forward stroke on the right to keep you in the eddy. Leaving the eddy would be similar. Set the angle, apply motion with a forward stroke or a sweep stroke, tilt as you do a crossdraw, then finish off with a forward stroke on your right side.

►EDDY TURN SOLO 1A   1B   1C   1D

►EDDY EXIT SOLO 2A   2B   2C   2D

Problems encountered in back ferrying

At the risk of boring my readers, I must again emphasize that the most common problem when back ferrying is riding too deep in the upstream end. I find I am rarely able to convince people they are riding too heavy in the stern. If they do make an effort to rectify the problem, the next time they load they again ignore the problem or forget it exists.

Recently we were reading a rapid with a huge rock right in the middle. From the right shore, we could see it split the rapid into two channels. The right channel looked good but the approach was from the center of the river. It was obvious that we would have to work hard in a back ferry to make the right channel without being carried into the rock. I couldn't see the left channel because of the huge rock, so I made the decision to take the right channel. We did a back ferry and made the right channel with no problem (diagram 1). The other canoe, which was riding low in the stern, failed to get into the back ferry position; instead, it was carried sideways toward the rock (diagram 2). The paddlers elected to power across the current toward the right channel. They outmuscled the current, missing the big rock by inches, and finished the maneuver with a spectacular crossbow draw that kept the stern from hitting the rock. They made a great recovery from a bad situation and then teasingly berated me for choosing the right channel instead of the left. They claimed the natural flow of the river was to the left. I'm not sure I convinced them that the problem was not in choosing the wrong channel but in loading too heavy in the stern, making the back ferry very difficult to execute properly. If the stern paddler is heavier than the bow paddler, the whole load should be positioned right behind the bow paddler. In some cases, the stern paddler still has to move forward onto the knees to get the stern up. This is particularly the case when running without a load.

It's tough to be a keel
The keel, if the canoe has one, takes a lot of blame for a bad ferry. "Yeah, it was the keel that did it. The current grabbed the keel and swung us around so we couldn't control it." If you have a keel, then it is all the more important to unweight the stern for a back ferry. Though it really is more difficult to pull the stern over against the current with a keel, once you are in the back ferry position, the keel actually assists in the ferry, since the sidewash on the canoe is increased because of it. Personally, I prefer a canoe without a keel, but don't blame the keel if you can't make a ferry.

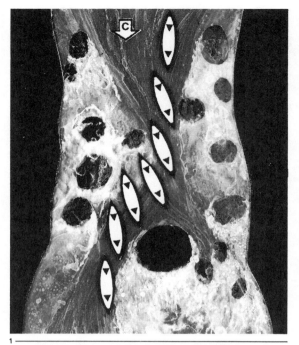

1

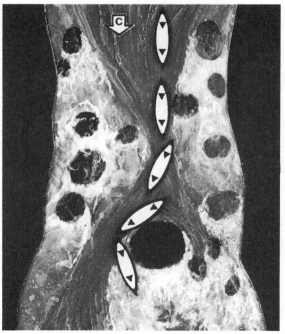

2

Landing in a current: a matter of life and death

During the filming of my canoe film series, *Path of the Paddle*, we had one particularly harrowing trip on a river in full flood in the spring. It was the Petawawa River, which rises in the northern section of Algonquin Park and flows southeast into the Ottawa River. Normally it is a river used by a moderate number of people. But on this holiday weekend, people descended on the river in numbers I wouldn't have dreamed possible a few years ago. They came in all kinds of canoes, most of which were unfit even for taking a bath. As whitewater canoes, they were devoid of any redeeming qualities whatsoever.

We had just set up to begin filming beside a very turbulent rapid when we looked upstream to see a horde of canoes descending upon the landing place above the rapids. As the first canoe approached we knew immediately by its angle that it was going to be an interesting sight. The bow hit shore first, and before the bow paddler could jump out and grab shore, the current swung the stern out into the current. The stern took his paddle out of the water and grabbed for the gunwales as the bow dove in desperation for the shore. He made it and hung on as the canoe swung around and into shore. They had made it with considerable luck. The next canoe bore down on the first canoe, which already was occupying the only good spot to land. The second canoe shot past and hit the shore just downstream, executing the same hair-raising landing. A couple of other canoes had landed above the first two canoes, where there was more room for error. The fifth canoe hit right below us, bow first. As the stern swung out into the current, the stern paddler lost his balance and upset the canoe which dumped him and his wife into the icy cold water. We raced to the water's edge to grab them but almost instantly they were swept into the

main stream. Three-quarters of the way down the rapids, they were swept into a whirlpool by the shore. It was not a dangerous whirlpool (not the kind that can suck you under), but they were unable to get to shore. They were obviously succumbing to the cold water as my cameraman, Ken Buck, and I reached the rock just above them. Since I was in a wet suit, it was no hardship to jump in and swim to them with a rope. By the time Ken pulled them out of the whirlpool and in to shore, they were in pretty bad shape from the cold water.

This was the first of five canoes that we helped that weekend, and we later heard that there were many more that had close calls. Ken rescued the same canoeists just mentioned once again with his canoe the following day, and we heard they upset yet again before they finally made it to a bridge and gave up. By asking around, we found that three-quarters of the wipeouts were caused by an inability to execute a safe landing. But the most tragic one occurred on our second last day.

We were camping just below a set of rapids and had just got the fire going. As I was scooping a pail of water from the river I looked up and saw a bright orange object at the base of the rapids. I groaned aloud and said to Ken "There's a packsack out there that some poor guy's lost. I better go and get it before it sinks." As I neared the object, my heart nearly stopped. The orange packsack took on the shape of a life jacket and the purple shape within it became a man's face. For a split second, all the energy drained out of me. I yelled to Ken to come quickly in the other canoe and for Paul to stoke up the fire and get the sleeping bags ready. Another canoeist was already on the way and reached the man soon after I did. Because of the icy water, we first attempted to get the man into the canoe. My canoe swamped in the attempt just as Ken arrived and began mouth-to-mouth resuscitation.

The three of us got him into the other canoe and paddled to shore as fast as we could. Ken kept up the mouth-to-mouth as we carried him from the canoe and covered him with sleeping bags. Despite many hours of concerted effort, he did not recover. We can only conclude that it was the cold water that killed him. His partner arrived on the scene not long after we got him to shore and, despite his obvious state of shock, joined in our efforts to revive him.

Later that night, with the body lying beside a tree in a sleeping bag, his friend told of their efforts to land above the rapids. The bow had hit shore first. The bow jumped out but as the stern swung away from shore, the stern paddler fell out and was swept through the rapids.

Running rapids is a calculated risk. There will always be an element of danger when people venture down rivers and through rapids. Despite the risks there is something in us that makes us want to do it. Skill and knowledge are two of the things that can cut the risks considerably or even bring them into the range of acceptablity. Well-designed canoes, good life jackets, and cold-water wet suits can cut risks still further. But it is not possible to completely eliminate all risks, and even if the element of danger could be completely eliminated, there is a question whether very many of us would really want it that way.

Landing in a current...

The greatest tragedy is people dying in a rapid or falls they had no intention of running, all for the want of a little knowledge and skill. When we asked some paddlers how they came to be on the Petawawa River when it was at such a dangerously high flood level, they replied that they had sought advice and were told that it was okay as long as they were careful! No piece of advice could be more useless than that. If you don't know how to land above a rapid in a swift current, no amount of caution is going to help. The man and his wife who were pulled from the river three times had no intention of running any rapids and couldn't have been more cautious. It was their skill that was lacking, not their caution. You have to be careful where you go for advice.

One of the main purposes of my films and this book is to give paddlers some kind of yardstick against which to measure their capabilities. If the readers do not know how to paddle a straight course, do a pivot turn, a sideslip and a safe landing, they are not ready to venture on to a river with dangerous rapids in high water conditions. If the readers do not know how to do an eddy turn or a ferry across the current, they are not ready to run rapids more difficult than Class 1. If these skills are not refined, certainly these canoeists should not be given the responsibility of leading a group of children on a canoe trip with rapids along the route.

In one of my canoe films, *Solo White-water*, there is a shot of an extremely wild, dangerous set of rapids with a long rock-studded approach. In the approach, the river gradually picks up speed as it narrows and races around a tight bend, where it drops off into a cauldron of foaming white-water. The foaming water is so full of air that a canoe wouldn't stay afloat even if it were possible to remain upright.

As we were portaging, Ken struck up a conversation with a fellow who told him that the last time he came down the river, he barely made it to shore before the drop-off into the rapids. Four canoes of kids that he was guiding shot by and into the rapids. The canoes capsized but somehow all the kids survived the swim. The thing that shocked Ken was the spirit in which the fellow related the incident, almost as though it was some sort of lark. I shudder to think of people like that guiding children down dangerous rivers.

▶BACK FERRYING (SETTING) TO SHORE

Landing wrong

Let's have a look at how a landing can go wrong. You are approaching a difficult stretch of rapids and decide to land. You head for the river left shore (photograph 1). As you approach, the bow enters the slower water by the shore while the stern is still out in the faster water of the main current. The stern begins to move away from shore despite your efforts to pry it over (photograph 2). Your bow paddler leaps out and hangs on (photograph 3). The bow now becomes a pivot point as the stern continues to be carried downstream. Because it is now empty, your weight pushes the bow out of the water and your stern deep into the water. You are sitting in the canoe where it is only eighteen inches (45.7 cm) wide. It is roughly equivalent to trying to balance yourself on a log (photograph 4). Quite likely you've made a grab for the gunwales instead of leaning on your paddle in a

downstream brace (photograph 5). The canoe is now broadside to the waves as you swing around. In this situation, you are very vulnerable to capsizing. If you do upset, it's swimtime in the rapids and big trouble unless you immediately swim clear of the canoe to avoid being pinned against a rock.

If this should ever happen to you, to avoid capsizing and to make the most out of a bad situation, quickly move forward against the thwart and go into the downstream brace position until the canoe swings to shore (photograph 6).

LANDING WRONG 1

2

3

LANDING WRONG 4

5

6

Landing correctly

Landing in a current with back ferry

You are approaching a dangerous looking stretch of rapids (photograph 1). You decide to land on the river left shore. Your bow paddler, instead of paddling furiously in the direction in which you want to go, prys the bow toward the right. This enables you to easily get your stern over to the left to begin the back ferry (photograph 2). With vigorous backpaddling the canoe is ferried over and approaches the shore stern first (photograph 3). The stern enters the slower water by the shore. The bow, which is still out in the current, is pushed to shore by the current with no effort from the bow paddler (photograph 4). You reach out from the upstream end and grab onto shore first (photograph 5). Only now does the bow paddler reach out and make contact with shore (photograph 6). He is careful not to pull the bow in closer to shore than the stern or the current would grab the stern and swing it out and away from shore. The stern paddler gets out first and hangs on to steady the canoe for the bow paddler. The stern paddler must leave the canoe quickly because with the stern riding deeper than the bow, it will be grabbed by the current.

Landing in a current with eddy turn

A safe landing also can be accomplished by an eddy turn. This landing can be done even if there is no available eddy into which to make the turn. The water close to shore flows slower than the water in midstream. You can capitalize on this difference in flow rate. As the bow enters the slow water near shore the stern is carried downstream, assisting in the turn. When the turn is completed, the bow paddler holds the bow tight to the shore, gets out first, and hangs on to steady the canoe for the stern paddler. The stern paddler (downstream end) must not get out first or the bow will dig in and be pulled around by the current.

Fortunately, most landings on rivers can be done where there is little current, but in high water your life can depend on your ability to land and disembark properly. Once again, allow me to emphasize that it's the upstream-end paddler that gets out first. If you do a shore eddy-turn landing, you end up with the bow paddler upstream. It is then the bow paddler who gets out first. In this case, it's a good idea if the stern paddler simultaneously slides forward to avoid being perched on that narrow beam at the stern. Remember that the canoe is eighteen inches (45 cm) wide at the stern seat and thirty-six inches (90 cm) wide near the middle.

Using the current to turn the canoe around

Always let the current work for you instead of you working against the current. For example, if you are facing upstream by the shore and want to turn the canoe around, stick the bow out into the current. The bow paddler leans downstream on a high brace as the current carries the bow downstream. You hold the stern in the slower water by shore with a backsweep until the turn is completed.

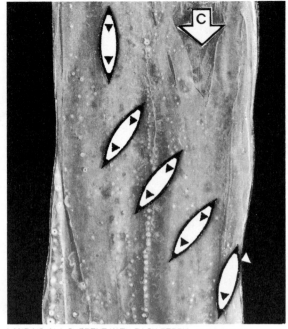

LANDING IN A CURRENT WITH BACK FERRY

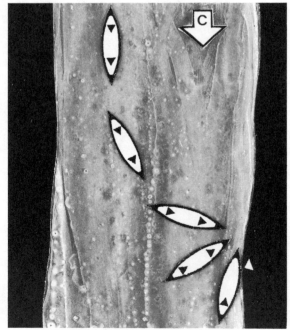

LANDING IN A CURRENT WITH EDDY TURN

▶LANDING IN A CURRENT WITH BACK FERRY

LANDING IN A CURRENT WITH BACK FERRY

LANDING IN A CURRENT WITH BACK FERRY

The partner

It is difficult to correct the mistakes of an unskilled partner in dangerous rapids. Training sessions should take place first on flatwater and then in very easy Class 1 rapids. You often will find yourself paddling with someone who isn't as skilled as you thought. You are faced with a rapid that is beyond the skills of your partner. You can either portage, run solo, or take your chances with your partner.

The difference between good and bad bow paddlers

It is possible to know all the strokes and all the right moves and yet still not be a very proficient whitewater paddler. Some bow paddlers just can't appreciate the problems of the stern paddler and can make it almost impossible for the stern paddler to clear his or her end of the canoe or put the canoe where it's supposed to go. The difference between a good and not so good bow paddler is very subtle and hard to explain.

First, a good bow paddler chooses the course. He or she has a much better view of the rapids ahead. Besides being closer to the action, the bow paddler cuts off most of the view ahead of the stern paddler. The stern paddler is forced to view everything at a much shallower angle. He or she can't look down into the water just ahead. Even stern paddlers who prefer to choose the general direction must trust their bow partner to avoid hidden rocks.

Bow oblivious of stern problems

Let's assume you are running a rapid of moderate difficulty. You are paddling in the stern, descending slowly steadily backpaddling to allow time to choose a course and position the canoe. The bow paddler decides to go to the right of boulder A. Drawing or prying the bow over in that direction, the bow paddler succeeds in clearing the rock. You are unable to clear the rock and glance off it. The bow paddler assumes you have just made a bad job of it. After all, if the bow had no trouble in missing it, why couldn't you?

What the bow paddler fails to understand is when the canoe is descending slower than the speed of the river, which is the case when backwatering, one must consider the sidewash. The force exerted by the water along the side of the canoe when the canoe is angled to the current is considerable. When the canoe is aligned parallel to the current there is no force either way.

In deciding to go right with no warning to you, the bow paddler angles the canoe in this direction. This maneuver exposes the right side of the canoe to the current which is rushing at it at about two or three mph. (3-5 km/h). Therefore the stern is actually forced over to the left and downstream. Not only do you have to fight the current to get your stern over to the right to clear the rock, but you also have less time to do it because the current has pushed you downstream and closer to the rock. A strong stern paddler might be able to overcome the force of the current and clear the stern by using a lot of energy.

Increase the speed of the current and there is no way the stern paddler can overpower it and clear the rock. Increase the speed of the current still further and the canoe will hit the rock broadside amidships. The canoe will be held on the rock while the water rushes in and swamps it. If the canoe turns and faces upstream, exposing the open top to the full force of the current, the canoe will wrap around the rock. Again, it's goodbye canoe and the bow paddler will still think you did it.

It could be argued that a good stern paddler would have made sure that the bow paddler was aware of the sidewash problem before attempting the rapids. However it's sometimes difficult to tell just how good a bow paddler really is until you get under way. Quite often the stern paddler is not aware of sidewash either and has no idea why he failed to avoid the rock. In this situation, the two paddlers end up blaming each other and neither one knows the cause of the problem. You can hear paddlers like this chewing each other out from miles away. I have seen situations where, given a saw, the canoeists would have made two canoes out of one and gone their separate ways. Recently I witnessed a husband who was paddling in the stern get a paddle full of water right in the face from an irate wife who had taken a volley of abuse all the way down the rapid.

Bow and stern paddlers work as a team

With an experienced paddler up front, a back ferry should go something like this. The canoe is descending slowly with both of you backpaddling. The bow paddler decides to go right but instead of moving right, the bow moves left and slows the canoe down with a strong backpaddle and at the same time indicates the upcoming shift to the right with a yell or the nod of the head to the right. The bow paddler should be sure his intentions are clear to the stern paddler. By moving the bow left instead of right, your bow paddler increases the sidewash on the left side of the canoe. The canoe is being pushed to the right, the direction in which you want to go, and you haven't even done anything yet. You see the bow paddler's move and what the canoe is doing and you know what the bow wants to do. You draw or pry the stern over to the right. It's so easy because the sidewash of the current on the left is forcing the canoe to the right anyway. As the bow clears boulder A, your bow paddler kicks the canoe over to the right and you kick your end to the left. The canoe is now aligned to go by the rock without exposing the side of the canoe. With the canoe aligned there is no sidewash either way.

A good bow paddler can make it extremely easy for a stern paddler. (Paul, my son, and I have reached the point where I can sense his intentions as soon as he makes his move. He rarely has to tell me where he's going to go. This sense of one-ness between bow paddler and stern paddler takes time to develop.) When we canoe as a family, Joyce, my wife, paddles in the stern of one canoe with Paul in the bow. My daughter, Becky, paddles in my bow. Joyce is not a whitewater paddler. She can take it or leave it. Given the choice, she would usually opt for the portage. Paul is such an exceptional bow paddler that he enables Joyce to descend rapids of moderate difficulty with confidence. He controls the angle and rate of descent and chooses the course. Joyce has learned to perform the corresponding strokes in the stern and the two make an excellent team. She has no desire to paddle with anyone else. Although not a whitewater fanatic, she is sufficiently competent to enable us to go on whitewater trips as a family.

BOW OBLIVIOUS OF STERN PROBLEMS

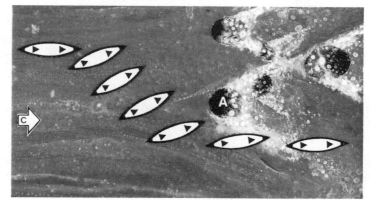

BOW AND STERN PADDLERS WORK AS A TEAM

BACKWATER PRIES AND DRAWS TO SET ANGLE

The partner...

Bow over-correcting

There is one other way in which the bow paddler can make it very easy or extremely difficult for the stern paddler. There is nothing worse than a bow paddler who over-corrects or makes a move and persists in it long past the point where the maneuver was needed. This is often what happens when the bow paddler is just learning and the stern paddler is choosing the course. The scenario goes something like this.

The canoe is moving into a section of rapids where it will have to move right to miss rock A and left to avoid rock B. In this case, the stern paddler (you) is choosing the course. You pry the stern over to the right, then call for a draw to the right. The bow paddler who doesn't know what's going on and whose only aim is to please, does so with great enthusiasm. Even after rock A has been well cleared your bow paddler is still drawing right as if your lives depended on it. You yell "That's enough, that's enough!" By the time the bow has got the message and discovered rock B, it's much too late to call for a pry or cross bow to the left. You wipe out on rock B and the bow begins to wonder if you really know what you're doing.

Anticipating problems ahead

The previous scenario should have gone something like this. You are paddling in the stern. You see rock A and decide to go right. You kick the stern to the right, then ask the bow paddler to draw right. The bow does so, not understanding why at first. But then as rock A approaches, the bow paddler realizes the reason for going right, and allows the bow to slip by within inches. There is nothing to be gained by missing the rock by six feet when six inches will suffice. Now when you see rock B and kick your stern over to the left, asking your partner to do the same, the bow is able to oblige because you haven't gone too far right. The

canoe is aligned and responsive to the pry or cross draw. A really good bow paddler will attempt to actually draw the bow right in behind the rock which makes it very easy for you to clear the rock. Now we are getting into the fine subtleties of what makes a skilled team. Let's take a look at what makes a good bow paddler.

Assisting stern in violent maneuvers

The canoe is bearing down on rock A. The bow paddler sees the rock at the last minute. There is no time to ferry right. The bow paddler throws the bow over to the right just in time to avoid the rock. You attempt to draw the stern over to the right but are having difficulty because the canoe is now angled to the current and the sidewash along the right side is pushing the canoe toward the rock. However as soon as the bow passes the rock, the bow paddler reaches beyond the rock and draws the bow in tight behind the rock. This immediately straightens the canoe in the current, freeing it of the sidewash and you now easily avoid banging the stern on the rock. A bow paddler who executes this type of maneuver really knows what's going on. This method of drawing the bow in behind the rock is necessary when running shallow, rock-studded rapids where there is no room for a back ferry.

Descending rapids slowly

A slow descent is the key to getting through a difficult rapid. And when I say slowly, I mean very slowly. The way to do this is by backpaddling. If you backpaddle hard enough, you can actually stop the canoe in relation to the shore and go back and forth across the current to find an opening. This type of maneuvering calls for very aggressive backpaddling. I find that many people think they are backpaddling and going slowly but in effect they are just drifting at the speed of the current. They are stationary in the water but the rocks and shore are

moving by quickly. You should practice backpaddling until you end up going back upstream in relation to the shore. This is much harder to do than you might think. The harder you backpaddle, the faster you move upstream against the current and the harder is the effect of the sidewash on your canoe. Remember, if your stern is riding lower than the bow, you won't be able to control your direction. The current will shove you around out of control.

When you can stop your canoe in relation to the shore and backpaddle back upstream under complete control, moving right and left whenever desired, you know with certainty that you are getting good. You have gained complete mastery of your craft and can put the canoe anywhere you want because you've learned to buy time. You can pick your course at will. You can grab an eddy instead of firing by and seeing it when it's too late. You can do an eddy turn or set your stern over into the eddy because of your powerful backpaddling. In some situations, you can even get yourself out of a blind alley by moving back upstream to pick a better channel. Paul and I have often salvaged a bad situation with strong backpaddling.

This happened a couple of times on the upper part of the Nahanni River. We were descending a set of rapids that started out not too badly, but more and more rocks started to appear until we were having great difficulty finding a deepwater channel. We decided to go to the left of a rock but almost immediately realized our mistake. There was nowhere to go. The channel was not navigable. Our bow already had passed the rock on our right so we were committed to this course. However, we had been backpaddling very hard as we moved down the channel and with just a little more effort we were able to move the canoe back upstream until the bow cleared the rock. Paul kicked the bow over to the right and we moved down the right channel, which proved to be deep enough to float us through. Paul threw me a glance which said, "We did it but I don't believe it." What I have just described is only possible in a rapid of no more than four mph (6 km/h). No one can backpaddle faster than that.

Speed of the canoe in relation to the shore

The speed at which you are descending a rapid in relation to the shore is the velocity of the water minus the speed at which you are backpaddling. In a current of five mph (8 km/h), if you are backpaddling at three mph (5 km/h), you are actually descending the river at two mph (3 km/h). If you really put some muscle into it and backpaddle at four mph (6 km/h), you would then be moving down the rapids at one mph (2 km/h). Conversely, if you are descending a rapid with a five mph (8 km/h) current and you are paddling forward at four mph (6 km/h), you would be descending the rapids in relation to the shore at nine mph (14 km/h). The price of a mistake at this speed is very high indeed.

BOW OVER-CORRECTING

ANTICIPATING PROBLEMS AHEAD

DRAWING BOW IN TIGHT BEHIND ROCK

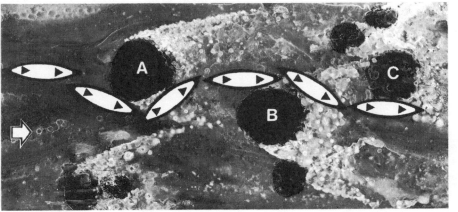

ASSISTING STERN IN VIOLENT MANEUVERS

Running rapids under control

I know many canoeists who, knowing very little about what is written here, luck through rapids all the time. The tough, almost indestructible materials of which canoes are made today make this possible. The excitement factor of running rapids on luck and a prayer is very high because of all the harrowing near misses and wipeouts. However, apart from the safety factor, running rapids under complete control can actually be more fun. Playing the rapids when in complete command of your craft is a very satisfying experience. There is, of course, added excitement as you graduate to more difficult rapids on which to test your increasing skills.

An experience I had recently is worth mentioning as an example of a situation with not too much risk but where the canoeists were not learning much because they weren't particularly aware of what was going on. In a bigger and faster river in a remote area, their ineptitude could have resulted in disaster.

We were canoeing in spring flood on a small but fast river. Paul and I had been invited to accompany a party of three other canoes. One canoe had two young and very enthusiastic paddlers. A couple of older fellows who were average paddlers were in the second canoe. The third canoe was paddled by a friend who had done a lot of whitewater canoeing and a bow paddler who was still a learner. Because of the cold water, Paul and I were wearing wet-suit tops.

The first few sets of rapids were tricky but everybody made it through just fine. I could tell the paddlers were inexperienced but they were certainly having fun. The price of a wipeout would be a cold swim, but each stretch of rapids wasn't very long so recovery would be easy. I also noticed that the two young paddlers were blaming each other for the bad moves, a sure indication that the bow paddler wasn't doing set-up maneuvers to make things easy for the stern paddler. Moreover, the stern paddler obviously didn't know how to compensate for the bow's lack of skill.

My biggest surprise was the experienced paddler's lack of understanding about flowing water. He was being swept right into the holes in the middle of the river. On several occasions, his canoe went through sideways, half full of water. He and his bow paddler were having a great time but if the holes had been bigger, they would have rolled or sunk in the foam. The other two canoes were doing much the same thing. One canoe finally swamped in a hole. The canoeists were forced to swim to shore and with the aid of their recovery line pulled the canoe to shore after them.

Paul and I were avoiding the holes and rollers by choice. We both agreed it was too cold to go swimming even with wet-suit tops. As for offering advice, we were in that tricky situation where, not being in charge of the trip, we didn't feel comfortable about telling anyone what to do unless asked.

Everyone was having fun and enjoying the near swampings and near mishaps.

Finally, after just missing a particularly large hole, the two younger canoeists asked Paul and me what they were doing wrong. I explained that their problem was an inability to read the direction of the current and make a move above the holes early enough to avoid being carried into them. In addition, they didn't know how to do a back ferry. They were attempting to miss the holes by paddling forward and steering around them. Instead, they were hitting the holes fast and at a bad angle, sometimes even broadside. How did Paul and I manage to avoid the holes, while they were swept into them? Here's a typical situation that will help demonstrate the difference between controlled and uncontrolled rapid running.

Being aware of current lines
We are descending the rapids favoring the river right on current line 4. From where we are, it appears that we can paddle right down the river passing the hole on the river right. But I know that nearly the whole width of the river will be funneling right through that hole. I look downstream following the current line and confirm my suspicion that if we were to follow this course on current line 4, we would be swept into the hole. Since we have figured this out in lots of time, we go into the ferry-right position and move over to current line 1, easily avoiding the hole and curling waves.

Being unaware of current lines

Our two young canoeists also approach the rapid on current line 4. They look down the rapids and assume they can paddle straight ahead; instead they are carried by the current toward the hole on current line 4. They finally realize what is happening, and begin to paddle very hard to steer to the right around the hole. But the canoe turns even more broadside into the oncoming hole. The bow is now in current line 3 and the stern is in current line 4 or even 5, which is flowing faster. The stern is swept downstream faster than the bow, turning the canoe broadside. Despite their efforts, they can't avoid the hole and end up going into it broadside. They wallow through and are pleased with themselves that they didn't upset or swamp. I can tell that they consider this a successful run. Actually, it was successful only because the hole wasn't too large. A really big one would have meant trouble, even a dangerous situation.

After explaining these principles and how most of the river was funneling into the holes to the two young canoeists, we told them to stay very tight on our tail and go into the back ferry position. They were absolutely delighted with the results. They started back ferrying all over the place enjoying the new control they had gained over their canoe. The other canoes continued to wallow into the holes. Their crews were allowing the river to dictate their course. Somehow they managed to survive each mishap. That is not running under control.

Paul and I nipped into the edge of some of the holes just to liven things up for ourselves, but we chose the time and place to tangle with the waves, not the river. However, if you want to fool around in holes, your canoe should be equipped with floatation.

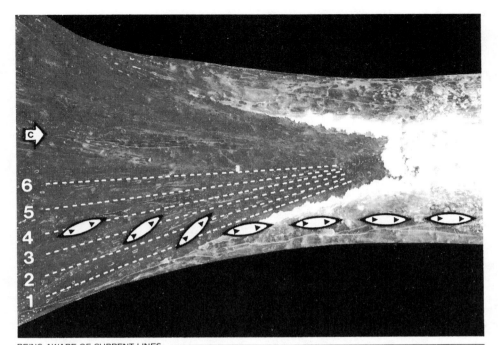

BEING AWARE OF CURRENT LINES

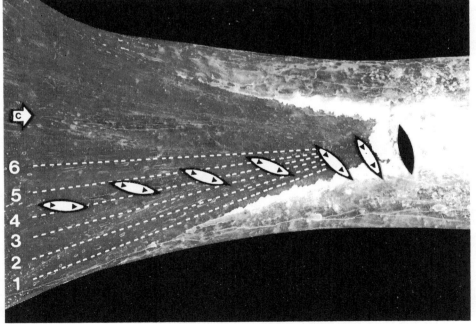

BEING UNAWARE OF CURRENT LINES

Current lines on the Nahanni

I would like to include one more situation that should impress upon you the need for lining up properly on the current line above big rapids. Wally Schaber and I had agreed to run a rapid for a camera crew filming for John and Janet Foster on the Nahanni River. The waves in the rapids could be avoided altogether by staying left. The rapids along the right side were mountainous. Our plan was to run down the left side of the waves (current line 4), venturing just far enough into them to make the shot interesting but not into the center (current line 6), where it would be unlikely we could stay upright even with a spray cover.

We approached the rapids on current line 6 (which we thought was current line 4). It looked like we were perfectly lined up to skirt down the left side of the big stuff (dotted line). But as we approached, we realized that we were on current line 6 and drifting into current line 7. Wally called for a hard left. I disagreed because there wasn't time to reach current line 4 at the speed with which we were being swept towards the rapids. I indicated that we should take our chances to the right on current line 8 which seemed to lead into waves that were smaller than the stuff in the center of the river where the monstrous rollers were. Wally agreed and we back ferried into current line 8. It looked as though we had salvaged a bad situation until we became aware of a hard straight line extending out from the right shore into the big waves in the center. We both knew it was a drop-off and the closer we got, the higher we knew it was going to be. We also knew there would be a monstrous diagonal curling wave beyond—the hardest possible wave to survive. We instinctively edged left to make a trade-off between the waves on the left (current line 7), and the drop-off on the right (current line 8). We figured the drop-off would mingle with the waves and be less

severe. We were backpaddling like crazy to delay the impending disaster. The waves looked worse than the drop-off so we decided to go over the drop-off as close as possible to the waves. We were very close. The curling wave began to reveal itself beyond the straight hard line of the brink. It was big alright, bigger than anything I had ever seen, and curling diagonally—an almost impossible wave to get through without rolling over. One moment I was suspended in space beyond the brink, the next minute I was dropping into the hole. On the way down I laid out to the right, parallel with the water, with all my weight leaning on the blade. If we were going to upset I knew it had to be to the left. I disappeared into the wave. I couldn't see a thing. The canoe was rolling. I could feel the right gunwale come up under my armpit. It stayed there for what seemed like a long time. I surfaced with the canoe still on edge. Then the canoe began to right itself. Somehow Wally, who was bracing on the left, had held himself in the canoe and refused to fall out. We stroked forward to propel ourselves up and over the wave and pulled into the eddy. We had made it but we couldn't believe it. We figured that the cameraman must have gotten the shot of the century. Unfortunately, we had dropped out of sight behind the wave and he didn't see much until we hit the eddy. As I look back on that venture, that wave was the biggest that I had ever attempted. The moment was an exciting one but not that dangerous. The water was big, deep, and cold but we were near an eddy and the jet boat was standing by. We would have been rescued from the cold water very quickly.

Fooling around like that on a wilderness trip with all our gear on board would be stupid. A canoe that upsets on the Nahanni

River might never stop. It just keeps going unless it's carried into an eddy. Wally and I both expressed this concern to the filmmakers, so they would explain that we were canoeing for fun with a rescue crew standing by. We insisted that this explanation be included in the commentary if they were going to use these wild rapid-running sequences. Films can make things look like such fun without revealing the consequences of a mistake.

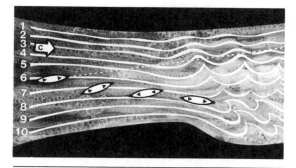

Aggressive technique: running rapids under power

Recently I was invited to give a canoe workshop on Vancouver Island, British Columbia. When I arrived I found there was an accomplished whitewater instructor among the group. We teamed up to demonstrate eddy turns. As we bore down on a wild-looking whirlpool-type eddy directly above a nasty-looking rock-studded drop-off, I suggested we change paddle sides so I could make the entry into the eddy with a nice safe bow cut and brace. He overruled the change and insisted on a bow pry entry. I thought to myself, "Oh man, I sure hope that guy back there knows what he's doing."

It was my first big maneuver with a stern paddler with whom I had never paddled before. With considerable apprehension, I threw in the most violent bow pry I've ever attempted. It was all or nothing. Much to my surprise, the canoe leaned way over toward the eddy and spun right around on my paddle ending up high in the eddy. My first feeling was one of relief and a touch of pride at a pry eddy entry very well done. Then, as I glanced back at my partner who sat there smiling, I realized that it was mostly his doing. He must have been leaning out there in the most solid brace imaginable. There was no way I could have tipped that canoe. If I had done the pry badly, the grip of the paddle might have been torn from my upper hand or I might have been catapulted overboard, but there was no way that canoe could have upset.

From then on I was happy to be more of an observer of his style and teaching methods than run the workshop myself. He insisted that we take the eddies on whatever side we happened to be paddling. Two canoes dumped in the eddy just described, which could have been serious. During the day, four of the six canoes upset at least once. A couple of canoes swamped powering too fast through the haystacks. I came away very impressed with his aggressive style and teaching methods and would probably agree that he turns out a superior brand of whitewater canoeist, if they survive. But an alternative to the aggressive bow pry eddy turn is the offside duffek. This puts the bow paddler on the downstream (relative to the current being entered) side of the canoe, which means that the canoe is more likely to have the correct tilt. The bow paddler rotates his torso, keeps the paddle vertical, and opens the face of the paddle to catch the current. This provides bracing action throughout the turn. An offside duffek or offside brace complements an aggressive style of paddling that often cuts across the flow of the current. One thing about being overly cautious when powering the bow into the eddy is if you aren't close enough to the eddy to get your paddle into

OFFSIDE DUFFEK

the calm water of the eddy, you'll end up doing your draw in the main current and fire right by the eddy. You end up running the rapids downstream backwards.

Haystacks, Natch Rapids, Petawawa River

105

Running rapids under power

Running a rapid under power (paddling downstream aggressively) increases the difficulties but makes possible a very stable brace. With the canoe traveling fast, the paddle blade planes on the water. If you keep the leading edge up, the paddle can't sink because of the force of the water on the underside of the blade. Remember that with the canoe traveling at the same speed as the current the paddle has to be sculled back and forth to provide support or it will sink. As your whitewater skills improve, you might decide to run fast for the thrill and exhilaration of a downstream run, or try your hand at some whitewater racing.

In downriver slalom racing, gates are set up in difficult places. The canoeists must run the gates and get to the bottom of the rapids as fast as possible. Penalties are collected each time a gate is touched or missed. Racing has resulted in the development of many strokes and techniques that the wilderness canoeist can utilize. The potential for the improvement of skills is unlimited. It is important to be aware of the possibilities, be willing to learn, and be aware of your limitations.

There are situations even on wilderness trips where running under power is desirable and fun. The under-power sideslip to the left and right as well as under-power pivots and braces were described in the section on flatwater paddling. Now let's consider where these aggressive techniques might be used in whitewater canoeing.

You're descending a deep, fast, wide rapid. The difficult areas are widely spaced. You run down chute A and see trouble ahead at rock B. The river right side looks good at chute C, which has a small hole at the end of it. There is lots of distance between you and chute C so you decide to power across rather then back ferry into position. This will give you more momentum to punch aggressively through the hole.

Paul refers to this as the "go for broke" method. As we come through chute A (photograph 1A) and make the decision to head for chute C under power, the paddler on the right, in this instance my son, Paul, does a cut and a draw. I do the same on the left (photograph 1B). The canoe pivots instantly because of the force of the water on the open face of our paddles (photograph 1C). We then power across, aiming high because we know the surge of the current will cause us to drift downstream (photograph 1D). As we reach a point above chute C, Paul does a pry to pivot the canoe. I do the same (photograph 1E). This is a fast, aggressive method of descending a rapid in a lightly loaded canoe. It is only suitable for rapids with widely spaced obstructions.

Sideslip under power

Sideslipping under power is also a useful maneuver. The canoe approaches rock A (photograph 2A). The channel B becomes obvious, Paul, who is in the bow paddling on the right, does a cut. I do a jam (photograph 2B). The canoe moves quickly to the right because the speed of the canoe increases the effectiveness of the strokes. As the momentum slows, Paul follows with a draw and I do a pry (photograph 2C). The canoe continues the sideslip and enters the chute (photograph 2D). The underpower sideslip requires fast decision making because the canoe is moving in relation to the shore and rocks at eight or nine mph (13 or 14 km/h).

There is one great advantage to moving downstream at a speed greater than the speed of the current. You can lean your weight out on your blade in a low brace. With the leading edge of your blade up, the paddle planes on the water. There is no need to scull. The feeling of stability is quite remarkable.

Keep in mind that when traveling fast you will bury deep into waves rather than being buoyed up by the water. The aggressive technique usually requires the use of a spray cover in large rapids. In wilderness travel, spray covers are a nuisance if there are many portages. The slower-than-the-current backpaddling technique is usually sufficient to avoid taking in excessive amounts of water.

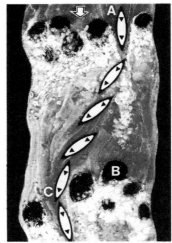

RUNNING RAPIDS UNDER POWER

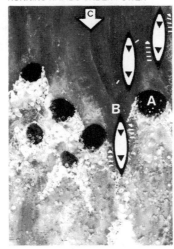

SIDESLIP UNDER POWER

RUNNING RAPIDS UNDER POWER 1A

1B

RUNNING RAPIDS UNDER POWER 1C

1D

RUNNING RAPIDS UNDER POWER 1E

1F

SIDESLIP UNDER POWER 2A

2B

2C

2D

Running haystacks and rollers

Some of the best canoeing is to be done during spring run-off when the rocks are all buried and the main problem is staying afloat in the haystacks and big rollers. There are several things you can do to avoid swamping in the big stuff. One of them is to equip the canoe with a spray deck and turn it into a covered whitewater canoe. However, many of us stay by choice with the open canoe. There are other ways to keep the canoe afloat.

One thing you can do is ferry to avoid hitting the worst part of the haystack. You can also backpaddle aggressively to slow your descent. Enter the wave very slowly to allow the bow to rise, then power out of the wave before you sink at the stern. It's a matter of timing. The best way to get an open canoe through the big stuff is to run empty, with the paddlers positioned in the center of the canoe. The unweighted bow and stern will bob lightly in the waves instead of plunging through them. The bow paddler braces against the center thwart while the stern paddler braces against the stern thwart. In case you are not yet convinced take a look at section 2. This is the same rapid in the same highwater conditions, only this time we are running in the normal bow and stern positions. We hit the same wave, disappear into it, and reappear swimming.

I've often seen bow paddlers move back behind the bow seat with the stern paddler remaining on the stern seat to raise the bow high. This is not a good idea for two reasons. With all of the weight concentrated near the stern, the canoe becomes tippy. There is also a danger of swamping at the stern. The rapid shown here is a good example of a rapid where it is safe to play. It is turbulent but deep with no rocks protruding above the surface. The rapid is very short and there is nothing dangerous downstream. It's almost one mile (1.6 km) before the next rapid. The water is chilly but not frigid.

▶TWO PADDLERS IN CENTER

TWO PADDLERS IN CENTER

TWO PADDLERS IN CENTER

▶TWO PADDLERS ON SEATS

Holes and haystacks at the end of a rapid

On the Rouge River in Quebec there is a rapid of moderate difficulty that has large haystacks at the end. These cannot be avoided in highwater conditions. However the rapids open into a deep quiet pond before continuing into the next set. The canoeists who wipe out in the haystacks have lots of time to get themselves and their canoe to shore. The price of a wipeout is a pleasant swim. There are no rocks downstream to damage the canoe or injure the swimmer. With good PFDs, a throw bag stashed safely away in the stern, and water temperatures that are not too cold there is little danger. If these same haystacks were located at the top of the rapid, it would be an entirely different situation. Instead of a Class 3, the rapids would have to be rated as a Class 4. A wipeout at the top would mean a long dangerous swim through the rest of the rapids. It's a matter of understanding the combinations that the river can throw at you. It's easy to dodge a left jab, but it's the uppercut which follows that will get you.

Practicing the eddy turn
Improving your skills comes through practice and pushing yourself past your limit. The place to do that safely is in the haystacks at the end of a rapid. Becky sets the angle of the canoe with a draw (photograph 1A). With the angle set, I do a sweep stroke to create the motion that will carry the canoe across the eddy line (photograph 1B). Becky continues with a draw stroke as she tilts the canoe downstream. I continue to do a sweep stroke while leaning into the turn, until the canoe is facing downstream (photograph 1C). Note — Becky and I could be a little more generous with our tilt.

Practicing the upstream ferry
A little farther downstream where the current isn't quite so strong, we angle the canoe upstream toward the eddy line to attempt a ferry. The bow crosses the eddy line but Becky forgets to brace (photograph 2A). The current grabs the bow and over we go (photograph 2B and 2C). Of course that's my version. Becky's version is that I hit the eddy line at too great an angle and that I was not braced enough in anticipation of crossing the eddy line. She's partly right.

I should have entered the current at a more shallow angle and pried the stern out into the current as the bow crossed the eddy line. Becky should have been in a high brace before we hit the main current.

►PRACTICING THE EDDY TURN 1A

1B

1C

►PRACTICING THE UPSTREAM FERRY 2A

2B

2C

Running a tight bend

Around a bend with the eddy turn
As you approach the bend hang tight to the inside shore. You can anticipate an eddy just around the corner. The bow paddler takes the paddle side toward the inside bend to prepare for the bow draw into the eddy (high brace). As well as staying out of the danger zone on the outside of the curve, rounding the bend with the eddy turn puts you in a good position to avoid trouble downstream.

Setting or back ferrying around a bend
Another method of taking a bend is to side-slip or set the canoe over. As you approach the bend, slow down and set an angle to back ferry to the inside of the corner. Remember that your back-ferry angle should be relative to the current, not the shoreline (canoe B in diagram). This maneuver depends on strong backpaddling to avoid running into the rock face.

Running a corner without looking it over from shore is very dangerous. Allowing the current to carry you around the outside of the bend puts you at the mercy of the river. On the other hand if you are familiar with the river, you know the bend is free of sweepers, and if you're looking for a wild ride, the outside of the bend is the place to be. In an open canoe you must be able to estimate whether or not the large waves in the main current will swamp the canoe. Around a sharp bend there is always the danger that the bank could be undercut, the canoe will swamp against the cliff face and be pulled and that you will be too. To avoid this end, scout the corner first then begin your back ferry or setting early so you can easily stay to the inside of the corner. Keep the stern closer to shore than the bow. If the stern does swing out and around, don't blame the canoe or the river. Blame yourself.

Sweepers
One of the most deadly obstacles you will face on the river is an obstacle like a downed tree where the water flows through rather than around it. They are called sweepers, also strainers, and are one of the canoeist's worst enemies. They often are located on the outside of a sharp bend where the shore is eroded away by the current. If you allow the current to carry you around the outside of a bend you are a perfect set-up for entrapment on a sweeper. The water flows through the branches leaving you and the canoe pinned. There is the possibility that you could be pinned against the branches underwater, or pinned against the branches by the canoe. If your efforts to avoid the sweeper fail, your best defence is to climb up onto the tree as you hit it. Recovering the canoe if it becomes wedged in the branches is extremely difficult. Sometimes the canoe will roll under the sweeper.

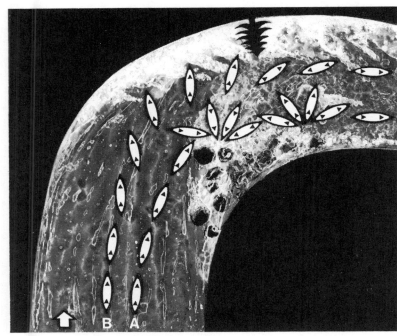

AROUND A BEND WITH THE EDDY TURN (A)
SETTING OR BACK FERRYING AROUND A BEND (B)

SWEEPERS

Wind and rapids

Wind and rapids don't mix very well. A rapid of moderate difficulty can become dangerous when running against strong and gusty winds, especially for the solo paddler. There is a rapid on the Petawawa River called Rollway Rapids. It is a potentially dangerous rapid because it is long with many large rocks just above and below the surface. The deepwater channel is there though, if you can find and follow it. I have enjoyed this rapid many times but on this particular day I was a bit concerned about the gusty wind conditions. I loaded a heavy pack in front of me to hold the bow down. The weight would make the canoe behave more sluggishly but I preferred this to being blown off course at a critical moment. Some of the deep water Vs are only four or five feet (120 or 150 cm) wide.

Everything went well until I approached a particularly turbulent stretch with only one narrow V. There is a drop-off on the left and large rocks on the right. I was lined up perfectly with the V when a sudden violent gust of wind wrenched the bow to the right. I could easily have corrected this with a bow pry but the bow was already past the first rock. I was at the point of no return and could only power between two rocks. As I shot through, I leaned the canoe to make it narrower at the waterline. It was split-second timing and luck that got me through. Wind has caused me problems on other occasions but I have always been able to use a counteracting stroke such as a bow pry or draw. The effect of wind when paddling double is not as great but it still is a factor. Take the wind into consideration when reading a rapid and trying to decide whether or not to run it. Sometimes a wind can make standing waves larger and sharper-edged.

Lake waves against river current

There is one situation where a wind can be very dangerous; in fact, for a couple of paddlers it was very nearly fatal. I was paddling for a film crew at a location where the Montreal River flows into Lake Superior. We were filming a sequence of paddling in large waves for a film to be used at Toronto's Ontario Place. The waves were supposed to look spectacular so I chose this location. I have discovered that where a strong current from a river meets large wind-blown waves on a lake, the waves can rise to mountainous proportions. To give away a trade secret, you can look like you are paddling in them by canoeing around the perimeter and shooting with a low camera angle. But, you have to be very careful to stay in the waves of the lake without being lured into the mountainous sharp-edged waves caused by the river. They are dangerous because they are stationary while the lake waves roll up onto the shore. If you upset in the river waves, you would be carried out into the lake and held there where the current equals the wind. In other words, the current is carrying you out and the wind is blowing you in. The only means of getting to shore is to swim out of the current and allow yourself to be carried to shore in the lake waves.

We got our shots, then the director, Pat Crawley, grabbed another canoe and joined me in the waves to sport around for the rest of the afternoon. We found that we could come and go at will by riding in on the waves and riding back out on the edge of the current, always being careful not to get into the big waves in the center of the current where a wipeout would be inevitable. The waves were terrifying to behold. To the camera crew watching from shore it looked like a lot of fun, and it was.

After supper, we were relaxing when we heard that two men had nearly drowned.

Two of the crew members had decided that it looked like such fun they would give it a try. They took one of the canoes, paddled straight down the middle of the current, and into the mountainous waves. They swamped on the first one and were carried out into the caldron. They were held there where the current carrying them out equaled the force of the waves rolling to shore. One fellow through luck or intentionally, swam out of the current parallel to shore and was carried in on the lake waves. The other fellow stayed with the canoe and had all but drowned when the lodge owner rescued him in a powerboat. Even the rescuers had a difficult time in the sharp-edged waves.

I relate this story as an illustration of the dangers of wind and current and what can happen when you get a combination of the two. I have never forgotten this incident because it made me realize the danger of making something look easier than it really is to an onlooker.

One of the greatest dangers to inexperienced canoeists is the temptation to run a rapid they have seen someone else run. A difficult rapid skillfully run looks so deceptively easy. Unfortunately the price of failure in a turbulent rapid can come high. One of the criticisms of my whitewater film is that it all looks so easy that people will be encouraged to grab a canoe and go try it. This is why it is essential for a prospective canoeist to see the basic film first to get some idea just what is involved in handling a canoe.

A test for running a complex rapid in low water

A rapid can have every conceivable problem and yet be runnable under control with the use of back ferries, front ferries, eddy turns, setting, power sideslipping, and the slow backwater descent. The first problem is to recognize the difficulties and plan a strategy. Now that you are familiar with all the maneuvers, try your hand at planning your strategy for Big Thompson Rapids on the Petawawa River. Study the diagram, work out your strategy, and draw it in with a series of canoes indicating which end of the canoe is the bow.

A. old log dam
B. portage over rock island
C. rock
D. deep water V
E. eddy behind rock
F. impenetrable rock garden
G. deep water V
H. eddy behind large rock
I. fast current
J. small haystacks
K. rocks with souse holes
L. ledge
M. deep water V

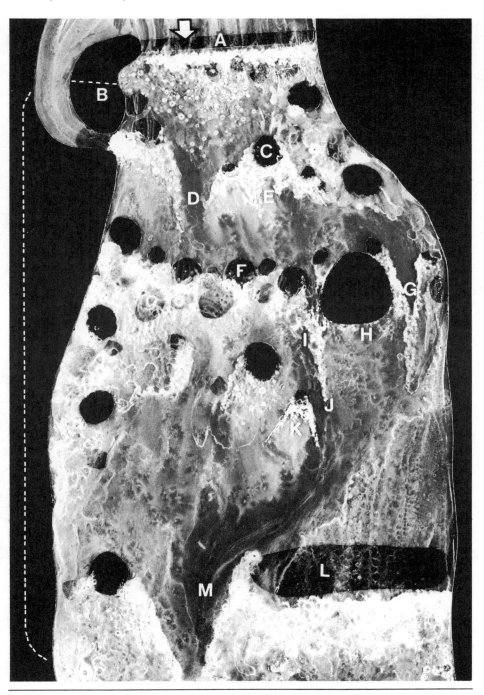

Solution: running a complex rapid in low water

Land on the river right side of island B and portage around the old log dam A. Put the canoe in the water below the dam and run downstream V(D), eddying out in eddy E, to avoid being swept into rock garden F. Peel out of the eddy and run downstream V(G), eddying out once again in eddy H behind the rock island. Eddy exit into current 1 (*see* photograph 1), set the ferry angle (photograph 2) and run the haystacks J until you pass hole K (photograph 3). As soon as you pass hole K, you go into the back ferry position (photograph 4) and back ferry all the way over to the right to avoid being carried over ledge L (photograph 5). Cease the back ferry when you are lined up with downstream V(M), (photograph 6) and take it through M to complete the run. Then congratulate yourselves on a good run. In this style of run you don't fight or attempt to beat the river, you work with it, utilizing the various elements that make a rapid what it is.

One of the things that often happened when we were filming on a well-traveled river such as the Petawawa was that canoeists would see us run rapids such as Big Thompson that are usually portaged. Having seen us make the run, they would figure that it must be safe. They would pile into their canoe, point the nose downstream, and go. The current would carry them down into the rock garden, through which they would ricochet from rock to rock, banging and thumping their way down. In shallow rapids, it's often possible to make it through without all the fancy maneuvers. But it's not as much fun as having complete control of your canoe.

Because the dam has deteriorated, this description of Big Thompson Rapids differs from the actual rapid.

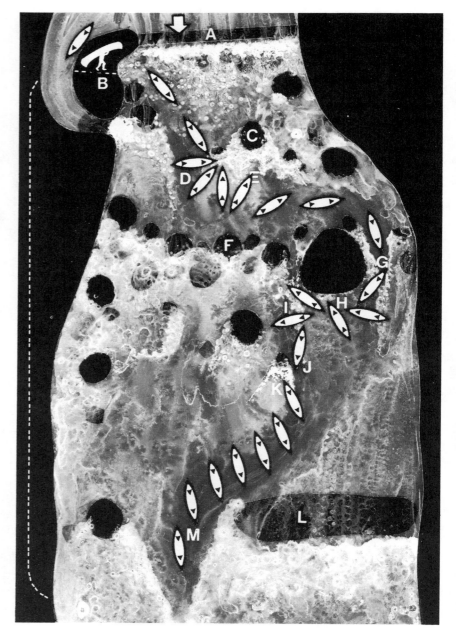

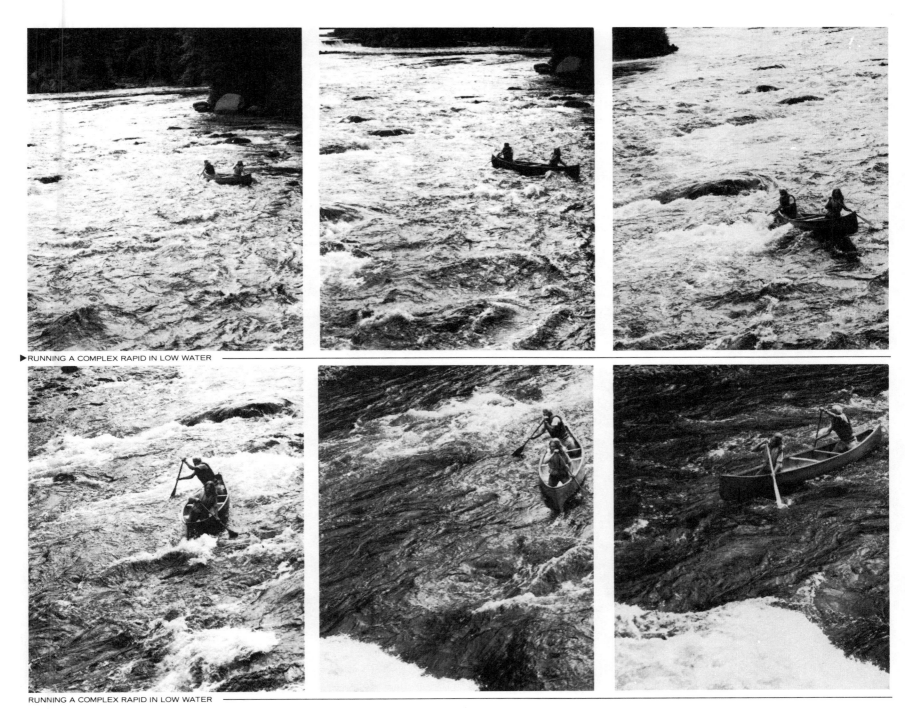

▶RUNNING A COMPLEX RAPID IN LOW WATER

RUNNING A COMPLEX RAPID IN LOW WATER

A test for reading whitewater

Here are some authentic problems that you could find on a river. See how you score at picking your way through these rapids. Try to imagine how it would look from the river, keeping in mind that you can't see around corners. A cliff indicates that you can't portage your canoe on that side. The dotted line indicates the portage but in many cases parts of the rapids are runnable if you start or finish at the right places.

First time through assume that you are being confronted with these rapids at your present skill level. The next time through assume that you are very proficient at the eddy turn (eddying out), eddy exit (re-enter mainstream), back ferry (setting), front ferry, and can perform a good solid high and low brace.

For the most likely solutions turn the page, but no cheating! For a third time through you might assume that you are leading a group of canoeists who are just learning. They know the various maneuvers but cannot always perform them well.

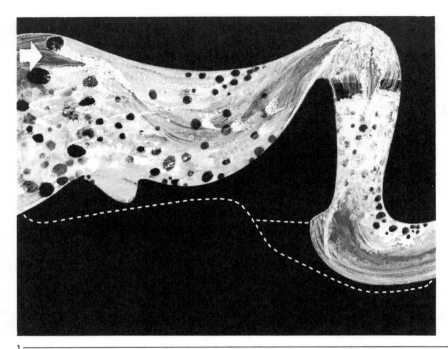

1

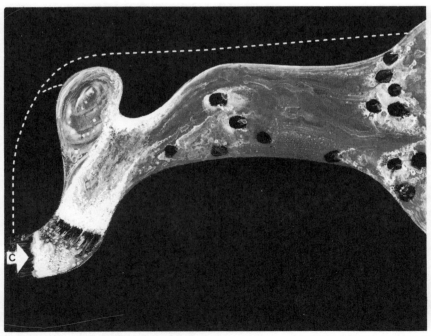

5

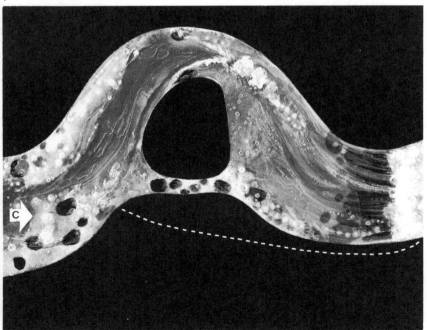

6

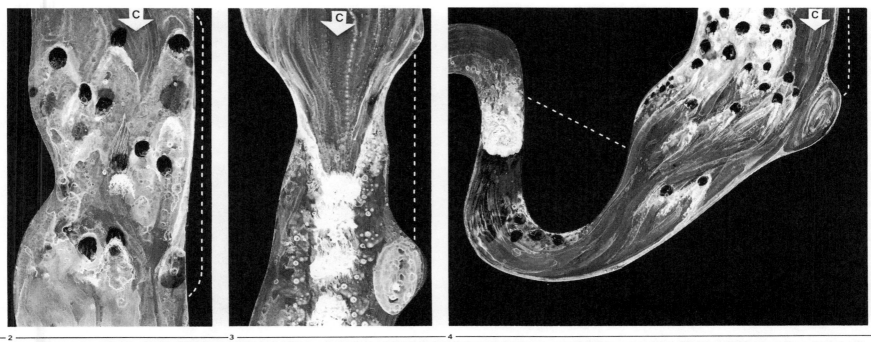

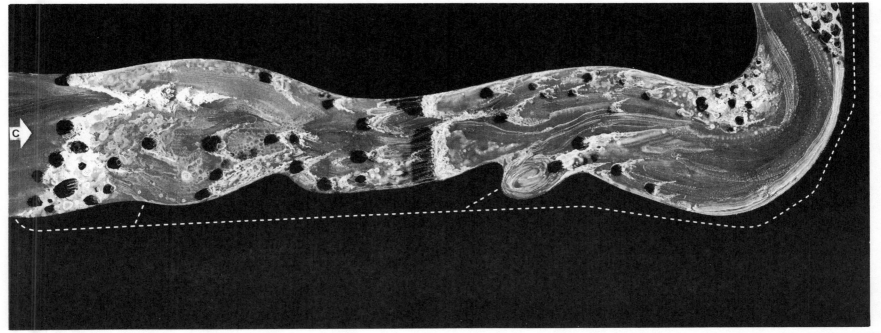

Solution: reading whitewater

1. Running the deep water channel at A is dangerous because the rock garden at B renders the back ferry to the landing at C impossible. The swiftness of the current and absence of an eddy at D makes a safe landing at E very difficult. It's game over for an open canoe in the foaming aerated water at F.

2. A strong back ferry makes it possible to follow the deep water channel.

3. Staying very close to shore in a back ferry position makes it possible to avoid the souse hole.

4. A strong front ferry is required at A to get from C to D to avoid being swept over falls B. They have to execute a flawless ferry to D to get to the portage around B.

5. Portaging to the shore eddy at A makes it possible to enjoy the rest of the rapids after the falls. However, with the full force of the current hitting point B, an aggressive eddy exit into the full force of current C is essential.

6. An eddy turn at A is not all that difficult but with certain death waiting over the falls at B, a landing and portage at C makes a lot of sense.

7. A wipeout in the huge haystacks at D would mean a long dangerous swim. An eddy out at B gives you a chance to look around the bend at C.

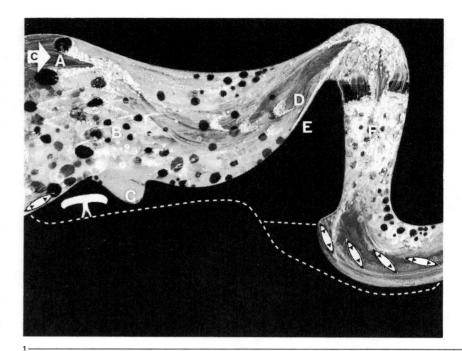

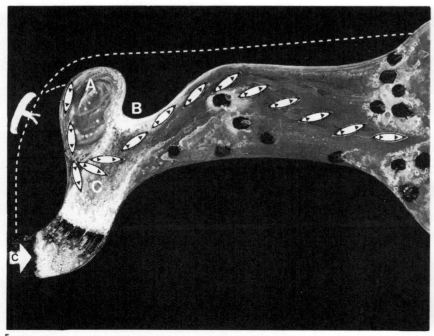

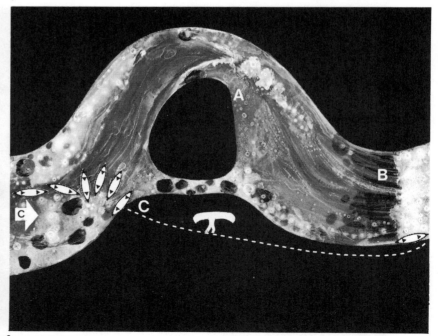

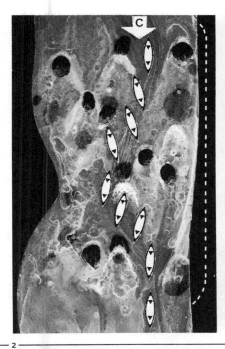

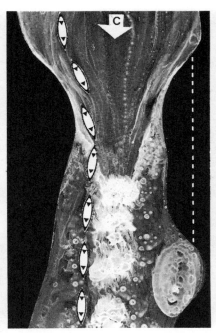

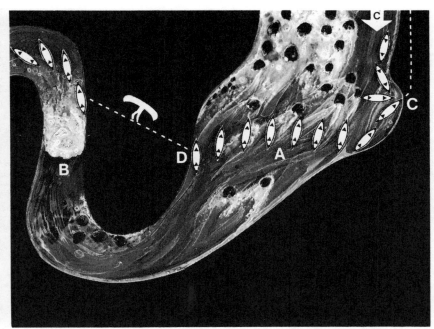

2

3

4

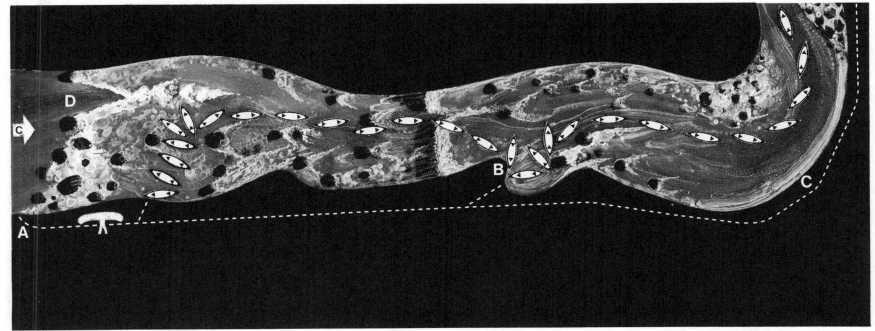

7

Petawawa River

Magnetawan River, Ontario

Denison Falls, Dog River, Ontario

Blue Chute, French River, Ontario

Little Thompson Rapids, Petawawa River, Ontario

Magpie River, Ontario

Petawawa River

Petawawa River

Magpie River

Brink of Virginia Falls

◄ Above Virginia Falls,
Nahanni River, Northwest Territories

Virginia Falls

129

Natch Rapids, Petawawa River

Natch Rapids, Petawawa River

Cascade Falls, Lake Superior

Petawawa River

Little Thompson Rapids, Petawawa River
◄South Nahanni River

133

Magnetawan River, Ontario

English River, Ontario

Petawawa River, Ontario   Fourth Canyon, Nahanni River ▶

134

Old Woman Bay, Lake Superior

8 WIPEOUTS, OR WHEN THINGS GO WRONG

Not many books deal with what to do when things go wrong. When it comes to wiping out in rapids, I can speak with authority. I have made every possible mistake at least once—as well as many variations of the same mistakes!

One of the problems associated with improved whitewater skills is the inevitable desire to run more and more difficult rapids. Getting better doesn't necessarily mean fewer wipeouts; what it often means is the wipeouts will be bigger, better and more spectacular. At least that's the way it seems to be for me. Let's take a look at some of the ways you can wipeout.

The most common wipeout is swamping. You collect water along the way until the canoe no longer responds to the paddle, and down you go. Or you plunge into a standing wave or hole and come out the other side awash. Rolling over on a diagonal curling wave is another common method of wiping out. Fetching up against a rock and allowing the upstream gunwale to dip so the canoe fills with water is the worst way to go. Going over a ledge or into a hole broadside will do it every time. Any way you do it, the results are always the same. You end up swimming, unless it's a very shallow rapid. Keep in mind that even in a shallow rapid, it's not advisable to stand in the current. Always swim into an eddy behind a rock before attempting to stand up. One of the greatest dangers you will face swimming through rapids is getting your foot wedged between rocks. In a current, your upper body will be forced downstream and held under water. Even in a moderate current, you will be unable to pull yourself upstream to free your foot. Only a pull from upstream can help you in this situation. Even if you have traveling companions, their aid might be too late if, in fact, they are able to reach you at all. So don't attempt to touch bottom. Swim into the eddy behind a

rock, then stand up. A rescuer on shore may be able to reach you with a throwline and then pendulum you into shore. At the very least you can rest in the eddy and reassess the best direction to swim.

Proper swimming position is lying on your back, feet downstream to fend off rocks, and backpaddling with your hands to control your descent. A sculling motion will help, as well, to keep your bum near the surface, avoiding shallow rocks.

A fast self-rescue technique is to use a heads-up front crawl and swim directly toward shore. This is a necessity if it is very cold or there is a hazard downstream such as an undercut rock, falls, pothole, or a strainer. If you cannot avoid a strainer, (page 111) use a heads-up front crawl to propel yourself up and over the tree trunk before the current catches your feet and tries to push you under the tree.

Emergency Knife
When you start messing around with long ropes, an emergency knife that's easy to get at is an absolute must. Did you ever try fishing around in your pocket for a jackknife while being dragged down a rapid, entangled in a tracking line? For general camp use you can't beat a belt knife or multipurpose jackknife, but in a crisis could you count on it being sharp? For this reason you should have an emergency knife attached to your PFD that is very accessible and used *only* for emergencies. Another good safety feature that you can attach to your PFD is a whistle, which can be blown three times to signal distress.

Throw bag
I swear I only need to pick up a rope, and it feels like it's attacking me. I can stand there and carefully coil a rope, fold it neatly in half, stuff it in the stern of the canoe, count to ten, remove the rope and pull it out

straight, and it will look like an army of elves spent a whole day tying knots in it. I've never been able to figure out how they get there.

To avoid getting knots in the rope and the more serious hazard of entanglement in a loose rope, most people use throw bags exclusively. You may find it helpful to have several different sizes and lengths. Perhaps a sixty- to seventy-foot (18 m-21 m) self-rescue line attached to the stern of your canoe,

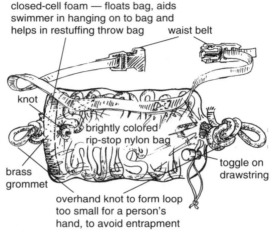

closed-cell foam — floats bag, aids swimmer in hanging on to bag and helps in restuffing throw bag

waist belt

knot

brightly colored rip-stop nylon bag

brass grommet

toggle on drawstring

overhand knot to form loop too small for a person's hand, to avoid entrapment

floating rope, either:
3/8 inch (9 mm) polypropylene, bulky, easy to hang on to
1/4 inch (7 mm) Spectra, more compact, stronger

as well as a thirty- to sixty-foot (9 m-18 m) throw bag for rescuing swimmers. Throw bags are available from outdoor gear stores, or you can sew your own from this diagram. For more information see *River Rescue* by Les Bechdel and Slim Ray.

Recovery rope on the Petawawa

On one of our filming trips, Ken Buck, the cameraman, Paul and I hit the Petawawa River, near Petawawa, Ontario, right at the peak of spring flood. The water was very cold, so we weren't fooling around this trip. We were filming a stretch of rapids called Rollway, the same rapids we had filmed in the fall to show the difference water levels make in the difficulty of a rapid. My intention was to show the rapid in full flood, then cut to the same rapid in low water so viewers could actually see the rocks that were causing the waves.

We had completed the filming of Rollway Rapids and had portaged the canoes to a point three-quarters of the way down. There was no way anyone could run the upper part in flood. But from here on it was easy. The rapid narrowed to a rocky slit at the bottom, where I had never experienced anything but easy haystacks. As a precaution, I was to run first with an empty canoe and wave if it was okay. The second canoe would follow. Then we would go back and portage the packs and valuable film equipment. I put on my wet-suit top and pushed off. Anyone who runs large rapids in spring flood without at least a wet-suit top is brave, crazy, or a little of both. As I neared the narrows, I couldn't believe my eyes. The river was backed up to an incredible height, and the water was pouring through the gap like water pouring out of a pail. There was no danger of hitting any rocks, but the wave that was thrown up looked like Mt. Everest. I didn't even have time to line up with the apex of the V.

I knew I was going to hit the diagonal curling wave. I thought maybe, just maybe, if I braced real hard into the wave, I'd make it without rolling over. The bow smashed into the wave, and instead of breaking through, it was thrown to the left. The rest of the canoe hit the wave broadside and over I went. I remember thinking as I waited to surface downstream how *fast* it all happened, especially in contrast to how long it took to surface. When you wipe out on a big wave, you are carried under, but you always come up. You just need patience, that's all. Don't fight for the surface. You'll bob up beyond the wave in time to grab a breath before you are pulled under again. It's all a matter of timing. If you fight too hard for the surface, each time you go under, you'll tire yourself out.

At the end of the haystacks I swam over to the canoe, reached under the stern, pulled out my recovery line and headed for the nearest shore, with the end of the rope clenched in one hand. The rope payed out without tangling. Halfway to shore, I began to realize just how cold the water was. My wet-suit covered only my upper body. It was not a well-fitting suit, and it allowed some cold water to leak in, but I knew it would be sufficient for a fast exit from the water. I hit the shore and tried to reel in the canoe, but the current was very strong. I had to run to keep up with it while I worked it out of the current. As I ran along the shore, jumping over or around the bolders, I saw a tree ahead. I knew that if I could cinch the rope around it, the canoe would stop in the current and swing to shore. There was another big rapids coming up, and I was anxious to recover the canoe before getting to the brink. It was an extremely difficult rapid in normal conditions, so I could only imagine what it would look like in full flood.

I ran around the tree in an attempt to cinch the rope but succeeded in getting it around only once. There was no rope left in my hands to secure it. I held on until the end slipped through my fingers and shot out into the river. I ran along the shore to cut it off, dove in, swam out to the canoe, reached under the stern, and found the rope. This time I had to pay out the rope through my hands to find the end of it because I wasn't using floating rope. Unfortunately I payed out the rope right past the end, and I had to

start all over. By now I was nearing the danger point of exposure to the cold water, but I figured I was good for one more try. I swam back to the canoe, found the rope, and headed for shore again. The river had widened, so when I reached the end of the rope I was still about twenty feet (6 m) short of the shore. I tried to tow the canoe, but I began to feel numb, I realized I was losing control of my body. I dropped the rope, said goodbye to the canoe, and headed for shore. I remember being furious at the canoe for its lack of cooperation. I reached shore none too soon, climbed up the bank with some difficulty, and stood shivering uncontrollably as the canoe drifted towards the next rapids. As I followed it along the shore, I kept hoping it would get caught in an eddy — but no such luck. As I rounded a point I looked toward the rapids and saw a canoe pulled up at the head of the portage. I took the liberty of borrowing it and completed a canoe-over-canoe rescue just above the brink. To save time, I paddled to shore with my canoe across the gunwales of the borrowed canoe. Fortunately, the owner had no objections to my rescue operation. As it turned out, there was so much water going through the next set of rapids that the canoe would not have been damaged. But I have no idea how I would have caught it because the river flows swiftly for a considerable distance below the rapids.

Before rejoining Ken, who was on the other side of the river and far upstream, I kindled a fire to thaw myself out. I always carry matches in a waterproof container. You can also buy waterproof matches or waterproof them yourself by dipping them in shellac or pouring paraffin wax over them. Ordinary cardboard matches are not suitable for the outdoors. In very difficult weather, I also carry a small candle. It's invaluable when starting a fire with wet tinder.

It was some time before I stopped shaking. I knew enough about the dangerous effects of immersion in cold water to be very concerned. The discomfort I was feeling told me that I had stayed in the water much too long, even with the wet-suit top. Chilling the body to the danger point is known as hypothermia, a condition that can result in death even after reaching shore. As I soaked up the warmth of the fire, I resolved that from then on my recovery rope would be the floating variety and long enough to reach shore. If you get ideas about tying a floating ball to the end of ordinary rope, you can forget it. It doesn't work. The rope will sink and catch under rocks. When you try to pull it in, the ball will catch and you'll have to cut the rope. During the filming of the canoe-swamping sequence, we fired an old canoe through a long turbulent rapid and neglected to remove a nonfloating hundred-foot (30 m) line. The line caught on a rock and held the canoe under water in the middle of the rapids, where it was totally irretrievable. For all I know it's still there.

Bailer

For running rapids and paddling in waves, a good size bailer is indispensable. It can be made from a plastic detergent bottle, an antifreeze container or any plastic container. You just cut the bottom out of it, but be sure to fasten the screw top tightly. Tie it to the canoe with a short cord that is thin enough that it would break if you became entangled. Even better is to use a carabiner to clip your bailer to a pack. It's safe and easy to access, and ensures that you won't lose your bailer.

Broadsiding onto a rock

I once overheard a student ask her instructor what to do if a canoe swings broadside into a rock. He replied "You don't let that happen." In actual fact, it happens all the time. It's happened to me more times than I care to admit, both while paddling solo and double. It's much easier to get out of trouble when you're paddling solo.

Let's assume you are paddling double and there is a rock coming up fast. One of the common errors the bow paddler can make is choosing the wrong side of the rock. Let's say the main surge of the current is to the left but the bowman goes right (see illustration 1). The stern is forced around, turning the canoe broadside, and it hits the rock amidships. The canoeists both lean away from the ominous-looking rock (illustration 2), the gunwale dips toward the upstream side, and the water pours in (illustration 3). The canoe, now facing upstream, becomes a giant scoop receiving the full force of the current. The canoe will fold around the rock and in this position is almost irretrievable (illustration 4).

The bear trap

To be caught between the canoe and the rock could be fatal (illustration 5). The force exerted by the canoe against the rock in an eight mph (13 km/h) current if it's facing upstream can go as high as two tons (tonnes). The canoe will fold around the rock (photograph 6). When you find yourself swimming down a rapid, your first priority is to get clear of the canoe. Swim away, out to the side of the canoe, then scull with your hands to slow down so that you remain upstream and off to the side of the canoe. If you only get upstream, you will wash into the canoe should it get caught on a rock or in a hole. Downstream of a swamped canoe is the most dangerous place you can be.

Recovery from broadsiding

Now let's look at it again and see what can be done to avoid losing the canoe in a broadside situation against the rock. You are approaching a rock in midstream (photograph 7). Your bow paddler blows it by passing the rock on the right when most of the current is going left (photograph 8). You try to draw your stern upstream, but the current is too strong. The canoe swings broadside. You yell to the bow paddler to lean downstream, toward the rock, to avoid the possibility of the current pulling the gunwale down and filling the canoe. He is already doing just that as you hit the rock. Realizing the canoe is against the rock forward of center, he steps out onto the rock (photograph 9). If the canoe were against the rock back of center, the stern paddler would jump out. As soon as the bow is unweighted, as the stern sinks deeper into the water, the current grabs it and swings it downstream, pivoting it clear of the rock, with the bow paddler hanging on for dear life (photograph 10). *Your* dear life because you are positioned where the canoe is only eighteen inches (50 cm) wide — a precarious perch in a bad situation. He runs his hands along the gunwales as the canoe swings downstream, and feeds it into the eddy (photograph 11), from the rock, he yells he is sorry about taking the rock on the wrong side and then climbs aboard, but all is forgiven because of the spectacular rescue he pulled off (photograph 12). Actually, the photographs show a mild version of broadsiding on a rock in a gentle current. I wasn't very enthusiastic about risking our canoe in anything bigger.

There are many variations of this problem and many situations that are a lot worse than the one illustrated here. If the rock is covered, you can sometimes get off without getting out of the canoe, as long as the bow paddler moves back to unweight the bow. The current will then grab the stern, which is riding deeper now, and swing it downstream into the eddy. Remember to always keep the upstream gunwale high by leaning downstream, toward the rock. The tendency is to lean away from the rock every time. It's a reflex action you must learn to overcome. If you don't, the canoe will fill in a split second.

A very serious problem occurs if the canoe is pinned against rocks at both ends. You must attempt to lift one end over the rock or slide the canoe forward until one end is free of the rock, and then pivot the canoe off the other rock. In either case, you have to get out of the canoe and onto the rock. Remember, if the canoe fills and pins you against a rock, it's a matter of life and death. Never position yourself downstream of the canoe. It's not the weight (mass) of the canoe that will kill you. It's the weight of the water pressing against the canoe. This is why the covered canoes and kayaks are equipped with air-filled floatation bags. Canoeists who are out to fool around in the big stuff sometimes also equip their open canoes with floatation bags or inner tubes. This is impractical for wilderness canoeing.

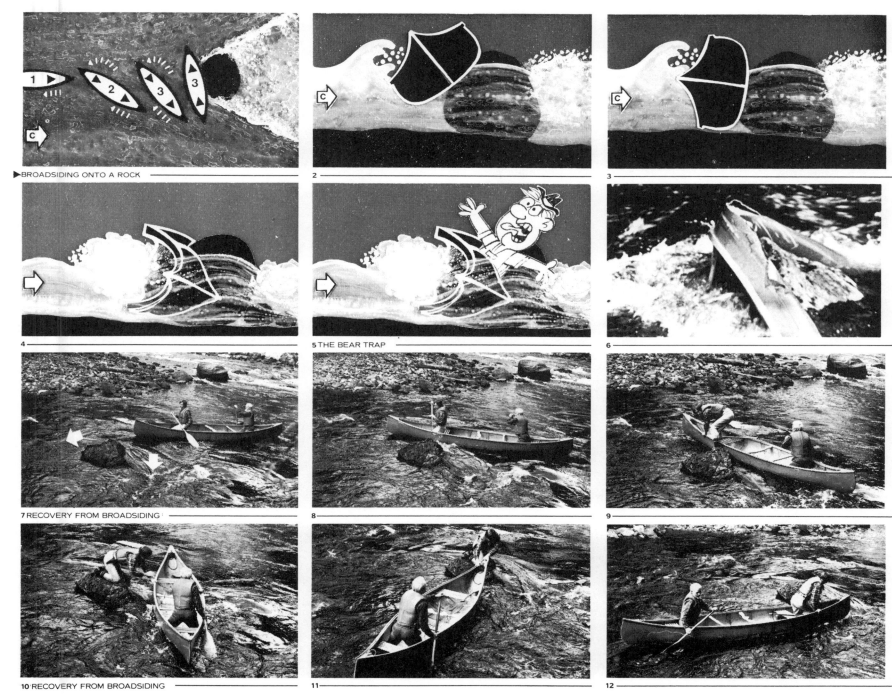

BROADSIDING ONTO A ROCK

2

3

4

5 THE BEAR TRAP

6

7 RECOVERY FROM BROADSIDING

8

9

10 RECOVERY FROM BROADSIDING

11

12

141

Recovering a pinned canoe

In the film *Solo Whitewater* there is a scene where the canoe fetches up broadside against a rock. For a split second, I committed the cardinal sin. My hands went for the gunwales, a reflex action. I recovered and was able to backpaddle off the rock because the canoe hit the rock forward of the pivot point. An interesting fact about a rock sticking above the surface in a rapid is that there is usually a cushion of stillwater in front of it. The canoe didn't actually make contact with the rock. But if it had swamped, it sure would have. The canoe would have bent around the rock—a situation in which the canoe is usually irretrievable.

Pinned Canoe on the Nahanni River
On our Nahanni trip we pinned a canoe twice. The first time, it happened to Paul and me. We had decided to line through a boulder field rather than run a nasty stretch on the outside of a curve. I looked over the boulder field and imagined I could see some semblance of a channel through it—a contorted channel, but nonetheless a channel. I instructed Paul to shove the canoe in the direction of the first gap as I proceeded down the rocky shore with the tracking line. He looked at me as though he didn't understand or couldn't believe my request. I assured him it would be okay. I've floated

canoes through the most impossible places without damage. Again he gave me that "I don't believe it" look. This time I ordered him to give it a shove. He gave me an "Okay, it's your canoe" shrug, lined it up, and fired it through the gap. That's about as far as it went. The bow passed on the wrong side of the next rock, swung broadside, and water poured into the canoe, pinning it against the rock.

Because I had run downstream with the tracking line, I was not in a position to yank the canoe back upstream when it began to swing. I should have left Paul in possession of the stern rope until the canoe was well on its way. Then he could have pulled it back upstream when it went on the wrong side of a rock. Within seconds the canoe was swamped and pinned. It's a panicky feeling when you know that the water in that canoe plus the eight mph (13 km/h) current exerts a force of at least a ton (tonne) against the canoe. We all knew that our destination lay 350 miles (560 km) away.

Barrie Nelson, one of the five canoeists accompanying me on the trip, waded out to the canoe with me following to attempt a rescue. First we cut the tether line on the packs. Because everything was laced on one line this wasn't too difficult, even though they were underwater and he had to grope around to find the rope. We handed the packs ashore, along with the paddles. The next problem was where to tie the recovery rope. We decided to tie it to the

thwarts, then pass the rope under the canoe and over it, so the pull from upstream would roll the canoe over and free it from the tremendous force of the current (*see* photograph 1). This effort was totally futile. Terry Orlick, Bob Edwards, and Paul (three of the other members of the party) tried pulling from all angles, including downstream. I couldn't get up much enthusiasm for any of these maneuvers because I knew that six men were not going to move that canoe! By now it was folded neatly around the rock. Meanwhile Alan Whatmough, our sixth canoeist, was hacking down a tree. As he looked up I indicated we needed one twice as big. He abandoned the first tree and moved to the bigger one. Anytime anyone even made a move to position himself downstream of the pinned canoe, he was faced with a volley of abuse. If that canoe had ever come loose, it would have been a deadly juggernaut. Just imagining anyone pinned between the rock and that canoe was enough to send chills up my spine. By now Alan had the tree down and was trimming the branches. He was working very fast, but it seemed like forever as we stood waist deep in the cold water. Alan dragged the pole to a position upstream, jumped in, and floated down to us (photograph 2). Together we placed the pole

under the bow and levered it on a rock. The canoe moved upward slightly, but the green pole bent with the weight (photograph 3). Bob chopped down an even bigger pole and positioned it amidships. With Bob, Terry, and Paul heaving on the second pole and Barrie, Alan and I heaving on the first pole, the canoe slowly began to rise (see illustrations 1 and 2 on next page). We were lifting an eighty five pound (39 kg) canoe containing almost a ton (tonne) of water against an eight mph (13 km/h) current. All of a sudden the canoe broke free and drifted over the rock. The canoe swung to shore because of the recovery rope that had been secured to a huge rock. The bottom of the canoe was buckled so badly that it almost touched the center thwart, but it was not beyond repair (photograph 4). To our great relief, our visions of paddling three-to-a-canoe in the other two canoes, plus hauling all our gear, faded. I have heard of many instances where the canoe was not recoverable. Without the use of levers, our canoe would have suffered the same fate. We put the bow and stern on two rocks, and Alan, who claimed to know something about body work, stamped and pounded until the canoe began to assume a reasonable facsimile of what a canoe should look like. Unfortunately, it was ripped in two places.

Second pinned canoe

The next morning Paul and I pushed off into a set of rapids just one hundred yards (90 m) below where we got stuck the previous day. It was tricky but we got through okay and continued on down the river into a second and third set. We eddied out just before a turn, where we would have been lost to the view of the other canoes. We looked back upstream just in time to see Terry and Alan racing back along the shore and around the bend. That could only mean a wipeout for Barrie and Bob. Because they didn't come floating around the bend, it also meant the canoe was pinned. "Where were they? Why didn't they float down around the corner?" Paul and I made a frantic ferry to their side of the river, and grabbed the hundred-foot (30 m) safety rope, the axe, and the saw. It seemed like an eternity as we worked our way along the boulder-strewn shoreline. We rounded the bend and there stood Barrie and Bob, right smack in the middle of the rapids, up to their waists in the foam. I yelled to Terry "Where's the canoe?" He shouted over the roar of the rapids something that sounded very much like "They're standing in it."

The recovery was going to be very difficult, maybe even impossible. They were on their own out there in the freezing water. It would have been difficult to get out to them, although it would have been possible by swimming down to them from upstream. But it goes without saying that everyone was hoping they could free it by themselves. By the time Paul and I arrived, Terry and Alan had thrown out a rope. Bob and Barrie secured the packs to it so that they could be pulled ashore. On a river like the Nahanni, which flows for miles and miles without slowing down, it is imperative to hang onto those packs, even at the risk of one's life. It was with great relief that we saw those four packs and three paddles safely on shore. The next job was to get a pry pole out to them to lever the canoe up and off the rock. I felled a six-inch (15 cm) spruce, trimmed it, tied it to the safety rope, and threw the other end to the stranded canoeists. The rope is thrown upstream and well past them. Thrown in this manner, they can't miss it as it drifts down on them. Bob caught the rope and pulled the log out. Barrie untied the rope, coiled it carefully, and flung it back, but forgot to hang onto one end. The rope fell short and drifted downstream, never to be seen again. The pole was worked into position, but there was no rock to use as a lever point. The only large rock was the one that the canoe was pinned up against. To pry off would have meant positioning themselves on the downstream side. We all knew this was out of the question. Instead, they worked the pole under the canoe and created a lever effect by lifting up instead of prying down (see illustrations 3 and 4 on next page).

▶SECOND PINNED CANOE UNDERWATER

Much to our delight, the canoe popped free and swung toward shore. Staying upstream, we waded out with grasping hands to greet the canoe. As soon as we got hold of it, we raised the upstream end. Raising it in this manner, eighty percent of the water flows out, making the rest of the recovery very easy.

We left the battered canoe on the rocks and went back to the job of getting Bob and Barrie safely to shore. They could choose to swim ashore or come ashore on a rope. The water was extremely fast between them and the shore, which would mean being swept downstream and possibly picking up some bruises or more serious injuries. We tied a stick to the other safety line and flung it well past Bob and Barrie and upstream, so it would drift down to them. Bob untied the stick and proceeded to loop the rope around his waist. I whistled and indicated "no". I made a small loop on my end, indicating he should do the same. I also indicated that he should not loop it over his wrist but only grasp it in his hand in case he was pulled under and had to let go. If he lost his footing, he would be pulled under and would be held there unless he chose to let go. Of course, we could have let go of our end, but floating downstream tied to one end of a dragging rope is not a good situation to be in. If the rope had caught on a

rock, Bob would have been held under and drowned, unless he could cut the rope. The only way I would tie myself to a rope would be if the only other option was to be swept over a fifty foot falls! Only then would I trust myself to the rescuers and their ability to pull me to shore.

Bob made the loop, grasped it with both hands, and stepped into the full force of the current. To decrease the force on Bob's body, the three of us hung onto the shore end of the rope, rather than lashing it around a rock or tree, and we were able to move gently downstream. Bob almost lost his footing a couple of times, but he made it safely to shore. Then we repeated the same procedure for Barrie. No one thought to check, but the entire operation must have taken at least half an hour, so they were both extremely chilled. Barrie admitted he was beginning to lose control of his legs and arms. In fact, he later told Terry that he was on the fringe of giving up and letting the river take him. This really scared me when I heard it because his cheery disposition, even during the difficulties, gave no indication he was in trouble. A fire was kindled, and our warmest clothes were distributed between Barrie and Bob. The hot sun made it unnecessary for them to climb into their sleeping bags. The heat of the sun and hot drinks were the external and internal sources of heat they needed to keep from going into hypothermia.

One thing I noticed — and some of the others admitted to it — was my feeling of panic at the prospect of not being able to recover the canoe or losing a pack. If we'd had to choose between losing one or another of the nine packs, there wasn't one of them that we would have been happy to do without.

As before, Alan put his boots to the canoe and restored it to health. Like the other canoe, it also was ripped in two places. They were bad, jagged rips. Alan pounded the edges flat and used aluminum solder to fill the holes. Then we applied a layer of epoxy and topped it off with duct tape. With a little stretching of the truth, you could say the canoe was as good as new. At least there was never any problem with the holes breaking open for the rest of the trip. Our only problem was trying to explain what was under those strips of tape when we returned the canoes to Wally Schaber, the outfitter who rented them to us.

In all my years of canoeing I had only pinned a canoe once before. Here our group of experienced canoeists had done it twice within a hundred yards. You never know when it might happen and it's important to remember that it can happen to anybody — a rather sobering thought.

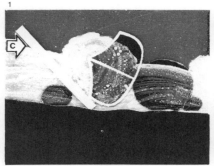
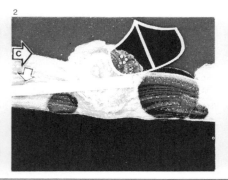

▶USING A TREE AS A LEVER

Preventing damage to a swamped canoe

As soon as a canoe swamps, it is vulnerable to severe damage or pinning and wrapping around a rock. In shallow rapids, don't stay in the canoe. If you stay in a swamped canoe it will continue to sink as your weight pushes it down. If it hits the bottom the damage to the canoe will be tremendous regardless of the material, because of the force of the current on it. You are much better off to swim to shore with a rescue line and pull the canoe in. When you reach shallow, slow-moving water, about knee deep, you can then do a shallow-water empty. In shallow rapids, the danger of being pinned between the canoe and a rock is just as great as it is in deep water. Don't attempt to save the canoe unless you are upstream of it.

Shallow-water empty

Stand beside the canoe in water just over the knees (photograph 1A). Rest the canoe on its side until it is perpendicular, grasp the center thwart with one hand, reach down into the water, and grasp the submerged gunwale with the other (photograph 1B). Now stand up slowly and the water will flow out, leaving the canoe bone dry (photograph 1C). You must tilt the canoe past the perpendicular to allow all the water to flow out. If you don't, you'll be attempting to lift the water in the canoe, and it can't be done, no matter how strong you are. Lift the near gunwale briskly as you drop the canoe onto the water (photograph 1D).

Most people simply empty the canoe over a rock, but it's hard on the canoe and sometimes you can't find just the right place. The method described here is very easy, once you get the hang of it. Practice it in shallow water. If there are two canoeists, the emptying can be done by each one

grabbing an end. The nice thing about the one-person empty is that the other canoeist can worry about the packs.

Empty on a dock

There is a right way and a wrong way to empty a swamped canoe on a dock or on shore. Lift the bow onto the dock (photograph 2A). Do not attempt to lift it any further. The two or three hundred pounds (100-150 kg) of water in the stern puts a tremendous strain on the canoe. Roll the canoe over (photograph 2B). Pull it up onto the dock upside down (photograph 2C). Right the canoe and return it to the water (photograph 2D).

▶ SHALLOW-WATER EMPTY 1A

1B

1C

1D

▶ EMPTY ON A DOCK 2A

2B

2C

2D

Preventing damage to a swamped canoe...

Canoe-over-canoe rescue

The first time I was called upon to use the canoe-over-canoe rescue was on Big Traverse Bay in Lake of the Woods, Ontario. It's a big enough body of water that you can't see across it. I was in charge of eight campers in three canoes. We used to travel three to a canoe for economy, but it's a practice I don't like and, in fact, am now very much against. We were running with an onshore wind between islands in a pretty healthy-looking swell. I wouldn't have been out there if there'd been any danger of being blown off shore into a large expanse of water, which would have been the situation with an offshore wind. The waves were breaking but only where the water was shallow and not too cold.

Everyone was loving it until all of a sudden a canoe overturned. It was a sickening feeling, since I realized that I had allowed the boys to push themselves beyond their capabilities. I was completely responsible for their safety. All of a sudden those waves looked a lot more ominous than they had a few moments before. As I brought my canoe alongside the boys', I checked to make sure they were in control of themselves. Much to my relief two of the boys were making light of the situation, probably to hide their embarrassment. The other boy looked a bit worried, so I got him to hang onto my canoe. I got hold of the bow of the overturned canoe and instructed the boys to hang onto my canoe. I then did a canoe-over-canoe empty, returned the canoe to the water, and hung on tightly to the gunwale while the boys climbed into their canoe and recovered their packs. The waves added to the difficulty of the operation; however, the boys had been trained to know how to assist, so we didn't have too much trouble.

The canoe-over-canoe empty is demonstrated by Derek Brown, one of Paul's canoeing companions. Derek brings his canoe alongside mine (see photograph 1). He asks me to hang onto the stern of his canoe. Reaching down into the water, he grasps the gunwale of my canoe about four feet (1.5 m) from the end and lifts. The canoe rolls easily and breaks the air lock (photograph 2). Lifting from the very end of the canoe is difficult because of the water trapped inside. He then runs his hands along the gunwale to the end and lifts the bow up onto his gunwale, keeping my canoe upside down. He now feeds my canoe across his until it is half way across (photograph 3). His canoe is now very stable and cannot be capsized. I could easily climb aboard or he could help me if I were weak from the cold. Next, he grasps the near gunwale and lifts (photograph 4), rolling my canoe right side up (photograph 5). My canoe is then fed into the water (photograph 6), and turned sideways to his (photograph 7). He locks gunwales (photograph 8) while I climb aboard (photograph 9), and doesn't let go until I am in paddling position (photograph 10). If I were having difficulty climbing in, Derek could help me by letting my canoe tilt so the gunwale would be closer to the water, making it a shorter distance for me to pull myself up.

One of the problems of doing the canoe-over-canoe rescue is that nearly everyone learns to do it in calm water. In reality, one seldom needs to empty in such conditions. The canoe-over-canoe procedure is of little use until you've learned to do it in high winds and waves, and in the swirling currents below a rapid. The episode on Big Traverse Bay made me very thankful for my instructor, who had taught me to do it in difficult conditions. It is even possible to do a canoe-over-canoe rescue when both canoes are swamped using this method.

Shake-out

The shake-out is a method of emptying the water out of the canoe in deep water. The difficulty depends on the canoe. Canoes with a lot of tumblehome are difficult to empty in this way. Shallow canoes without tumblehome are easiest. The hardest part of the shake-out is getting started. Some people find it impossible to shake out a completely swamped canoe. You might find it easier to swim to the bow or stern and empty some of the water by pushing down and forward on the end of the canoe (see photograph 1). Timing is important. You must push the end down and forward, so the water flows out, then lift it up quickly before the water flows back in. I find it easier to begin the shake-out this way. After about half the water is emptied, I then move to the center to complete the shake-out (photograph 2). As you push down on the gunwale, you must propel the canoe away from you until the water splashes out over the side. Then quickly raise the gunwale to prevent more water from flowing in.

The best way to learn the shake-out is to practice while standing in shallow water. Then, when you've learned the principle of it, move to deep water. The shake-out is only of real value if you can do it in swirling currents or waves. I've seen people empty a canoe in less than thirty seconds using this method.

▶CANOE-OVER-CANOE RESCUE

CANOE-OVER-CANOE RESCUE

CANOE-OVER-CANOE RESCUE

▶SHAKE-OUT

Wipeout while filming

Most of my worst wipeouts happen while filming. You don't run a rapid the way you normally would when filming. It is necessary to do things so the camera can catch the action clearly. If you are demonstrating a stroke, there's no point in doing it on the side opposite the camera, or the viewer won't see a thing. I often paddle on the side opposite to the one I normally would have chosen and sometimes end up swimming.

On one occasion I was running a rapid with the camera bolted to a crash helmet on my head. I was so busy keeping the camera pointed in the right direction that I hit all the wrong places, and the canoe slowly filled and sank. On that occasion I waited for the longest time to come up. I had completely forgotten about the ten pounds (5 kg) of camera gear on my head. As it turned out all the camera operator on shore could see was a camera bobbing down the rapids. I was underneath wondering why I didn't surface. Finally, a very strenuous dog paddle kept me up long enough to make shore. I should have worn two life jackets to compensate for the weight of the camera.

Wipeout on voyageur film

The biggest wipeout I ever had was during the making of the voyageur film. We landed above Culbute Rapids on the Ottawa River near Petawawa, Ontario. Culbute roughly translates "ass over teakettle" in English. It really was a very large rapid. There was a hole in the middle of the rapid, followed by three huge waves. I took one look at it and knew that no canoe could get through — not even our twenty-five footer. To make matters worse, the river was full of logs. I didn't doubt we could avoid them in the canoe, but I didn't like the prospect of swimming with them in those churning waves if we swamped or upset. Our canoe was a twenty-five foot (8 m) canvas-cedar canoe, painted to look like a birchbark canoe. It

had those high, sweeping ends typical of the fur traders' canoes. The film was a re-enactment of the fur brigade days. The men were an authentic-looking bunch, picked for their canoeing skills, from the backwoods of Quebec. They were a good crew, experienced in whitewater racing. The man in charge of the stern was a marvelous character who played his role to the hilt. He was well informed about the history of the fur trade and was loving the whole thing. I was just beginning my career in film making and was hired as the second camera operator. I was doing all the filming from within the canoe. The main camera operator was filming from shore.

The director asked the stern if he thought he could get through okay. With great contempt, the stern expressed his disdain for the rapids. They were nothing. His men would paddle through; there'd be no problem at all. I politely pointed out that the huge breaking wave and hole would be difficult to avoid. With a wave of the hand, he dismissed these hazards completely. He would avoid them with no problem. I suggested that the whole river seemed to be funneling right into the hole and that it could be a problem avoiding it. I also expressed a concern for the logs. He assured the director that we would push them aside. "And if we wipe out and end up swimming with them?" I questioned. The stern again insisted that there was no problem because we would not upset. The director looked at me and I said "I think you're going to get some very interesting footage."

So it was go. We climbed in and I positioned myself right behind the bow so I could shoot the approaching doom. I knew that the hole and the curling waves were going to look three or four times as big from the canoe. The river was wide and the hole a considerable distance from shore. I knew it was bigger, much bigger, than it looked. The director's final instructions to me were to get the expressions on the men's faces

as they approached the rapids. I protested that it was much more important to film the approaching waves. But the director insisted that he wanted their faces as we approached the brink. I replied that these old pros would be expressionless. It would be a waste of film. After having made it clear what he would do to me if I didn't get their faces, I agreed that it would be a good idea.

We shoved off and started down the approach to the rapids. The river narrowed as we neared the brink. I looked at the current we were riding and followed it into the rapids. Just as I figured, we were heading right for that hole. We were right of center when we should have been very close to shore to have even a hope of missing that hole. I resigned myself to the impending doom, pointed the camera at their faces, and started shooting. Their faces ranged from a mixture of calm anticipation to boredom. But as the roar of the rapids increased and the canoe began to pick up speed, I could detect a growing interest in what lay ahead. As I panned from face to face I realized they were becoming several shades whiter. My feelings of impending doom were now shared by all. I remember saying to myself "That must be some wave." I held the camera on the faces until, sensing the approach of the wave, I spun around, still looking through the viewfinder. I picked up the bowman and a wall of water beyond. I could feel the canoe dropping down, down into the hole. We hit the wave and the bowman landed in my lap as the water cascaded over us. He struggled back to his seat and this time held onto the gunwales. The second wave hit. Using his body like a shield, he caused the water to spray off to the sides, but it poured in over the gunwales the full length of the canoe. We were wallowing. We hit the third wave and the canoe slowly disappeared into it. The canoe rolled over to the left and everything disappeared in the foam. The camera was not waterproof, but I kept shooting just in case.

I surfaced, caught a breath, and disappeared again. I fought my way to the surface to find people and equipment all over the place and logs everywhere. I grabbed onto a log but there was no buoyancy in it. I let go and I was carried under again. I slipped the camera strap from my wrist and held on only with my hand in case I ran out of air and had to drop the camera. I knew I'd need both hands to get to the surface. Again I reached daylight, this time to find I was past the last of the big waves. I glanced around and saw that the canoe and everyone else was heading for the right shore. But the left shore was much closer. I struck out for the left shore, dragging the camera. To my surprise, I found that I was being carried downstream at an alarming rate. I knew there was another stretch of rapids not far from the first. I swam as hard as I could, still considering the possibility of dropping the camera. Then, to my relief I touched bottom. Also to my relief, it was a small-boulder bottom. After several attempts, I got to my feet. The water was up to my thighs but the current was very fast. I tried to take a step toward shore but lost my footing. I got back to my feet and realized I couldn't move against the current. It was

too strong. There were logs drifting by, some small, some large. There were four-, eight-, and twelve-foot logs. I knew that some of them would surely hit me; it was only a matter of time. They wouldn't hurt me, but I figured they would be just big enough to push me over. Meanwhile, I was yelling to the director to bring a rope. Glancing downstream, I could see the plunging whitewater of the next rapid. It was a big one!

The rest of the men had made it into an eddy on the right and were trying to swim the canoe to shore. They had made the right decision. They weren't as close to the right shore as they were to the left, but they were on the edge of the current. What I didn't know was that the whole main surge of the current was between me and the left shore, despite the fact it looked closer. I was on the outside bend of the river, standing in the full force of the current, with no eddies between me and the next rapids. The director was running along the shore toward me. I remember seeing that the camera operator, true to form, was still shooting. The others were losing their battle with the canoe. They couldn't hold it. It was swinging out into the current again. I looked up and saw some logs that looked very much like they were going to hit me. One did, but I steered it aside. Another one pushed me over. I shoved it past me, out of the way, and stood up again. To my surprise, the water was deeper. This meant that I was on the downstream side of the bar. The water would get progressively deeper. The director was getting closer, but I could see he didn't have a rope. It was my responsibility to see that one was on hand, so it was my own fault. This was in the days when I did most of my canoeing by myself. I was oblivious to the various safety measures one should take when messing around in big stuff. But I was learning fast.

Wipeout while filming . . .

Another log knocked me over and again I got to my feet. This time I could barely stand in the force of the current. A sixteen-foot length drifted toward me, and this time it *was* swim time! I considered abandoning the camera and swimming for shore, but I knew I wouldn't make it in time. The log pushed me over and I was on my way to the rapids. I had time to think. I decided that I would take a deep breath when I could. The rapids were narrow, so they would be deep. There was no danger of hitting any rocks. I looked to my right and there was the canoe. It was far enough away not to present a danger to me. I resisted the temptation to swim to it. That twenty five foot (8 m) canoe would easily exert a pressure of several tons if it hit a rock. I wasn't the least interested in putting myself in a position where I could be caught between the canoe and a rock, even though the rapids were deep. I would take my chances by myself.

I hit the first wave and was carried under. I resisted the urge to fight for the surface. When I floated to the surface, I grabbed as much air as I could before going down again. I found myself being carried up and down in some kind of rhythm with the waves and experienced no kind of distress whatsoever in getting my breath. Looking back, if I had been panicky and gasping for air at the wrong times, I could have been in trouble. As I floated out past the last haystack, I saw yet another set of rapids coming up. This set has an ancient cribbing to guide the logs. It would be much more violent than the last rapid. I figured enough was enough and was headed for shore for all I was worth, flailing the water with the camera still held firmly in my left hand. Much to my relief, I felt myself cross the eddy line. My descent toward the third rapid had ceased. Between myself and shore lay a solid mat of logs about forty feet (12 m) wide. But at least they were stationary in the eddy. The logs were too small to bear my weight, so I shoved them aside and made a path to shore.

The director arrived just as I touched shore. When he saw that I was okay, his state of panic subsided sufficiently to enquire despondently about the camera. Of course, I knew that it wasn't the camera he was worried about, but the shot that was in the camera — going through that hole and the expressions on the faces of the men. I raised my left arm and as the camera, or rather what was left of the camera, surfaced you should have seen the expression on the director's face. It was an expression that would warm the heart of any camera operator. We both knew that as long as the body of the camera wasn't ruptured, the film, even though it was wet, could be processed and the shot salvaged. The camera itself was totaled. It had dragged on bottom when I was attempting to stand up in the shallows. When the shot was processed the footage was great, although the camera had stopped after the first wave. That really was some wave.

The fellows recovered the canoe before it went through the final chute. It was badly damaged but not beyond repair. Having survived the wipeout, most of the men were in a state of euphoria. One was nursing bruised ribs; a log had come up from the depths and belted him in the mid-section. The wind was knocked out of him and he was lucky that he had been close enough to the canoe to hang on. One man was in bad shape mentally. He had nearly drowned and probably would have had it not been for his brother. The man was a poor swimmer. He had ended up under the canoe, become disoriented, and couldn't find his way free.

He spoke of how he knew he was going to drown. His brother, who was a strong swimmer, had looked for him as soon as we went over. Not being able to see anyone, the brother worked his way along the gunwale of the canoe, sweeping his arm under it as far as he could reach, found the drowning man, yanked him free, and threw him up onto the overturned canoe. The canoe swept into the eddy and when the men were unable to get it to shore, his brother towed him to safety.

It was interesting for me to hear that, even though all these men had raced in down-river races (not slalom) for years, none of them had ever tipped before. They were not familiar with the problems of a large body of water like the Ottawa River. As for life preservers, we weren't wearing the standard whitewater ones because it was a historical film. Everyone was in authentic dress, including me. A couple of us wore the belt preservers and the rest had on a balloon type, which was supposed to inflate when squeezed. When we were all reassembled on shore, they told the director, with considerable good humor and mirth, exactly where he could put his life preservers. There, hanging from each person's belt, was this little balloon. Some were about an inch in diameter, some two or three inches and the largest about six inches. I was glad that I had been wearing a belt type. As useless as they are, they're better than nothing.

I remembered that as we approached the brink, one of the men had shouted out something in French. I asked the camera operator to translate it for me. Loosely translated, it was "Hey boys, watch the ducks perform." I think they all knew we were going swimming when they saw that hole coming and realized we were heading straight for it. It's an insane business, this camera work, but only a camera operator knows the sheer joy of having the shot in the can when it's all over. And next time you'd do it again.

It's from such experiences, from doing things I would not normally do, that I've learned much about rapids. It was here that I fully realized that a line of current twenty feet (6 m) from shore, one hundred yards (91 m) above a hole can end up in the center of the river going right into the hole. To avoid that hole you must be within three feet (1 m), or almost touching, the shore and drawing hard to avoid being carried into it. And the other lesson I won't forget is that you don't always swim to the nearest shore. Swim into the nearest eddy. That's the fastest way to stop your downstream descent. Also remember that if you don't keep your stern closer to shore than your bow, there is a tendency for your stern to swing out and downstream of the bow, putting you broadside. The reason is that water flows slower close to shore because of friction on the bottom and side of the rapid.

A word about tying in the packs. I used to lash them in securely until I had to do a canoe-over-canoe rescue in a very fast river. Three miles (5 km) and about ten rapids later, I still hadn't managed to right the canoe, let alone do the empty. I think there might be merit in relating the incident in its entirety.

Barrie Nelson, Blake James, Alan Whatnough, and I were canoeing the Colonge in springflood. Much to our disappointment, we were sharing the river with thousands of logs. The further downstream we traveled, the thicker they got. We rounded a bend and found the river almost completely blocked by a huge logjam. The water seemed to be flowing under the logs, one of the most dangerous situations a canoeist is likely to encounter. Blake and I threw our canoe into reverse with backwater strokes. I pried my stern over toward shore in a back ferry while Blake did a sculling draw as though his life depended on it. Which in fact it did, not to mention mine. As I turned around to warn the others, they shot by and broadsided against the jam. The upstream gunwale dipped and the canoe filled with water, spilling the canoeists out of the canoe and into the river. I watched with horror as the canoe disappeared beneath the dam, expecting to see the bobbing heads of Alan and Barrie follow it any minute. In that terrible moment, everything seemed to move in slow motion. I thought I was going to see them disappear forever as they were swept into the logs, but instead I saw them both make a grab for the logs on

the face of the jam. The relief Blake and I felt as they scrambled up onto the logs was indescribable. And you can imagine our delight when the canoe reappeared beyond the jam.

We dragged my canoe over the logjam, and I took off after the runaway canoe. I caught up to it but couldn't roll it right side up to begin the canoe-over-canoe rescue. The packs, lashed tightly in the canoe, combined with the swirling currents, making it impossible to roll the canoe upright. I couldn't even lift the end high enough to reach under and pull out the recovery rope. I followed it down endless sets of rapids, attempting a recovery between each rapid. It finally swung into an eddy, and I completed the recovery by riding my canoe up onto it and gently nudging it to shore. I emptied and began the long wait for my companions to make their way along the shore.

I now use only one short rope on the packs, just to prevent them from floating away. One end of the rope is secured to the thwart and then passed through the straps of each pack. The other end is tied to the last pack. This way, only the last pack need be untied to release them all. The canoe can even be emptied without untying them at all. The tether rope must be short to avoid any possibility of becoming entangled in it.

After our experience with the logjam, we lost our enthusiasm for the river. We continued for a while, but after a couple more jams, we decided that logs present an unnatural hazard to canoe travel. We terminated our trip at the first logging camp we found and hitched a ride out on a truck.

Solo versus double

There is considerable controversy whether very large rapids can be run more easily in an open canoe solo or double. Some canoeists believe that you have more control and stability with two paddlers because a brace can be done on both sides of the canoe at the same time. They also feel that with a paddler in each end of the canoe there is more control for turning and sideslipping and more power for back ferrying. This is probably true but with two paddlers instead of one there are two people to make mistakes and lose their balance. The solo paddler also has more buoyancy. With his weight in the middle of the canoe, the bow and stern bob lightly in the big waves instead of plunging through them. In addition, the solo paddler can favor one side of the canoe, leaning out on a solid brace making it almost impossible to tip to the nonpaddle side.

My personal opinion of the merits of solo versus double in the big stuff has vacillated. Years ago when most of my rapid running was done solo I felt much more comfortable in large rapids by myself. Then as I began running rapids with other paddlers, I began to appreciate the merits of doubles. I was completely won over to the advantages of doubles when I recently teamed up with Wally Schaber, an excellent whitewater canoeist, on the Nahanni River for a couple of runs for a camera crew. The crew asked Wally and me to get together for a run through the worst part of Hell's Gate (see first sequence of photographs). They wanted to spark up their footage with a little excitement, and since they said they'd be standing by with the park ranger's jetboat, we jumped at the chance. Personally, I wouldn't mess around with anything as dangerous as Hell's Gate without a rescue boat. It is not difficult to get through if you stick to the proper route and avoid the huge waves, but it's dangerous if you get into the big stuff. With the jetboat standing by, Wally took us through the wildest and most

difficult route he could find. The waves were by far the biggest I had ever paddled in. As we hit the waves, I braced way out on the right, Wally braced left and that canoe went through them like a barge. We did three runs, looking for the wildest waves each time. With our spray cover secure and leaning out on our braces, we didn't even come close to upsetting. Wally asked me later if I thought solo would be as easy. I thought for a long time, then finally admitted that I would be reluctant to try it solo. The solo paddler can only brace on one side. With the extreme turbulence, I believe I would have been hard pressed to prevent the canoe from rolling to my off side.

However, since then one of Wally's guides on the Nahanni River, Dirk Van Wyck, ran solo through the big waves and I've had to review my thinking again. What really put the clincher on the advantages of solo is seen in the second sequence of photographs. Wally is threading his canoe down a Class 4 rapid in an open canoe. Time and time again he disappeared completely from view only to reappear again with the buoyant bow and stern riding high in the water rather than plunging through the waves. Somehow he kept the canoe upright and afloat. Several times the canoe was perpendicular to the waves but his downstream brace kept the canoe from rolling all the way over and held him in the canoe. Wally agreed that paddling double in an open canoe in this situation would have been impossible.

A few days later Wally and Louise Gaulin attempted to run Cache Rapids, which has some of the largest waves found on the Nahanni. In the third sequence of photographs you can see their solid braces are to no avail. Not even their spray cover could save them from a wipeout. The waves can be avoided easily with a good back ferry but with the jetboat standing by, Wally and Louise ran right through the biggest waves

for the camera crew. Here (photograph 1) the canoe descends into a deep hole and explodes into the air while Louise frantically trys to reach the water for a brace (photograph 2). There's not much of Wally showing, but to hear him tell it, he was applying that brace just as hard as he could to prevent the canoe from rolling left. It's all to no avail. As Louise comes down from the clouds the canoe begins to roll (photograph 3). Notice that she is still attempting a brace instead of grabbing the gunwales. This is the sign of a great whitewater paddler. The water engulfs Wally in the stern, caves in the spray cover, and it's swim time. Still Louise hangs in there with her brace (photograph 4). Louise surfaces, gasping for air (photograph 5). She had considerable difficulty freeing herself, which is one of the very serious drawbacks of spray covers. After this episode, we all agreed our spray cover arrangement was not ideal. Wally and Louise stayed with the canoe for buoyancy in the huge rapids. If there'd been any danger of hitting rocks, they'd have swum clear of the canoe. The Park Services jetboat was standing by for a rescue, which is the only reason they attempted the rapid through the most difficult part. Otherwise, a run like this in wilderness conditions would be very risky, even foolish. Usually the large waves can be avoided altogether. This is true of all of the Nahanni except the canyon below the falls and the first fifty or sixty miles (80 or 96 km) of the Upper Nahanni, which is solid nonstop runnable rapids.

►HELL'S GATE, NAHANNI RIVER

►PICANOC RIVER, QUEBEC

►CACHE RAPIDS, NAHANNI RIVER ►

CACHE RAPIDS, NAHANNI RIVER

Floatation

In recent years canoeists have been running open canoes through rapids that once were considered strictly the domain of the rafts and kayaks. Even the Grand Canyon is being run on a regular basis by open canoeists. The trick that makes this possible, apart from new canoe designs, is the use of floatation, primarily in the form of air bags.

A swamped canoe is incredibly dangerous and extremely unmanageable because of the weight of the water confined within the hull. With the addition of floatation, the swamped canoe will ride much higher and therefore hold less water. With enough floatation, you can maintain sufficient control of your swamped canoe to navigate the remainder of the rapid, and if your canoe is set up for it you can even do an Eskimo roll in the event of a capsize.

There is a catch however. The room that is normally used for packs in the canoe is taken up by floatation. On a wilderness trip there is little available space for the luxury of floatation. On trips where I know the rapids are of only moderate difficulty, I don't bother with it or use very little. However, even a little bit helps. For wilderness trips you can use air bags that are designed to fit the ends of your canoe. They are lashed in behind the stern paddler and in front of the bow paddler. D rings glued to the hull provide excellent lash points to hold your air bags in place. You may ask yourself, is the expense and effort really worth it? Well, keep in mind that with increased skills and tough modern materials, people are running bigger and bigger rapids, rapids that would have been portaged in the days of the wood and canvas canoe. A swamped canoe, no matter what it's made of, is dangerous.

For the really big rapids, or "hotdogging," the more floatation the better. Some canoeists leave only the area where they are kneeling clear of floatation. With this much floatation you can't sink or swamp, you can

only upset. In an upset, you may be able to roll it back up or, failing this, right the canoe and climb back in. Then either bail the water out or paddle to shore to empty it. If you prefer a spray cover, you have two advantages: you don't lose storage space for your packs and no water comes into your canoe. The disadvantage is that in an upset you have a terrible problem recovering your canoe.

For playing around in large waves and for instructional purposes when no packs are being carried, there are several methods of adding floatation. The easiest and cheapest way is to fill one or more large truck inner tubes and wedge them into your canoe. Be careful you don't burst your canoe, though, with too much pressure. When running solo you need an inner tube both in front and behind you. If you only position one in front of you, your stern will sink making the canoe uncontrollable. When running double using one large tube, position it a bit toward the stern paddler to prevent the stern from sinking if the canoe is swamped. They do have a drawback in that they are relatively heavy compared with air bags — a fact you will quickly be made aware of when it comes to portaging. For wilderness canoeing you can buy air bags that open to hold your gear. You insert your packs, close the bag and pump it up for maximum buoyancy. For hotdogging or one day runs they can be installed empty.

The most important point to remember about floatation is that it must be secured extremely tightly in your canoe. If it isn't, several things may happen. The air bags could just pop out between the ropes and float away; the bags might lift off the bottom of the canoe, allowing your canoe to sink deeper; or the bags might float to one side of the canoe, causing an extreme list. If your floatation-equipped canoe does capsize, you will find it harder to right than one without floatation. You must reach under the canoe, grab the far gunwale and pull it

down while pushing up on the near gunwale. After you install floatation, take your canoe out in calm water and fool around with it. When you swamp, if one end sinks, you haven't installed the floatation properly.

Floatation is a problem if you want to run both solo and doubles. You have to reposition the floatation. Be sure to leave a space for your head for doing a solo portage. An inner tube works well because of the hole in the center. Well, now that the secret's out, there goes the price of old inner tubes, right out of sight like everything else!

These two photographs illustrate two different approaches to floatation. In the top photo Paul is using truck-tire inner tubes, one behind him and one in front. Although a helmet is not mandatory when you are not using thigh straps, it's still not a bad idea. The second photo illustrates the latest outfitting, using lightweight nylon air bags installed in a solo playboat. An Eskimo roll is a standard self-rescue procedure in a canoe like this.

Spray covers for the Nahanni

In 1977, when we were making preparations for canoeing the Nahanni, Wally Schaber recommended that we equip our canoes with spray covers. He warned me that the canyons below the falls could not be portaged or lined. It was run or swim, and Wally claimed that without spray covers we would be swimming. The rest of us were skeptical, but we followed his advice.

We did the Upper Nahanni to the falls without much problem. After a couple of days of drinking in the overwhelming splendor and power of the falls, we made the portage to the bottom, where the first canyon begins. We pushed off with our spray covers securely fastened. Alan, who had been down the canyon before, was yelling at Paul and me to cross all the way to the left shore and hug the cliff. I was so busy drinking in the sheer beauty and size of the place that I wasn't paying too much attention. I really wasn't concerned because I knew that if I saw a big wave coming, Paul and I could back ferry across and out of its way.

The canyon was overwhelming in its size. I had real trouble comprehending its depth as I looked up at the towering canyon walls. But it wasn't until I glanced over and saw Alan and Terry hugging that left wall, and Bob and Barrie obediently following suit, that I began to realize just how huge that canyon was. They looked very small silhouetted against the cliff. I also became aware of some big stuff coming up, and Paul and I were headed right into it. We went into reverse, with me drawing and Paul prying for all he was worth. As we neared the wave, it became obvious that we were going into what I knew would be the biggest breaking wave I'd ever seen or would ever want to see. I yelled for Paul to go for broke, which means power diagonally across the river in an attempt to cross the current and clear the wave. As soon as we switched from back ferrying to powering across, we bore down on the wave at an alarming speed. Paul realized at the same time as I did that we weren't going to clear it, so he slammed on the brakes right on the brink and straightened the bow out with a draw. I yelled "Brace" just as we dropped into the hole, but I needn't have bothered. Paul was leaning out on the flat of the blade on the right, and I did the same on the left. He just about disappeared into the wave. The water rushed along the spray cover and hit me in the chest. At some point, we changed from the brace to a power stroke so we could propel the canoe up and out of the wave. The realization that we had somehow stayed upright and afloat in there brought on a feeling that can best be described as euphoric. There is no way an open canoe would have made it through that wave. And there was more to come. The other two canoes were in big stuff on the left and were going through beautifully. The waves came from all directions, but with the spray covers fastened and a solid brace, everyone was doing fine. After the initial shock, we started enjoying the run and I began taking pictures between taking the waves. It was all over so soon. We wished we could do it again. Up to that point we had paddled two hundred miles (320 km) and there was no way back up the river. We eddied out and bailed out some water that had leaked in. The spray covers had worked magnificently, and right there we had six people converted to the merits of using spray covers for running big rivers like the Nahanni. We felt very sorry for anyone trying to come through what we had come through without them. During the portage around the falls we had seen a couple of canoes that were not equipped with spray covers, and we wondered how they would make out. As it turned out, a few minutes later a canoe came floating around the corner, upside down. We recovered the canoe and pulled it up on the shore. We watched and waited but no one came floating through, so we assumed the paddlers got to shore. The other canoe somehow made it through.

We learned later that four open canoes without spray covers wiped out in the canyon within a period of six days. We also heard that on one occasion the rangers began picking up packsacks and plastic pails floating down the river. With the use of a helicopter and jetboat, they found the owners. One man was on one side of the river and his wife was on the other. Their dog had taken off and was found only days later. The man wanted to collect all his stuff and continue, but his wife quit right there. They flew out on a charter flight.

Most of the canoes that swamp on the Nahanni, or anywhere else for that matter, are far too small and too shallow for any kind of wilderness travel with a load. These small, shallow canoes are just not suitable for rivers like the Nahanni — or for anything more than Class 1 rapids. For most conditions, my deep, large-volume prospector canoe doesn't need a spray cover, but it's nice to have for high-water conditions and for sporting around in the big stuff.

Covered canoes

In whitewater racing, such as slalom and downriver races, the object is to get to the end of the rapids as fast as possible. The aggressive, running-under-full-power technique necessitates the use of closed canoes to avoid swamping. In a race, there is no time to sit in an eddy and bail out your canoe.

Closed canoes and whitewater slalom racing require a different attack on the rapids, as well as a different philosophy. Some of the stuff these racers do get through is absolutely astounding. Remember, though, that racing is done with qualified crews standing by, ready to lend a hand or pull off a dramatic rescue.

Whitewater racing techniques are not the subject of this book. However, a compromise between the closed canoes and the open-wilderness canoes can be made by equipping your canoe with a spray cover. Waterproof nylon spray covers can be installed to cover just the bow, or even the whole canoe.

The pros and cons of spray covers

Before you decide to get spray covers, I suggest you think about it for a while. On a river with many rapids and falls that must be portaged, they are more trouble than they are worth. To do the one-person carry necessitates opening or removing the cover. If you are contemplating rolling an open canoe equipped with a spray cover upright after an upset, forget it. It is all but impossible to pull off. I had intended to illustrate the Eskimo roll in a spray-covered open canoe. After an entire summer, neither I nor any of my canoeing and kayaking friends have been able to manage it. Spray covers have their uses, but an open canoe is still an open canoe, despite the covers.

On the plus side of the spray covers argument, you are less likely to swamp your canoe or have it damaged or destroyed on a rock. On the other hand, with a spray cover you will invariably be wanting to tackle the bigger stuff. You will be entering the realm of the covered canoes and kayaks. Once you start doing that, you will have to start taking more safety precautions, such as flotation bags, helmets, rescue crews, and so on. The paddlers with the spray covers do have more fun in high water. You can belt right down the middle into the big rollers in high-water conditions, when there is little danger of hitting rocks.

In the first set of photos Paul and I charge right through the large rollers with no danger of taking in water. However, just to cool your enthusiasm, take a look at the second set of photos. Here a friend, Alan Whatmough, and I tackle a monster wave under full power. We submarine right through the wave, but the spray deck gives way and down we go. We find out the hard way that spray covers attached to the canoe with Velcro are okay for average stuff but are not good for the aggressive, full-power technique needed in the really big rollers. This rolling wave was at the end of the rapid, so the wipeout only resulted in a refreshing swim. In large, dangerous rapids, a spray cover must be trustworthy.

It is becoming standard practice to wear a helmet when running whitewater, but it is especially crucial if you are using a spray cover. When you upset in an open canoe, you usually fall out to the side. Your head remains close to the surface. In a covered canoe, it takes a moment to free yourself from the spray cover, and in this moment you are upside down with your head exposed to any passing rocks. This is especially true if you are paddling a specialized whitewater canoe and you try to use an Eskimo roll to right the canoe.

▶FUN IN THE BIG STUFF WITH A SPRAY COVER

·FUN IN THE BIG STUFF WITH A SPRAY COVER·

▶SPRAY COVER FASTENED WITH VELCRO

SPRAY COVER FASTENED WITH VELCRO

Spray covers

The opinions that Dad expressed on spray covers in *Song of the Paddle* are still considered valid today, so I've reprinted excerpts here along with some new information and opinions. The subject of spray covers is a controversial one. There are times when they are a definite asset, and times when they are more trouble than they're worth. Spray covers have made many rivers accessible to canoeists of moderate skill. Yet those same rivers have been canoed by paddlers who used skill rather than spray covers to keep themselves afloat. Spray covers are not without their problems, however. Although they will keep the water out of your canoe, they won't keep you from upsetting. Covered or not, a seventeen-foot (5 m) canoe full of water weighs close to a ton (1000 kg). That's a lot of weight to pull out of a strong current. When you do get it into an eddy, a covered canoe is much more difficult to empty than a canoe without a spray cover. Unfastening one side of the cover makes it possible to tip out the water or bail it out of the cockpit.

Another disadvantage of spray covers is the difficulty they present for portaging. They add weight and make it difficult to see where you are going, so usually you have to remove them or go to the trouble of adjusting them. On a river with many portages and only a few rapids that require a spray cover, I would choose to leave the cover at home and portage the questionable rapids. However, for lake travel, spray covers add immeasurably to safety and comfort. In waves they will keep you dry and protected from the wind, while in rain you won't have to do much bailing. They also cut down on wind drag by streamlining the load. On the big, cold, portage-free rivers of the mountains I also prefer spray covers, but in the rock-studded rivers of the east, with their many portages, I use floatation and pause in the eddies to bail. Sometimes I use spray covers in the east when the rivers are in spring flood.

Closed Cockpits

One decision that has to be made concerning spray covers is whether to also equip them with spray skirts. The spray skirt fits tightly around the body and keeps the water out of the cockpit. Many people are afraid they will be trapped during an upset, and refuse to wear them. Their fears are valid. People have drowned as a result of becoming tangled in a spray skirt. Homemade rigs can be particularly dangerous. There are two kinds of spray skirts. One is worn around the waist like a skirt and the bottom of the skirt is secured to the cockpit cowling. Some canoeists are afraid that the skirt might not come free, so adjust it loosely. However, if it's too loose, it will cave in when hit by a large wave. This kind is not commercially available. The second type of spray skirt is secured permanently to the spray cover, comes up around the paddler's chest, and is held there with an elasticized closure. The paddler falls free of the skirt in an upset, but if he twists while tipping, the sleeve can bind and tangle him. At the very least this can be a frightening experience; at worst it can be fatal.

Open Cockpit

To avoid a large part of the danger of entanglement you may choose to use an open cockpit–style of spray cover. The advantage of this design is ease of access, even to the point of scouting from a standing position at the top of a rapid. It is more adaptable to different-shaped canoes, you aren't restricted to only kneeling, and there is very little danger of entrapment in an upset. The main disadvantage is that some water will come into the cockpit; the ease with which it will enter depends on the design. Featured on the facing page is the Black Feather Spray Cover. It has an open cockpit with a reinforcing rod in an extension of the cover, thus creating a windshield effect that sheds the water. Made of 400 denier nylon, this cover is built to last. The

extra grab loops on the bow and stern of the spray cover give swimmers something to hang on to while being rescued. The supporting rod is removable from the reinforced sleeve, so that the spray cover can be rolled up when it is not in use. A real plus is being able to access your gear from the center without removing the whole cover. The cover is attached to the canoe with ladder-lock buckles on short pieces of webbing that loop through a length of nylon webbing permanently affixed to each side of the canoe. Be forewarned — rescuing a canoe that has a spray cover is a major challenge; usually it means towing the overturned canoe to shore with a throwline. Test your rescue systems before you go on your trip.

SPRAY SKIRT

SLEEVE

COWLING

STERN COCKPIT

NAHANNI RIVER N.W.T.

CENTER SEAM

INTERIOR—FRONT COCKPIT

Installing thigh straps and toe blocks

If you really want to get serious about outfitting your canoe for the big water, you might want to install thigh straps, toe blocks, and knee pads. In an open canoe without thigh straps, your tilt is limited. In this case, the degree of tilt depends on how far you can shift your weight out onto the paddle. With thigh straps, you can pull the canoe over into a much greater tilt by lifting up on your far thigh. The toe blocks keep your leg pushed forward and tight against the strap. Using thigh straps, you become a part of your canoe. If you happen to upset, you slip your toes off the toe blocks and slide your knees back and out. It sounds more complicated than it is. Usually you will automatically bail out of the straps without thinking about it. Your thigh straps should have a quick-release system and you definitely need to wear a helmet when using any kind of thigh straps. The knee pads are mainly for comfort, but they also help you to keep from slipping around. The Royalex and Kev-

lar canoes with very smooth floors are absolutely hopeless. You slide around all over the place. These smooth-sided interiors make it imperative that you at least cement in knee pads for stability. Wearing knee pads is a bother and they can cut off circulation.

Whitewater Saddles

The lower-left photo illustrates a custom-outfitted playboat. Installing a foam saddle instead of traditional seats is an option. When a foam saddle is combined with adjustable foot pegs, contoured knee pads, and a double, rigid, thigh-strap set-up you feel really secure. Having just said how wonderful saddles are, I have to add that they are not suitable for every canoe. A saddle restricts your movement laterally and front to back. This is not a big issue in the short, narrow playboats, but it is a real inconvenience when you are trying to tilt your fully loaded sixteen-foot (4.5 m) pros-

pector for an eddy turn. When wilderness tripping, you need to be able to move forward and back for front and back ferrying. Some canoeists do put a saddle and straps in the bow and stern for tandem paddling, which enhances control and performance.

A word of caution

If you decide to use spray covers, thigh straps, toe blocks, and knee pads, you must realize that the danger of being caught in your canoe in an upset is much greater than it is with an ordinary canoe. It is essential that you train yourself to skillfully eject from your canoe after upsetting. Nevertheless, these refinements add a great deal to the comfort and control of your canoe. With this gear, you don't just sit or kneel in your canoe. You literally "wear" the canoe and it becomes a part of you.

THIGH STRAPS

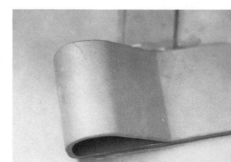

TOE BLOCKS

SADDLE AND STRAPS IN A SOLO PLAYBOAT

HANGING IN THERE WITH THIGH STRAPS

9 THE ALTERNATIVES TO RUNNING RAPIDS

Wading

While I don't dislike portaging and, in fact, accept it as an important part of wilderness canoeing, I see it as a last resort. I much prefer to wade or line a rapid I can't run. I often eddy out, line the bad stretch, and continue the run rather than portage a whole set of rapids that has only one or two tricky spots.

In very shallow rapids, it is sometimes easier to get out and walk or wade. Wading has many advantages over portaging. It can be very refreshing on a hot day. You can study the flow of the water around and over the rocks. After all, small rapids are the same as big ones only in miniature. You can feel the strength of the current in the Vs and study closely the sheer zone between eddy and main current. You can put your hand in a curling wave caused by a rock, or in a miniature haystack at the end of a downstream V. Then when you stand on shore to read the rapid, you will know what's happening under the surface. Even though you can't see the rocks, you will know exactly where they are. As you wade you are not only learning about rapids, but you are also making progress up or downstream.

Wading is a cautious way of approaching a dangerous stretch of water. By wading along the shore, hanging onto the canoe, of course, you avoid the risk of running fast-water down to the portage and being unable to get out of the current. Just be very careful not to get caught in any tracking lines. Another word of caution: wading in water much over your knees can be dangerous. If you were to wedge your foot between rocks and fall over, the force of the current would push you downstream and hold you there. In this situation, even water two feet (60 cm) in depth could be deep enough to drown you. Keep together, watch your partner carefully, and use common sense about where you wade.

Wading, Petawawa River

Tracking on the Petawawa River

Wading, Magnetawan River

Lining

Lining on two ropes

If the water is too deep to wade, the canoe can be guided down the rapids from shore on one or two tracking lines. The canoe is less likely to broadside in the current and swamp if a bridle is used (see photograph 1). The bridle prevents the upstream gunwale from dipping and taking in water.

There are many ways to tie a bridle. I prefer the method shown here. Take your tracking line, preferably quarter-inch (6 mm) floating rope, double back one end about six feet (2 m), and knot both ends together in the center (photograph 2). Drop the long end, pass the rope under the bow, and tie the two ends onto the leading edge of the bow seat (photograph 3). Check to make sure the knot is positioned right on the keel line at dead center (photograph 4). Perform the same procedure with the second tracking line at the stern, securing the lines to the stern seat. Some canoeists and authors suggest tying the line right at the waterline. I fail to see any advantage in this, only disadvantages. If you cross the river to track on the other side, you have to retie the bridle. If the rope is tied at the waterline, the canoe won't roll up and away from the surge of the current, and water will get in and swamp the canoe.

If you use two ropes you must descend slowly in order to maintain sidewash on the canoe for steerage around the rocks (photograph 5). If you walk at the same speed as the current, there is no sidewash at all. When the canoe is close to shore, the lines are short (diagram position A and photograph 6). To get the canoe out into the center of the rapids the lines are payed out, the angle of the canoe increased, and you walk slowly so that more sidewash may force the canoe out from shore (diagram position B and photograph 6). To bring the canoe in again, decrease the angle (photo-

graph 7) and shorten up on the lines (diagram position C and photograph 8). If you walk downstream too fast, you will decrease the sidewash on the canoe and it will move toward shore. Lining is a good way to get down an unknown river or to get to the brink of a falls without risking your neck. Be sure to stay clear of the lines. Never wind the rope around your hand in case you lose the angle on the canoe and are dragged into the rapids or over a falls.

Lining on one rope

It's also possible to line with one rope tied to the bridle near the stern. The advantage of this method is that you just give the canoe a shove and let 'er go. When the canoe heads for trouble, yank it into shore.

When lining with Paul I shove the canoe into the current, pay out the rope to the end, then pull the canoe to shore where Paul grabs it. While Paul coils the rope, I run downstream about the length of the rope. When I am in position, Paul pushes the canoe back into the current, pays out the rope, and so on. In this manner, we can leapfrog down the river at considerable speed.

You can either pay the rope out to its full length, then swing it to shore, or you can run along the shore giving the canoe lots of slack and let it descend at the speed of the water. Always be ready to yank the canoe back upstream if it hangs up on a rock. If you aren't quick, the canoe will swing broadside and swamp. It could wrap around the rock. To prevent this, always weight the downstream end. If the stern is pointed upstream, place the pack or packs in the bow so the canoe rides slightly higher in the stern. It's the same principle as back ferrying. When the canoe is held stationary in relation to the shore or rocks, the water will be rushing by at approximately five mph (8 km/h). If the upstream end is not lightened, it will dig in, swing sideways, and swamp.

If your aim and timing are dead on, it is possible to line without a bridle. In photographs 9 and 10, we see Wally Schaber firing his canoe through a rock-studded drop without a bridle. His ability with a tracking line has to be seen to be believed. For him (like me), the portage is absolutely the last resort. I am happy to report, however, that on our last run together, when he had to pull back upstream on his line, his canoe turned broadside and swamped. I waited a long time for that.

▶TOWING BRIDLE

▶LINING ON TWO ROPES

LINING ON TWO ROPES

▶LINING ON ONE ROPE

163

Tracking

Tracking upstream requires the use of two ropes. A very small river with little current doesn't require a bridle. A river that is fast and tricky requires a bridle at least on the upstream rope. A really tough current requires a bridle at each end to prevent swamping. The secret to tracking is to play the current. In a large rapid, you walk a fine line between moving the canoe upstream and swamping it. Whenever the canoe starts to dig in on a particularly nasty wave you must back off, pay out more line, or shorten the line in order to hit the wave at a different angle or in a different place.

Let's presume we are heading upstream in a tough current bow first. One bridle is tied to the forward edge of the bow seat and the other is tied to the stern seat. Most canoeists prefer the bow bridle to be further forward but I find by having it back on the bow seat, the canoe is much less likely to dig in on a large wave. You must also place at least one pack in the stern to raise the upstream end (the bow). Be sure to lash it in. Also lash in the paddles. You are now ready to tackle anything short of a waterfall. It is customary to have one person on each line but with practice (a lot of practice) one person can learn to handle both lines. Be sure there are no knots in the lines and never tie a knot at the end of the line. It could get caught between two rocks.

Choose a place where the footing ahead is pretty good, at least for a little way, so you can run ahead to get your angle on the ropes. Shove the canoe out into the current and run upstream paying out both ropes as you go. At about thirty feet (9 m), you hang on and adjust the angle of the canoe so it holds stationary in the current out from shore. If the angle of the canoe across the current is insufficient, the canoe will swing

back into shore and you will have to start all over again. If the angle is too great, there will be too much sidewash on the canoe and it will start to swamp or will be too difficult to pull upstream against the current. You can decrease the angle by pulling in on the bow rope or lengthening the stern rope. Be careful not to overcorrect. Now that the angle is just right you start moving upstream. Everything is fine until you come to a big rock that obstructs the progress of the canoe (see diagram position A). If you pay out more rope you can work the canoe further out into the center of the rapids. If you shorten the ropes, the canoe will move closer to shore. There is room for the canoe between the rock and the shore so you shorten the ropes.

The canoe moves toward shore and you continue upstream between the rock and the shore (diagram position B). You begin to realize the faster you move upstream, the further out into the river the canoe positions itself (photograph 2). This is because the faster you move, the greater the sidewash on the canoe. If you go slower, the canoe will move toward shore because of the decrease in sidewash. You can move the canoe around and past rocks by moving either faster or slower, as well as by lengthening or shortening the lines. Now you are approaching a place where your progress is blocked by rocks (diagram position C), but there is a very fast V or deepwater channel in the middle of the current. You pay out the rope and move faster. The sidewash increases and the canoe moves way out into midstream (diagram position D). The canoe hits the first haystacks and gets through okay (diagram position E and photograph 3). You move upstream easily now (diagram position F), and the canoe is held out in the current by the sidewash (diagram position G and photograph 4). You are approaching large haystacks at the base of a deepwater V. A haystack starts

piling up against the side of the canoe and threatens to spill into the canoe (diagram position H and photograph 5). You stand there straining against the rope, wondering whether or not to chance it. You decide to go for broke and move upstream hauling on the ropes. The canoe rears up, almost breaks through but water starts to pour in. Immediately you pay out the bow rope (diagram position I and photograph 6); the canoe rights itself and swings downstream on the stern rope (diagram position J and photograph 7). You run downstream carefully drawing the canoe to shore, stern first (photograph 8). It is important to use care because the upstream end is now the heavily-loaded stern. It is difficult to control the canoe with the weight in the upstream end. You pull the canoe in and grab onto the stern. To turn the canoe around just stick the stern out into the current, running your hands quickly along the gunwale until you reach the bow. The canoe will pivot around easily until it again faces upstream. You can now portage or try again.

You decide to try again. You are beginning to enjoy this. It's just you and the river playing a game. You know you can't fight the river. It will win every time. It is relentlessly powerful and never tires, never lets up. You decide the angle must be just right to break through and over that wave into the fast slick of the V. Too much of an angle and the canoe will swamp. Too little and the canoe will not get far enough out into the river to reach the V. You work out a strategy. You must move quickly with the canoe at a considerable angle to get it out into the V. Just before the canoe hits the big wave at the base of the V, you must decrease the angle and yank the canoe up and

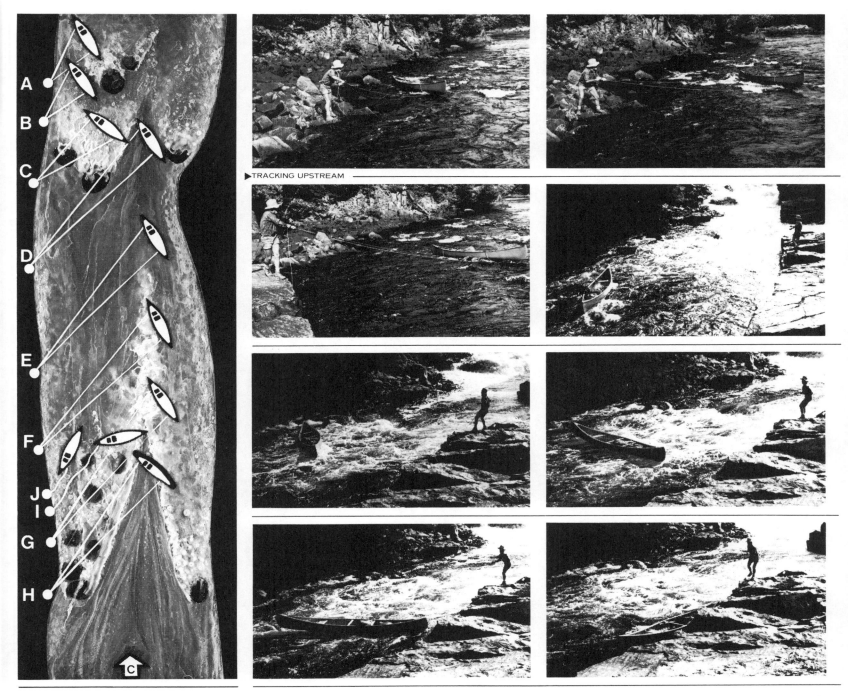

through that wave very quickly so it is aligned momentarily with the surge of the current. Once through the wave and into the slick of the V, you must pay out a little bow rope to increase the angle again so the canoe doesn't swing to shore and into the rocks. You try again and again until finally everything goes just right and the canoe breaks through the wave and into the slick. You let out the bow line a little, the canoe moves out and into the center of the slick, and forward and up over the top of the chute. You've won, but not by overpowering the river. You've won by understanding the currents and the effect they have on the canoe. It's like landing a big fish, you've got to use strategy. You know a lot more about rapids now than if you had portaged.

Tracking lines should be about fifty feet (15 m) long depending on the size of the river. Sash cord has a nice feel and doesn't tangle as easily as nylon but floating rope is a lot safer. Again never tie knots in the end of the rope or they will jam between rocks when you drag the ends, especially if you are handling the two ropes yourself. I always wear a small belt-knife when working with tracking lines. It is surprisingly easy to become entangled in a line. Most PFDs designed for paddle sports have a place to attach a rescue knife, and since you should always be wearing a PFD around moving water, your knife will always be handy.

Sometimes it's easier and faster to portage if there is a good trail. Often I line through anyway, even if there is a good portage, because I enjoy the river so much. I don't canoe a river to get from the top to the bottom. I canoe a river to experience it in all its moods. And a river is at its best when it disappears around a corner into a canyon. Of course, many canyons are not negotiable, even by tracking or lining. There must be a gravel or rocky bar on the inside of the corners from which to track. Before you

enter an unknown canyon, it's wise to check it out to make sure you can get all the way down by lining.

I have had the experience of entering a canyon only to find that the sides got steeper and steeper and the bars narrower and narrower until the only two options were to run the remainder or climb out. It was an excruciating climb to haul the canoe and packs up the sides to the top. If I had checked the canyon out, I would have discovered that I could have run the rest of the canyon. But running an unknown canyon is only for those with suicidal tendencies. If you've ever had the experience where you have been tempted to run a blind corner and instead checked it out and found a waterfall just downstream, you're not likely to be tempted again.

There is no way you can trust your maps to warn of waterfalls. When I'm running an unfamiliar river I must see at least a little blackwater before the river disappears around the bend so I know I've got enough room for an eddy turn to shore. Don't trust your life to your maps. The maps for the Dog River that flows into Lake Superior show five waterfalls. We counted twelve.

Tracking and lining are not easy at the best of times but it is the difficulty that makes this method of canoe travel an asset. Very few paddlers know how or are willing to expend the energy to track up a river. As more people take up canoeing and the rivers become more and more crowded, it is the tracking lines that will make it possible to journey into hidden places.

Poling and snubbing

Sometimes a rapid is too fast to run but not wild enough to track. Poling, or snubbing as it's called when you use the pole for going downstream, is a lot more fun and easier than negotiating the portage trail. In many areas of North America, there is as much poling done as paddling. The rivers with their gravel-bottom shallows are ideal for poling.

If you are descending a rapid and find that you can't backpaddle hard enough to control the descent of the canoe, snubbing with a pole will hold the canoe back better than the paddle. The pole can be about twelve feet (4 m) long. A sapling will do, but aluminum is the best if you are going on a trip that requires a lot of poling. A dull, pointed metal shoe can be attached to each end of the pole to keep it from brooming and slipping on the rocks. Normally you stand in the canoe for versatility and power with the pole. The important thing is weight distribution. Again we return to the old rule: weight in the downstream end. If you are snubbing downstream, you stand ahead of the center thwart or straddle the center thwart if you have some packs that can be placed in the bow (see photographs 1 and 2). You load heavy in the downstream end because you are traveling slower than the current. You don't want the current grabbing the upstream end of the canoe and

shoving it around downstream. The fine points of how to use the pole are rather difficult to explain; fortunately, it is easy to learn by trial and error and with common sense. Pick a river where the price of error doesn't come too high.

When snubbing you plant the pole ahead of you in the river bottom to slow down. The canoe will tend to swing, so you have to compensate constantly. You can plant the pole and push the canoe sideways all the way across the current like a back ferry to position yourself in the deep water. You use the back eddies to your advantage just as in paddling. As for falling overboard in the standing position it's all a matter of practice. Some people pick up snubbing faster than others. Some people never do get the hang of it. However, it's a neat way to get down a shallow, rock-studded rapid that is too fast to run but not big enough to portage. To travel upstream, again position yourself so the upstream end rides a little higher and pole yourself from eddy to eddy (photograph 3). Using the quiet eddies is the main secret to successful poling. Sometimes you have to pole very hard to fight your way up a V to the next eddy. It can take several attempts. There are many little tricks to keeping the canoe aligned with the current but they are difficult to explain. They will come with practice.

To force your way against the current, you can use short jabs, or plant the pole and climb it hand-over-hand. When you reach

the end of the pole, plant that end in the water and again climb it so that you are alternating ends. This way you avoid having to recover the pole after the push. Poling is a lot of fun and much easier than portaging and tracking, if the rapids are right. Practice in very slow shallows until you get the feel of it.

▶SNUBBING

POLING

Portaging

I've heard it said that portaging is like hitting yourself on the head with a hammer; it feels so good when you stop. Again I must say that for me portaging is the last resort, but it's not all that bad. Portaging can be a welcome change from paddling and a chance to stretch your legs. The trip back for a second load gives you perspective and a closeness with the land that you don't get from a canoe. Most of the animals I've encountered on canoe trips have been seen along the portage trail. If you still curse the portages, it might help to remember that it is the portages that separate us from civilization. The more portages you can put between yourself and civilization, the greater the wilderness experience. It's the portage that makes traveling by canoe unique. What other vehicle can you just pick up and carry on your head? It's easy to understand why portages were hated and cursed by the voyageurs. To them, reaching their destination was the only thing that mattered. To today's canoeist, the goal should not be the destination, but the journey itself.

When portaging it is important to check out the trail if it looks at all questionable or confusing. There is nothing worse than charging around in thick, mosquito-infested bush with a canoe on your head not knowing where you are going. On a long portage drop your packs at various intervals and go back for the second load to vary the trip.

It's difficult to get lost on a river trip, but not impossible. I once made a portage around a rapid and ended up on an inland lake. When I finally found the outlet, and it was only about one tenth as big as the river I was on, I figured something had gone wrong. I've also walked portages that seemed to just disappear. Sometimes it's not easy to backtrack and find the place you started from. On a strange river it's a good

idea to carry a map with you at all times as well as a compass. On ninety percent of all my trips I never look at my compass, but it's nice to know it's there. A compass is a must for backpacking side trips. On a twisting river you can sometimes locate where you are by using your compass to figure out your direction of travel and comparing it to the map. The inlet or the outlet to a large lake can easily be pinpointed very accurately with a compass reading. I would never travel anywhere without a detailed topographical map.

The hardest thing about a portage is picking up the canoe—especially if it's a heavy one. Getting it up on your shoulders takes technique rather than strength.

Portaging yokes

Some canoists don't use any form of portaging yoke. They just carry the canoe with the center thwart on the back of the neck. I occasionally do a short portage this way but traveling any distance makes my neck sore. I have a friend who carries a key-hole life preserver which he uses for a yoke.

Using the paddles as a yoke is very convenient because it gets the paddles out of the way and over the portage with the canoe (see photograph 1). The rope on the center thwart holding the blades is tied permanently so only the grip-ends need be secured. Notice that the blades are positioned so it's easy to get your head between them. You won't break your neck if you fall. Some canoeists tie the paddles so the tips of the blades rest on their shoulders.

A padded yoke is quite comfortable (photograph 2). I tie my paddles in even when I use this yoke to keep them out of the way.

A wooden yoke with the paddles tied in and a tumpline installed to take some of the weight off your shoulders is the most comfortable arrangement (photograph 3). However, the tumpline must be adjusted perfectly or it's agony. It's an all or nothing

arrangement. If done properly, it distributes the seventy-five pound (35 kg) weight over your entire body (photograph 4). When your head and neck become tired, you lower the weight onto your shoulders. When they get tired, you slip the tumpline back on and so on.

If the two-person carry is used, it makes sense for one person to carry with the stern thwart resting on his or her shoulders using the paddles as a yoke, and the other person carrying only the bow resting on one shoulder so he or she can see where you both are going. The person carrying the bow can also carry a pack because the bow carries only one-third of the weight this way, with the stern carrying two-thirds. The stern provides balance and stability.

Lifting the canoe

Grasp the near gunwale amidships with one hand on each side of the center thwart (photograph 5). Stand up and hoist the canoe onto your thighs (photograph 6). To end up facing in the direction of your right shoulder, grasp the center thwart in the middle with your left hand. Roll the canoe toward you with your left hand while you push down with your right and bend your knees to cradle the canoe on your thighs (photograph 7). In this position, you are able to grasp the far gunwale just forward of the center thwart (photograph 8). Now you can drop your left hand back onto the lower gunwale just behind the center thwart (photograph 9) or reach between your legs and cradle the canoe on your arm. You then roll the canoe onto your shoulder as you stand up. In the method illustrated, you heave the canoe up in one continuous motion (photographs 10 and 11) and step under the canoe as you lower it onto your shoulders (photograph 12). I use one knee to assist in heaving it up there. Finally, slide your left hand forward of the center thwart, grasp the paddles or gunwales and you're off.

To lower the canoe do the entire procedure in reverse. The important thing is to lower the canoe onto your thighs then onto the ground. Where you position your hands on the gunwales is very important for balance.

A very strong person can forego some of these steps and just lift the canoe using brute strength. I can heave my custom-made, sixty-pound (27 kg) Kevlar right up onto my shoulders from the ground. But to get a ninety-pound (40 kg) canoe up there, I need to use every trick there is.

If you have any difficulty lifting the canoe by yourself, have someone assist you. It is foolish to risk straining yourself. To make the one-person lift easier, you can roll the

canoe up over your head by leaving one end on the ground. When you get the canoe on your shoulders, hop your hands along the gunwales until you are in position at the center thwart. Lower the thwart onto your neck and you're ready to go.

▶PORTAGING YOKES

▶LIFTING THE CANOE

LIFTING THE CANOE

Lashing canoes together

Lashing two or even three canoes together to make a catamaran or trimaran is a marvelous way to add interest and excitement to a canoe journey. Only someone who has paddled for many days against a relentless head wind can really know the full joy of running before the wind. With two or three canoes lashed together and a large ground sheet or piece of parachute rigged as a square sail, the feeling as you lay back in the sun and watch the miles go by is euphoric. When you travel by canoe you earn every mile you travel except when you harness the wind or the current of a river. It's like getting something for nothing. Fortunate are the paddlers who enter a long lake and find the wind coming from behind.

There are things you should know about lashing canoes together to avoid inconvenience or even to avert disaster. First you need four poles. Right away you've got a problem. Cutting green trees in a park is illegal, that is unless you happen to be a logger. If you are and have a permit, then cutting down green trees is no problem. Thirty or forty truckloads of trees leave Algonquin Park day after day, year after year. If you are a canoeist, you will have to be content with poles that don't have any leaves growing out of them. On rarely traveled routes that are in remote wilderness areas I have no qualms about cutting green poles. But I would never cut them from the forest edge. I go well back in and select judiciously from a clump.

The poles for lashing canoes together should be about two to three inches (50 to 75 mm) in diameter and ten feet (300 cm) long. The two poles for the masts can be lighter and should be three to four feet (90 to 120 cm) taller than the dimension of the sail. The canoes are placed side by side on the shore with the bows facing the water. They should be three feet (90 cm) apart at the bow and four feet (120 cm) apart at the stern. This is very important or the water between the canoes will pile up and splash into them. Lay one pole across the two canoes along the back edge of the bow seat and one pole along the stern thwarts. Fasten the poles securely with square lashing so there is absolutely no play. They will be lashed at four points on each canoe. Tie the two masts together at one end only, and raise them. Tie the lower ends resting in the canoe to the outside edge of the bow seats. Run a forward stay from the top of the poles to the bow cleat so the poles can't fall back. Run a back stay from the top of the poles to the stern. The poles cannot possibly fall down. To raise and lower the sail, undo the bow stay. If the sail is triangular, one corner is raised to the top of the poles, preferably on a pulley so it can be readily raised and lowered. If the sail is square, a little ingenuity is required to get the best results. A yardarm can be rigged to hold the sail out to its full width.

If paddles are tied as lee boards, you can sail across the wind. I've never been able to tack into the wind with this rig but maybe somebody who knows more about sailing might manage it. One unavoidable problem is that the water from waves splashes from the bow of one canoe into the other canoe. You can deal with this by bailing from time to time or by rigging a spray cover.

A canoe catamaran is virtually impossible to capsize. The only danger is swamping or running aground on a shoal. It's a very unmanageable rig to haul off rocks or to empty once it's swamped. It is unwise to set out without having bailing pails on hand.

Rigging two or three canoes together is a marvelous way to travel the fast-flowing rivers of the mountains in stretches where there are no rapids. We rigged a trimaran on the Nahanni River and spent a couple of glorious days watching the spectacular scenery unfold around each bend in the river. We sunbathed, read, ate, and swam.

We could have rigged a sail from time to time but we had no desire to travel any faster than the current. We wanted to savor the river. Running rapids with two canoes lashed together is not a good idea unless the rapids are deep and free of rocks at or near the surface.

There is considerable enthusiasm for the catamaran among many western paddlers who claim it can get them through rapids that would be beyond the capacity of some of their moderately-skilled canoeists. They use spray covers to avoid swamping. It would be advisable to know your river and the nature of the rapids before attempting to float a catamaran rig through them.

Huge loads can be transported on a catamaran. The carrying capacity of a single canoe is about 700 pounds (320 kg). But two canoes lashed together could almost carry a ton (tonne). Prospectors and trappers often used two canoes lashed together to carry building materials for a cabin, or even a stove. They would dismantle and reassemble the catamaran at each end of the portage. I have often used the catamaran for safety reasons, when paddling with children, to take the risk out of paddling in waves. Their squeals of delight every time a wave splashes over them leave no question as to what a welcome diversion the catamaran can be.

Obviously one doesn't have to go to all this trouble to harness the wind. You can just tie a ground sheet to two paddles and hold your makeshift sail up to hitch a ride on the wind.

Catamaran

Two canoes lashed together

Trimaran on the Nahanni River

Sailing a catamaran

171

Coping with wind

Very few forms of transportation are more affected by wind than the canoe. Wind causes waves. The size and shape of waves depend on how big the body of water is and its depth. Lake Superior waves sometimes resemble an ocean swell. Shallow lakes such as Lake Winnipeg have waves that are steeper, closer together, and break more easily. They are difficult to paddle in. Even the most skillful open-canoe paddler can not get a canoe through a breaking wave without upsetting or swamping. It is very dangerous to set out from a lee shore in a wind to cross a lake. Along the lee shore there are no waves, no matter how strong the wind is blowing. The further from shore, the larger the waves will be. They could be breaking out in the middle of the lake, but you won't know until you get there and it's too late to turn back. It's a nasty situation. On several occasions I have been very apprehensive about the way the waves were building.

Be very careful that you are not led out into this sort of situation by a member of your party who isn't aware of this danger.

Several years ago we were canoeing the shore of Lake Superior. Ahead of us lay a huge bay about five miles (8 km) across. Our destination was the mouth of the Michipicoten River, which lay directly across the bay. There was a good stiff breeze blowing offshore. There were no waves where we were, but I figured the waves might be of considerable size on the other side. I suggested we should paddle the ten miles (16 km) around the bay staying close to shore. To upset far from shore in Lake Superior is almost certain death. Survival time in the cold water is very short. A canoe-over-canoe rescue in big waves is very difficult. If the waves are big enough to upset one canoe, you can be sure it's going to be difficult to perform a canoe-over-canoe rescue with the other.

We agreed to angle across the bay favoring the shore. If the waves weren't too big when we got halfway down the bay, we would cut across the remainder of the bay and head directly for our destination.

I was suspicious but agreed. We set out following the shore on a compromise course. However, the other canoe began to veer more and more out into the bay. The waves really weren't very big. It seemed ridiculous to be paddling around the shore in such puny waves. I felt a bit silly for being so cautious so I said nothing and followed the other canoe until we were heading out, directly toward the mouth of the river. The waves built very gradually, almost imperceptibly. It was a beautiful day. The sun sparkled on the crystal-clear water under a bright blue sky. Then a wave curled just a little. It was enough to jolt me out of my feeling of complacency. I looked back. We were barely halfway across. The wind was blowing stronger. I knew those waves were going to get bigger and bigger. There was no turning back. The shore to our left was just as far away as our destination. Any attempt to go that way would mean taking the waves broadside. We had no choice but to continue and hope the waves didn't become unmanageable. The other canoe was ahead of us and increasing the distance between us steadily. My friends were paddling my Chestnut prospector. We were in a Grumman. We couldn't keep up to them. I yelled to them to slow down so that we could stay together but they couldn't hear. We were becoming dangerously separated. If we upset, they wouldn't know unless they happened to look back. Looking back in big waves can cause an upset. They would have had a hard time getting back to us anyway. If they upset, we would be quite awhile getting to them. I stared down at the icy water and prayed. The waves stayed about the same size for the rest of the crossing with only a very occasional wave breaking, but only at the very top. A great feeling of relief came over me as we neared the shore.

And then I remembered the mouth of the Michipicoten. It is a big river. The current rushing into the lake would throw up mountainous waves when it hit the Lake Superior waves. I yelled and yelled but they couldn't hear me. Finally as the canoe neared shore, it changed course and paddled parallel to shore. My friend was aware of the possible danger. We all reached shore safely. Everybody thought it was an exhilarating run. I am not sure I was able to convince them that we had laid our lives on the line. There had been no escape route planned. We were at the mercy of the lake. In these situations, I leave my cooking pails out for easy access. However, in large waves bailing out a swamped canoe is not easy.

If paddling Lake Superior ever were to become popular, I feel very strongly that the death rate would be high. It is so difficult to convince people of the dangers of cold water. You never believe it until you are in it, and then it's too late.

Wave conditions can sometimes be avoided by paddling at night and in the early morning. Local onshore winds are created when the air over the land is heated by the sun. The warm air rises, bringing in the cooler air from over the water, which is then heated and in turn rises. Strong local winds are thus created which can result in wave action.

Sea anchor

When running with a wind, dragging a sea anchor can help to keep the stern from swinging around on each wave. A bridle is tied on the stern seat so the pull is at the keel for stability. Your largest cooking pail can be used as an anchor. The resistance of the open pail being pulled through the water keeps the stern upwind with little effort.

When paddling solo into a wind, paddle several degrees off the wind and lean the canoe so that you increase the freeboard on the windward side. To maintain control, you must move back or forward to trim the canoe and maintain steerage. A solo paddler who knows how to use his or her weight as ballast can paddle safely in much larger waves than double paddlers because of the buoyancy of the bow and stern. However, a solo paddler has much more difficulty making headway.

Lake Superior

Virginia Falls, Nahanni River

10 WHITEWATER AND WILDERNESS SAFETY Avoiding tragedy

One of the primary concerns of all canoeing organizations is safety. This has also been one of my main concerns while writing my book as well as when making my films on canoeing. There is a lot to know about the art of canoeing. It's a lot of fun learning how to canoe and even more fun when you begin to apply what you've learned. Knowledge and skill can reduce the element of danger and risk but it can never be completely eliminated.

One of the most exciting things about the Nahanni River is the Virginia Falls. All that breathtaking beauty and splendor and the raw and terrifying power of the water may be fully experienced without the restraint of guardrails and signs. As you stand on the brink of the falls staring straight down, common sense keeps you from stepping over the edge.

This is true for rapids and big lakes as well. The danger is relative to your level of skill and awareness of where the danger lies. The danger of a careless step at the edge of the Virginia Falls is obvious. Upsetting a canoe several hundred yards from shore in icy-cold water is just as deadly yet the danger is not as obvious.

To survive a mishap on a wilderness journey you must be able to think. It is necessary to appraise a situation quickly, consider the possible options, make a decision, and act. You must make the right decision because in many situations you may not have a second chance. With that one decision, you might have used up all your options as well.

The advice of most organizations concerned with water safety is to stay with your overturned or swamped craft, assume the heat-preserving fetal position, or climb up onto your craft until help arrives. What bothers me about this advice is that none of it ever follows the situation to a conclusion where no help arrives. They never say, "If no one comes, you're dead." Some literature suggests rather vaguely that the waves will wash you to shore. If that's your best hope, then you might consider the fact that you will wash to shore three to four times faster if you have on a PFD and assume the heat-preserving fetal or huddling position and let go of your craft. A swamped canoe drifts very slowly even in a big wind.

The reasons these organizations strongly recommend that you stay with your craft are based on sound research and cannot be argued with in theory. For example, it has been proven that swimming, even at a moderate pace, increases circulation of the blood causing a heat loss that is thirty-five percent greater than if the person stays still and assumes a heat-saving fetal position. This heat loss occurs because the swimming activity creates almost three times as much heat in the body. The body benefits from the increased heat for a very short time then the heat is quickly lost to the cold water through the extremities. This heat loss is very serious unless the swimmer has reached shore. If the distance to the shore is too great and the swimmer succumbs to the cold and loses consciousness, then certainly leaving the craft would be the indirect cause of death.

On the other hand if the paddler stays with the canoe and assumes the heat-saving position, he or she will stay conscious for almost twice as long — even longer if the canoeist can use the craft or packs for buoyancy and so get some of the upper body out of the water. If help comes, the canoeist will be alive to benefit from that help. Now we come to the part no one ever mentions. Suppose help does not come. Then the paddler dies.

Let's go back to the first scenario. If the canoeist was sensible, he or she would have contemplated the danger of the cold water and would not have strayed too far from shore in the waves. The distance from shore would not have been great enough to deplete the body's supply of heat when swimming back to land. The heat generated from the swim would actually be an asset. This example just concerns uncomfortably cold water.

With water at or near the freezing point, you could be incapacitated in a matter of a few seconds, as Dr. Joseph McInnis has detailed in *The Icy Facts on How Cold Water Kills*.

Exposure to severe cold is accompanied by a shower of nervous reflexes from the skin to the heart and lungs. Breathing is so hard to control that if small waves are breaking over the face they will almost certainly be inhaled. Cold water hitting the back of the throat can cause the heart to stop beating, and if the head is underwater, drowning occurs immediately.

Overbreathing, or hyperventilation, causes the body to lose large amounts of carbon dioxide. This diminishes blood flow to the brain, and certain muscles—such as those in the hands—can go into spasm.

In water like this it would be difficult enough just to hang onto your canoe or assume the heat-saving position. In light of this, I must say if I am in a wilderness area with no hope of assistance, I would rather die trying to swim to shore. I have arrived at this conclusion after much thought and many frightening personal experiences.

Avoiding Tragedy...

I believe that blindly following rules such as "never leave your overturned craft" do not necessarily apply in wilderness canoeing. It is a sound basic rule that must be tempered with preplanning and common sense. This preplanning also applies to running rapids. If the water is cold and the weather is warm, I will run a rapid of Class 3 difficulty. If I wipeout, I head to shore with the recovery rope in my hand and get out of the cold water as fast as possible. The warm sun will quickly restore my lost body heat. If the weather is very cold as you might expect in late fall, I would pass on the Class 3 rapids unless I had on a wet suit. I think that it is safe to say that in all of my many and varied wipeouts, the heat loss I suffered while swimming to shore was less than if I stayed with my craft and attempted to swim my canoe ashore or waited in vain for help.

It's a matter of common sense. A lack of it is what can kill you. The thing that keeps me alive is that I am a coward when it comes to cold water. I am not about to get myself into a situation where my life depends on someone just happening along to find me clinging to my overturned canoe. They might find my canoe, but I'll be sitting on the shore beside my fire drying out. If I'm not sitting before a warm fire then my fatal mistake would have been my failure to contemplate their arrival. But then the question one must ask is, "Would they have arrived in time?"

A couple of years ago I was paddling along the shore of Lake Superior in a strong onshore wind. I'm not sure of the size of the waves but they were very big. When I look at some of the slides that were taken at the time, the distance from the peak of one wave to the peak of the next was more than two canoe lengths. That's about forty feet (12 m). It sounds like a foolish situation to be paddling in, but the waves were not breaking except on the shoals. These waves were like an ocean swell. Where they broke on the shoals and along the rocky shores, they exploded twenty to thirty feet (6 to 9 m) in the air. We were filming a sequence depicting a reenactment of a solo trip I had taken along the shore ten years ago. As long as I stayed out beyond the breakers and avoided going over a shoal where the really big waves broke, I knew there would be no danger. The wind was very strong but by loading heavy in the bow I was able to control the canoe and make headway.

We had been filming most of the day and after supper I decided to go for one more shot against the setting sun. From the safety of a cove, I rounded the point out into the huge waves. I slowly fought my way out into the waves off from an extremely scenic rocky cliff. Ken was getting some great shots and I was enjoying it immensely. Suddenly ahead of me I saw a huge wave approaching out of nowhere. It was a freak giant. I watched it coming, then felt my heart sink as it walled up. It towered over me and began to curl at the top. I knew if it broke I would never be able to break through it without swamping. It looked like a tidal wave coming at me. Then it broke in a cascading sea of rolling white. I straightened the canoe and hit it hard in an effort to power through. The wave picked me up like a leaf and carried me backward until I felt the canoe sink at the stern. As the canoe filled and rolled and the ice-cold water engulfed me, I knew exactly what I was going

to do. In fact, I was already swimming for shore before I hit the water. There was no debating the issue in my mind, no second thoughts. I knew that my only hope of survival was to get to shore as quickly as I could with a minimum amount of heat loss. In that cold water I had a very limited amount of time to save myself. I had to save myself because there was no hope of rescue. There was nothing Ken could do from shore. As I swam for the shore, I knew I was in big trouble. I had to get there as fast as I could without exhausting myself. Gradually I overcame my feeling of panic as my body adjusted to the cold water. I slowed my stroke to pace myself. How I longed for my wet-suit top! I should have worn it but I just didn't believe it was necessary. Where did that freak wave come from? I thought I had appraised the situation flawlessly.

I had about two hundred yards (185 m) to go. Getting to shore was only my first problem. My second problem was in front of me—a sheer cliff with waves pounding into it. However, I knew there was a cove where the waves washed right in between two rocky sentinels onto a boulder beach. I had to line up with that cove. I swam for what felt like a very long time. Ken and my wife were frantic, but there was nothing they could do. Ken locked the camera on wide angle and left it running, then hurried down to the cove to be ready to assist me. I lined up on the mouth of the cove and kept coming. As I reached a point just off the mouth, I slowly became aware that I wasn't making any headway. I was staying in the same place in relation to the rocky sentinels at the mouth. I then realized much to my horror that the waves were pushing me in, but there was a backwash of water from the cove pushing me back out. I slowed my pace to think about my problem and save my energy. My next option was to swim about a quarter of a mile down the coast to a protected cove where I had first entered the lake in my canoe. It was an option I was not at all happy about. The cold was definitely getting to me. I decided to go for broke across that sheer zone of currents. Saving my energy I waited for a lull in the waves, then I headed for the cove swimming as hard as I could. I swam for what felt like an eternity, then I felt myself being picked up and carried in on a thundering roller. It passed me and I started to move back out but another picked me up and finished the job. I felt my feet touch bottom. Ken was waiting to grab me and haul me to shore. A warm sleeping bag and hot drinks soon stopped my shivering.

After an hour or so, I was back to normal and walked over to the beach. As I watched the canoe bobbing in the waves, I looked along the shore to where I had wiped out. I estimated the canoe had traveled about four hundred yards (365 m) — four hundred yards in about an hour. I had covered the two-hundred yards (185 m) or so to the cove in about five minutes. The canoe was not even approaching shore. It was being blown parallel to the shore. At the rate the canoe was going it would not reach the distant shore across the bay until morning.

Whether or not I hang onto my canoe depends entirely on the circumstances.

The tragedy of the St. John's Boys School disaster on Lake Timiskaming near North Bay, Ontario, where fourteen people lost their lives is that the occupants of the first canoe that upset believed help was on the way. However, when the second and the third canoes upset, all hope of help vanished. Some of those who set out for shore

after the third canoe tipped were already too far gone to make it. I can't help wondering how many of them would have made it if they had headed for shore as soon as they hit the water. No blame can be laid because they assumed help was coming. When the third and last canoe upset, the logical thing to do was head for shore. The old adage about never leaving an overturned canoe no longer applied when the last canoe upset.

If we have a tendency to be critical of the people involved in wilderness accidents we should maybe remind ourselves that all such accidents could be avoided by simply staying at home. For most of my acquaintances this little piece of advice would go over like a lead balloon. We know there are risks out there and we know that anyone can make a mistake. It may be an unavoidable mistake or a stupid one. It just makes sense to eliminate the risks as much as we can and to learn from the mistakes of others. The physical, mental, and spiritual enjoyment derived from a wilderness journey is worth all the risks.

I am deeply grateful to the counselors who gave their time and accepted the responsibility of taking me on my first wilderness journey. I am forever in their debt because what I experienced as a young camper shaped my entire life. They weren't the most knowledgeable canoeists but they did their best. We made mistakes but we survived. Their level of skills at that time would not be adequate for any well-run wilderness program today. When I compare those days with the present, I realize we have come a long way.

Lake Superior Wipeout — swimming to shore

Voyageur canoes

I have been asked many times to comment on the six- or eight-person canoes used for organized trips and historical pageantry. Reliving history by paddling a thirty- or forty-foot voyageur canoe can be a lot of fun, especially if you can dress up in an authentic costume. If you paddle one for any distance though, you'll soon realize that the bow and stern usually have all the fun. All that is expected of the paddlers amidships is forward power. However, it does get novices out in a canoe. With training, the amidship paddlers can attain a high level of skill and learn to maneuver the big canoe. The objective is to get the kids out in a canoe as quickly and economically as possible. One big canoe is cheaper than four small ones and the training time for a big trip is much less.

Problems arise when it is assumed that a big canoe is safer than a small canoe. If a small canoe wipes out, you have two people in the water and you can quickly do a canoe-over-canoe rescue, even in big waves. If a big canoe wipes out, you have eight people in the water and a very unmanageable canoe. It's a tall order to do a canoe-over-canoe rescue with a twenty-foot (6 m) canoe. The big canoes are also overestimated when it comes to stability. With eight people on board, there are eight chances for an upset. With a small canoe, with only two people there are just two chances for a mistake to be made. Another danger is when you assume the big canoes are capable of riding much larger waves than the small sixteen-footers, you can be lured into situations you would avoid if you were using the small ones.

One of the worst moments I have ever experienced with children in a canoe was in a twenty-foot freighter many years ago. It was a canoe of truly gargantuan proportions. I had loaded it with my Sunday school class for a short journey down the shoreline for a picnic. The water was calm, the distance was short. There was no way anything could go wrong. The kids had a great time. Some of them had never been in any kind of canoe before. On the way back one kid started fooling around. He was a good swimmer and as we neared the dock he dove overboard to swim the rest of the way. With the sudden release of his weight on one side of the canoe, it rocked. Everyone threw his or her weight to the other side to compensate and over went the canoe. As I hit the water, I was overwhelmed with panic. I had no idea how competent the kids were in the water. I hadn't even bothered to check their life jackets because I was so confident of the stability of the huge canoe. I had no idea if anyone was trapped underneath. I tried counting heads until I realized I wasn't even sure of the exact number of kids in the canoe. It was incredibly stupid of me not to know. Most of the kids were laughing and loving it but a couple were wide-eyed with fear. They were not at home in the water and swimming with their clothes on was an unfamiliar and frightening feeling. I did one underwater pass along the length of the canoe, then helped two kids to shore yelling to the others to count heads. They were totally and completely unaware of my concern until I reached shore and lost my temper. Only then did they realize I wasn't kidding around. Everyone was safe but because I hadn't counted heads before we set out, I still felt terrible after it was all over. Just supposing we had forgotten somebody and they were still down there.

In rapids, a swamping or an upset in a large six- or eight-person canoe is many times more dangerous than in a smaller craft. If a canoeist falls out on the downstream side, a twenty-foot canoe is a lot harder to swim clear of than a sixteen-foot canoe. If the swimmer is pinned by the canoe against a rock, the crushing power of the water would be greater. Rescue would be virtually impossible. These are factors that are rarely considered. Fortunately these incidents rarely happen but I am always aware of them when I run rapids in the big canoes.

There has been great interest in the big voyageur canoes. Several canoe companies make fiberglass replicas of the thirty- and forty-foot (10 and 13 m) canoes in simulated bark. The Voyageur Canoe Company in Millbrook, Ontario makes a beautiful, big, simulated birchbark canoe. The most authentic-looking canoe, though, is made by Chicagoland Canoe Base. The gunwales are all lashed and cedar ribs and planking are installed. The most beautiful voyageur canoes are the real thing. The photograph is a real birchbark canoe, forty feet (13 m) in length, made by Charlie Laberge. He is more or less responsible for the resurgence of interest in the big birchbark canoes. This canoe was used for the filming of Christopher Chapman's film *Impressions*, made for the Hudson Bay Co. The photo was taken out in the middle of Lake Nipissing.

Hypothermia

Most people who venture into the woods have some kind of fear they find difficult to overcome. It could be a fear of snakes, spiders, bears, lightning — the list is endless. It is ironic that the major killer of outdoor recreationists concerns us very little. It is called *hypothermia*.

I recently discovered the best description of hypothermia I have read. Having been close to a state of hypothermia more than once myself, I found the following excerpt from *The Icy Facts on How Cold Water Kills* by Dr. Joseph McInnis frighteningly accurate. This is the most dramatic form of hypothermia.

It is a warm afternoon in May. You are paddling a canoe, alone on a northern lake, the sun is shining and you feel secure and comfortable in your regulation life jacket. The shore is about 200 yards away. You are a good swimmer and paddler and you don't worry when the wind begins to blow. As the waves get bigger you turn the bow of the canoe toward shore, but a strong gust slams into you, your balance is lost and the canoe begins to tip. Your last thoughts before you hit the water are, "I'm wearing a life jacket. I'll be OK."

But will you?

A few seconds after you hit the water, it feels as if you had been pushed into boiling sulfuric acid. The pain is so intense you suck in your breath and begin breathing uncontrollably. No matter how hard you try, you can't stop breathing so rapidly.

An iron numbness rages through your skin and into your body and brain. Your arms and legs are on fire. Your thoughts, which only a minute ago were lucid and dreamy, are now in disarray. You can't believe this is happening. You reach out for the canoe and take hold of its overturned end.

Soon the shivering begins, starting as a tremor and turning into a violent shaking of muscles out of control. Apprehension mounts. Everything is such an effort. The shore looks a mile away. You begin to push the canoe toward the thin line of evergreens. Trying to kick, your legs move like a drowned man's.

The water is like sludge. Your arms and legs move slowly as if wrapped in chains. "Thank God for the life jacket," you murmur, as part of your internal soliloquy of hope.

As you move, the pain begins to turn into numbness. Your breathing becomes even faster and you have trouble keeping your head above the icy sting of the waves. Inside your hammering chest, in parts of your central nervous system, electrical anarchy is trying to take place.

The glacial cold has fired off reflex impulses to your heart and lungs. Your heart muscles are so overstimulated that if they undergo much more stress they will become ineffective.

You have been swimming for what seems like hours when something solid brushes against your feet. The rocks are slippery, your legs are wooden and they don't respond when you order them to carry you out of the water. It is the worst of nightmares when you are so close and yet so far from safety. You can almost reach out and touch the trees, but your legs are no longer yours. Their strength is gone and they won't work. Nothing works. Everything becomes blurry and the last thing you remember is the sun on the trees. And anger, a black fury, at the suddenness of what has happened, and at the water you thought was your friend....

What is hypothermia?

Hypothermia is a condition where the body loses heat faster than it produces it, resulting in a lowering of the body's core temperature. It is caused by immersion in cold water or exposure to cold air, aggravated by wetness, wind, and exhaustion. Your body begins to lose heat faster than it can produce it. When you are exposed to cold air while wearing insufficient clothing, exercising to stay warm will cause your body to automatically make adjustments to preserve normal temperatures in the vital organs. This will drain your energy reserves until they are exhausted. The cold will then reach your brain, depriving you of judgment and reasoning power. At this point you are in a state of hypothermia.

Next you will lose control of your hands. Your internal temperature is sliding downward. Your rate of body-heat production instantly drops by fifty percent or more. Violent, incapacitating shivering begins. There are two classifications of hypothermia: chronic and acute. The insidious thing about chronic hypothermia is that you probably won't know it's happening. It may take several hours of cold, damp weather to occur. If someone asks you if you are all right, you are more than likely to insist you are fine. Acute hypothermia caused by falling into ice-cold water can happen in a matter of minutes. A person who recognizes symptoms of hypothermia and insists on remedial action can save lives. The best defense against hypothermia is to learn to plan for and cope with all types of weather. Avoid situations that could lead to an upset or swamping in deadly cold water that you cannot get out of quickly.

How to avoid hypothermia

The best way to avoid hypothermia is to stay dry and well nourished and to consume adequate liquids, up to a gallon (five liters) a day. Wear clothing made of wool or pile, which retains body heat. When combined with a waterproof layer, such clothing will greatly diminish chilling that occurs through evaporation. Improper clothing loses about ninety percent of its insulating value when wet.

Beware of the wind. Even a slight breeze carries heat away from bare skin much faster than still air. Wind also drives cold air under and through clothing. Wind has a refrigerating effect on wet clothes by evaporating moisture from the surface. Cold water running down your neck and legs will flush away body heat without you being particularly aware of it. Falling into fifty degree fahrenheit (10°C) water is so unbearably cold that you know you are in trouble and will make every effort to get out of it. According to the Coast Guard pamphlet on hypothermia, "Even seemingly warm water temperatures may be particularly hazardous when exposure occurs for

Hypothermia...

a prolonged length of time." Many hypothermia cases develop not in cold water but in air temperatures between thirty-two degrees fahrenheit (0°C) and fifty degrees fahrenheit. It is difficult to believe such temperatures can be dangerous. Underestimating the dangers of being wet at such temperatures can be fatal. It is often very difficult to convince people they should stop and take the time to change into dry clothing or build a fire and dry out the clothes they are wearing.

It makes sense to put on rain gear before you get wet. The age-old problem with rain gear, however, is that body moisture is unable to escape. If you are working hard, it is possible to be just as wet from the inside as you would be from the rain without a raincoat or poncho. As soon as you stop working you begin to feel cold and clammy. You must either change, or build a fire and dry your clothes. Remember, though, you can get away with a lot more moisture if you are wearing wool or pile under your rain gear. Even though you might feel damp from the accumulation of perspiration, your loss of body heat will be much less. The rain gear also cuts down on the evaporation and convection created by the wind.

I have made an interesting discovery over the years. Wool socks and wool or pile clothing under a rain suit (pants and jacket), can act somewhat like a wet suit. A wet suit allows water to seep in. The water is quickly warmed by the body. Because of the tightness of the suit more cold water cannot get in to replace the warm water. The insulating quality of the wet suit prevents further loss of body heat. I have found pile clothing under a rain suit works in the same way if the ankles, waist, wrists, and neck are secured. The cold water rushes in and you

feel the wallop of the frigid water hitting your skin. However, if you are very active your body heat will soon warm the water in your clothing. Even though you are still immersed in cold water, your loss of body heat is much less than if you were not wearing the rain suit. It would be a ridiculous exaggeration to claim that you will be comfortable. However, this arrangement can greatly increase the length of time you can endure cold water when partially or even completely immersed.

When running rapids in spring flood conditions a wet suit is highly recommended. However, I must admit they are uncomfortably warm when paddling between rapids and are difficult to get on and off. The other option is a drysuit. Although more expensive and less durable than a wetsuit, a drysuit is far more comfortable. On hot, sunny days you just hop in the cold water to cool off. How much insulation you wear and how active you are will determine the conditions you can paddle in comfortably. A quality drysuit will keep the water out, but over time as your body sweats the moisture will condense, making the suit clammy.

Canoeists are especially susceptible to hypothermia because the best conditions for whitewater canoeing are found in spring flood when the water temperatures are very cold. Swamping and upsets are more frequent in these conditions and the length of time you are likely in the water is much longer because of the difficulty in getting to shore.

What you do or what your friends do in the first few moments after you emerge from the water can mean the difference between life and death. Every year people die from hypothermia. Many of these deaths are needless. If the proper precautions are taken immediately, lives can be saved.

Exhaustion can contribute to hypothermia in difficult weather conditions. Be sure

to stop and make camp while you still have a good reserve of energy. Violent exercise can keep you from going into a state of hypothermia but it's only a matter of time until exhaustion takes over and makes it impossible to continue.

How to diagnose hypothermia

Whenever your party is exposed to wind, cold, and wet, be aware of the dangers of hypothermia.

Temperature	Symptoms
98.6°F (37°C)	shivering may begin
96.8–95°F (36–35°C)	cold sensation, goose bumps, inability to perform complex tasks with hands
95–93.2°F (35–34°C)	intense shivering, muscle incoordination, mild confusion, may appear alert
93.2–89.6°F (34–32°C)	violent shivering, difficulty speaking, inability to use hands, stumbling gait, depression, irrational behavior
89.6–86°F (32–30°C)	shivering stops, incoherent, blue or puffy skin, inability to walk, may be able to maintain posture
86–80.6°F (30–27°C)	muscles rigid, may lose consciousness, slow pulse and respiration
80.6–77°F (27–25°C)	unconsciousness, no reflexes, no apparent heartbeat or respiration, death may occur before this point

Often the victim will have many of these symptoms yet deny being in trouble. Most people don't want to be a bother. Believe the symptoms, not the victim. Even mild symptoms demand some form of immediate treatment.

Treatment for hypothermia

1. Get the victim out of the wind and rain.
2. Strip off all wet clothes.
3. If the victim is only mildly impaired give warm drinks; get him or her into dry clothes and exercising vigorously. Putting the victim in a sleeping bag with a heat source is the second best option.
4. If the victim is semiconscious, try to keep him or her awake. Do not give any fluid unless victim is fully awake. (Any attempt to get warm drinks into a person who is unconscious or nearly unconscious could cause aspiration of the fluid into the lungs and result in asphyxia. Any hot drinks should be well spiked with a rapid energy source such as sugar to replace the carbohydrate that has been lost through the cold water, exertion, and shivering. You must have fuel to produce internal heat.) No alcohol should be given at this stage. (Despite the fact that alcohol does make the body feel warmer and provides some calories, it may well induce further cooling due to the dilatation of the superficial vessels of the body as well as the inhibition of the central heat-regulating mechanism in the brain.)
5. Leave the victim stripped and get him or her into a sleeping bag with another person (also stripped). If you have a double bag get two people into the bag along with the victim. In fact the more, the better. Skin-to-skin contact is the most effective treatment. It's important to realize that a person in a state of hypothermia has lost the ability to generate sufficient body heat to keep alive. Only external heat and heat in the form of hot drinks will save a victim of hypothermia. It is of absolute importance to avoid rough handling or transport of the severely hypothermic individual, as fatal ventricular fibrillation of the heart (heart failure) may be caused by reflex nerve action. Dr. Gerry Bristow has seen many situations where both the moderately and severely hypothermic individuals have suffered cardiac arrest in the form of ventricular fibrillation simply because of rough handling. In a wilderness situation this would be fatal.
6. As mentioned earlier, uncontrollable shivering is one of the sure signs that a victim is hypothermic. The shivering itself increases heat production approximately three hundred to five hundred percent and is a great ally, both in providing increased heat as well as a warning of the victim's condition. This greatly accelerated production of heat will immediately benefit the victim and can prevent him or her from going into a hypothermic state. However, at this rate the body will quickly deplete its heat reserves. It is essential to apply external and internal heat, such as warm sweet liquids, as quickly as possible to terminate this rapid depletion of resources. When shivering ceases, the victim is either on the road to recovery, which will be self-evident, or getting worse. (Mental blunting and uncoordination are usually observed at ninety-one to ninety-three degrees fahrenheit (33° to 34°C). It is best to watch the signs and symptoms in an individual rather than monitor his or her actual temperature. As hypothermia progresses, shivering is lost at a core (central body) temperature of about ninety-two degrees fahrenheit (32°C).

Consciousness is lost at approximately eighty-six degrees fahrenheit (30°C). At this stage, the victim's life is in great jeopardy. Even a slight further drop in body temperature will result in abnormalities of heart rhythm ending in ventricular fibrillation (heart failure). When this happens in a wilderness situation, it's game over.

Cold water is the villain in many water fatalities but it can also be an unappreciated life preserver if the victim can be quickly transported to a hospital before rewarming occurs. In recent years, doctors have discovered that drowning victims presumed dead can still be alive. In treating fifty drowning cases over the last two and one-half years, Dr. Niemeroff has successfully revived thirty-three persons without permanent brain damage. The average time under water for these cases is ten minutes. Most of these people are young and were involved in cold water. A sixteen-year old boy who could have been clinically dead, responded to treatment two and one-half hours after Dr. Gerry Bristow and a team of doctors began their efforts to save him. Dr. Bristow has pointed out that when dealing with individuals apparently dead from hypothermia, judgment of death can correctly be made only after failure to revive, *once rewarming has occurred.* The job of the rescuers is to get the victim to a hospital before rewarming occurs. Prevent further cooling by wrapping the victim in insulating material, with hot-water bottles or other external sources of heat placed near the groin, neck, and armpits to prevent further cooling. But do not rewarm the victim during transportation. The reason is that any attempt at warming the victim externally by the use of hot towels or immersion in hot water will send the very cold blood near the surface to the body's core, thus dropping the core temperature even more.

It is highly recommended that paddlers engaged in whitewater canoeing in cold-water conditions be knowledgeable in hypothermia and be trained in cardio-pulmonary resuscitation. Many revived near-drowning victims die within twenty-four hours of the accident. This is because residual untreated water remains in the lungs. Therefore, in all near-drowning accidents, the victim should be taken to hospital as soon as possible.

11 TYPES OF CANOES

BIRCHBARK

CEDAR AND CANVAS

CEDARSTRIP

STRIPPER

ALUMINUM

FIBERGLASS

KEVLAR

ABS

One of the questions that I am asked most often about canoeing is, "What is the best canoe to buy?" There really is no one answer. It varies with the kind of canoeing you intend to do and the philosophy that you might have toward canoeing in general. As any canoe manufacturer will tell you, it's a tough profession. All canoe enthusiasts have their own idea of what a canoe should be. I am no exception. I'm about as opinionated about the subject of canoe design and materials as anyone. Give me a chance and I'll bore you to death on the subject.

If you can find one and/or afford it, the birchbark canoe is the ultimate for those who are afflicted with an incurable love and passion for the beauty, grace, and history of the canoe. There is nothing to compare with the feeling of paddling into the golden mist of a fall morning in a genuine birchbark canoe. It's like a time machine that transports you back into the past when the land was unaltered by people. However, the birchbark canoe is totally impractical for the canoeist of today. Even if you can find one, it would be much too valuable for hard daily use. Birchbark canoes require constant maintenance and care.

Today, the main concern of most paddlers is the cost and durability of a canoe. I admit these are legitimate concerns; however, the performance and aesthetics of a canoe are also important. Although I could talk endlessly about the high-tech designs and theories of flatwater racing, whitewater racing, freestyle, playboating, and other specialized areas of the sport, this discussion will be limited to canoes used for pleasure canoeing, flatwater and whitewater canoeing, and wilderness tripping.

Canoe materials

Birchbark
AESTHETICS Ravishingly beautiful, if well-made.
DURABILITY Very fragile; needs constant maintenance.
COST The crown jewels, if you can find one.
HANDLING Paddles like a leaf.
WEIGHT Light when dry.

Cedar and canvas
AESTHETICS Next best thing to a birchbark canoe.
HANDLING Superb; best shapes and designs are found in these canoes.
DURABILITY Much tougher than most people think; must be stored out of sun and rain for longevity; need loving care and maintenance.
COST Expensive because of high cost of skilled labor.
WEIGHT Medium to heavy; very heavy when wet and waterlogged.

Cedarstrip
AESTHETICS Beautiful, graceful, regal; the elite of canoes; almost extinct; made by skilled craftsmen but very few are being made today.
HANDLING Paddles with the grace of a swan; usually too shallow for canoe tripping; built for looks, not practicalities.
DURABILITY Must be soaked to keep out the water; need care and proper storage out of the sun.
COST Very expensive.
WEIGHT Light to very heavy; some have narrow thick planking, some wide thin planking.

Stripper
AESTHETICS Can be very pretty depending on the maker; many people make their own; made on a mold with thin strips of wood that are fiberglassed inside and out to seal the wood between the two layers.
HANDLING Usually very nice.
DURABILITY Relatively strong; scrapes through to the wood; must be quickly sealed or serious damage could result.
COST Average to high.
WEIGHT Can be quite light.

Aluminum
AESTHETICS The pits.
HANDLING Sluggish, noisy; flatbottomed but very safe; great for carrying children; excellent carrying capacity; sticks badly on rocks, a great disadvantage.
DURABILITY Absolutely no maintenance; dents but can be repaired easily; rips can be mended.
COST Medium range.
WEIGHT Not as light as most people think — eighty-five pounds (38.5 kg) unless you buy lightweight canoe at sixty pounds (27 kg), which dents easily.

Fiberglass
AESTHETICS Terrible to good depending on the manufacturer.
HANDLING Depends entirely on the manufacturer.
DURABILITY Quite strong; many makes go hogged in time, which is one of the worst things that can happen to a canoe; little maintenance required.
COST Cheapest canoes are made in fiberglass, also the worst, so watch out; good one finished in wood costs more.
WEIGHT Moderate to heavy or sixty (27 kg) to eighty-five pounds (38.5 kg).

Kevlar
AESTHETICS Same as fiberglass.
HANDLING Same as fiberglass; depends on manufacturer.
DURABILITY Incredible tensile strength. Scratch resistant–should not be left in sunlight, which causes the material to break down.
COST Very expensive; twice as much as fiberglass; difficult material to handle.
WEIGHT Exceptionally light.

S-Glass
AESTHETICS Same as fiberglass.
HANDLING Stronger and lighter than fiberglass.
DURABILITY High compressive strength and impact resistance.
COST Similar to Kevlar.
WEIGHT It is usually laminated with Kevlar to create a light canoe.

Nylon
AESTHETICS Similar to fiberglass.
HANDLING Good tensile strength.
DURABILITY Similar strength to Kevlar.
COST Less expensive than Kevlar.
WEIGHT To be as strong as a Kevlar canoe it would be heavier.

Carbon Fiber
AESTHETICS Similar to Fiberglass.
HANDLING Very stiff.
DURABILITY High tensile and compressive strength.
COST Expensive.
WEIGHT Light and stiff when used as a composite.

Spectra
AESTHETICS Similar to Fiberglass.
DURABILITY Slightly higher tensile strength than Kevlar but harder to work with.

COST Similar to Kevlar.
WEIGHT Slightly lighter than Kevlar.

Royalex
AESTHETICS Difficult to mold into fine lines.
HANDLING Bottom can be too flexible. Each manufacturer specifies a different layup for each model; therefore performance varies a great deal. There is a sixteen-foot (4.5 m) and a seventeen-foot (4.7 m) prospector available in Royalex from Trailhead. Yes, Dad would have loved to have his favorite canoe in Royalex for those shallow, rock-studded rivers.
DURABILITY Can be folded in half and popped back with minor damage; repairable.
COST Expensive.
WEIGHT Heavy.

R 84 R Light
AESTHETICS Similar to Royalex.
HANDLING Performs as well as Royalex.
DURABILITY Will not withstand heavy use as well as Royalex.
COST Similar to Royalex.
WEIGHT Lighter than Royalex.

Polyethylene
AESTHETICS Usually not something to write home about.
HANDLING Bottoms distort over time.
DURABILITY Can survive extreme distortion and impact, more resistant to abrasion than Royalex, difficult to repair.
COST Less than Royalex.
WEIGHT Heavier than Royalex.

What to look for in a canoe

The ideal canoe for me isn't necessarily the best canoe for you. It's difficult not to let my personal preferences and prejudices show; however, the following information should help you find the canoe that suits your needs.

The diagrams in the left column are views of the tops of various canoes at the waterline. The center column shows the side view of each canoe and the right column shows a cutaway view in the center of each canoe.

Canoe 1

TOP A voluminous canoe with extremely high carrying capacity; good buoyancy in the ends; rides high on the waves rather than knifing into them; a difficult shape to push through the water; sluggish. SIDE Straight keel line is fast for lake travel; tracks a straight course; no good for quick turns or backferrying in rapids as current tends to grab the ends of the canoe which ride too deep in the water; gunwale drops too suddenly allowing water to splash in. CUTAWAY Flat bottom allows for shallow draft; great stability at the expense of speed. Most of these features would be found in a Grumman canoe which we used when our children were very young.

Canoe 2

TOP A very fast canoe at the expense of carrying capacity; cuts the water very well; knifes into and through waves instead of thudding to a halt on each one. SIDE Good rocker (lots of curve along the keel line from bow to stern); very easy to turn and pivot because bow and stern ride high; excellent for whitewater maneuvers; good depth amidships and at bow and stern; good curve of gunwale line. CUTAWAY Round bottom; very fast; easy to paddle but very tippy; good tumblehome (inward curve of canoe sides near gunwale); a very hot canoe. This canoe comes very close to the dimensions of the Chestnut cruiser canoe except for its extreme rocker.

Canoe 3

TOP A compromise between canoes 1 and 2; bow is sharp; has good sheer but flares out quickly for comfortable breadth amidships; reasonably fast with good carrying capacity. SIDE Again a compromise between canoes 1 and 2; not as much rocker as canoe 2 but sufficient for quick pivots and sideslipping in rapids; reasonable tracking characteristics in flatwater; gunwale curve just right; deep bow and stern. CUTAWAY Another compromise between canoes 1 and 2; bottom is round but not too round; reasonable stability and quite fast; sensitive to leans for paddling solo; excellent tumblehome for ease of paddling; good depth for lots of carrying capacity. All of these dimensions can be found in the Chestnut prospector, the all-round, almost perfect canoe.

Canoe 4

TOP No sheer at bow and stern (not sharp enough at waterline); too wide amidships. SIDE A real dog; hogged keel line (bow and stern riding deeper than center) makes sideslipping and pivots difficult; handles like a barge—a very common condition of many cheaper aluminum and fiberglass canoes. CUTAWAY No tumblehome which makes paddling a little more awkward; sides flare out and deflect waves better than tumblehome; V bottom is very fast. Canoes with no tumblehome fare better in rapids when swamped as the water tends to spill out when the canoe hits a rock.

Canoe 5

TOP An asymmetrical canoe; widest point is behind the center of the canoe. Tracks very well; therefore usually fast and efficient to paddle. SIDE Some rocker at the bow assists ease of turning, but straight keel line at stern doesn't compromise the tracking ability. Upward curve of gunwale and increased flare at the bow sheds waves. Difficult to sideslip or back ferry. CUTAWAY Quite stable with added flare toward the bow. Bow often has soft chine (a rounded bottom), while the stern will be V bottom that will also assist in tracking.

Gunwales

Often overlooked, an element of good canoe design is the gunwale. The gunwale consists of an inwale and an outwale (*see* diagram A). Whether your canoe is made of aluminum, fiberglass, Kevlar, or Royalex, wood gunwales are by far the most desirable. They give a good feel for the wood shaft of the paddle against the wood gunwale. Wood is easiest on your hands and makes the least noise. A good outwale has a rounded surface so your paddle shaft can be pried off it without denting or wearing the wood. I like the gunwales to be of white ash or oak, and no less than one inch (25 mm) deep. The gunwale in diagram B is strong and well-designed, but the outer edge is not deep enough. It is too close to a cutting edge and dents the wooden paddle shaft.

The gunwale in diagram C is an aluminum caplike affair that is pop-riveted on to hold it in place. These will be lighter than wood gunwales. But if rivets have been used, make sure they are very flat and not sharp-edged along the outer gunwale. A gunwale that is a molded part of the fiberglass hull is shown in diagram D. This system is usually indicative of a poorly made, flimsy, weak canoe. The gunwale in diagram E is made of vinyl with an aluminum insert. These are very strong and durable.

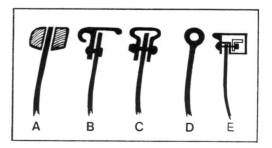

A   B   C   D   E

GUNWALES

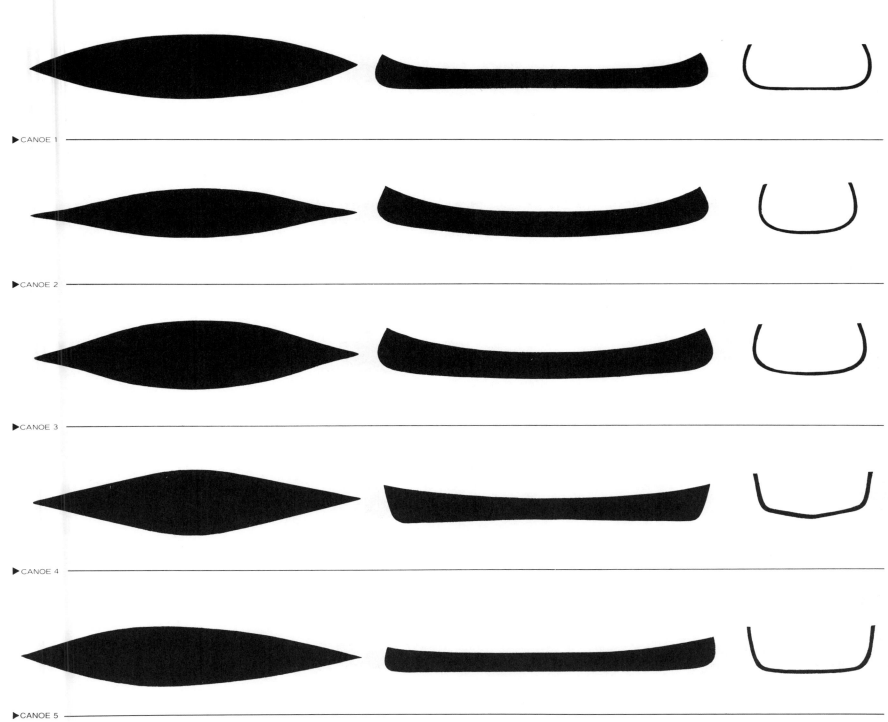

▶CANOE 1

▶CANOE 2

▶CANOE 3

▶CANOE 4

▶CANOE 5

185

Choosing the right canoe

I enjoy debating the various aspects of canoeing techniques, the advantages or disadvantages of a keel, and so on, but it is pointless to engage me in debate when it comes to choosing the perfect canoe. For me, it's no contest. The Chestnut prospector sixteen-foot (4.5 m) canoe wins on all points.

If the next question is "How do you get one?" the answer is "It isn't easy," especially now that Chestnut has folded and the Chestnut prospector is on the endangered-species list.

If you are fortunate enough to own a Chestnut prospector or some other wood-canvas canoe, you have probably been told that these canoes are too fragile for running rapids. I've been using mine in rapids for fifteen years now, and it's still got the original canvas. They are not as delicate as most people think. However, they do have to be handled with skill and care and they do require maintenance. Personally, I don't mind this. It's all part of the art of canoeing.

Perhaps I am partial to the canvas-covered canoe because it is only one generation removed from the birchbark canoe of the Native people. In an age when everything is so utilitarian, I insist on retaining some of the aesthetics of canoeing. My purpose in a wilderness journey is not only to get from the top of the river to the bottom, but also to enjoy the trip itself. My enjoyment is greatly enhanced by paddling a beautiful canoe.

The difference between a beautifully crafted canvas-covered canoe and an aluminum or Royalex canoe is the difference between a fine racehorse and a dray horse running a steeplechase. Both horses will get to the finish line, but the dray horse will have knocked down and trodden the obstacles in its path into the mud. On the other hand, you wouldn't hitch a racehorse to a plow. It's reckless to take a heavily loaded cedar-canvas canoe down a river in late fall in low water. The tough modern materials do have their place.

Dad went to great lengths to obtain his prospector canoes. Now there are many prospector-like canoes on the market, made from a variety of materials with varying degrees of success. Beware — just because a canoe is called a prospector does not mean that it will be true to the design features of the original Chestnut prospector. When appraising a "prospector" canoe, look for gunwales that curve up at the stern and bow, a graceful curve of the stem, a rockered keel line, generous depth amidships, and a sharp entry line at water level that flares out a few feet back to provide volume and tumblehome. There is a prospector out now that I think Dad would have been first in line to buy. It is made from Royalex and is available in a seventeen-foot (4.7 m) expedition model, a sixteen-foot (4.5 m) whitewater edition, and a sixteen-foot (4.5 m) lightweight model. Although the fine entry lines and subtle nuances of the original prospector cannot be reproduced in Royalex, these canoes do retain most of the handling characteristics Dad was so fond of. The seventeen-foot (4.7 m) Royalex prospector is a serious wilderness tripper's dream. A huge carrying capacity combined with the prospector's trademark sharp ends and subtle rocker make for a fast, maneuverable, and tough expedition canoe. At eighty-three pounds (38 kg) the seventeen-foot (4.7 m) is a bit heavy on the portage trail, but that is a common trait of most Royalex canoes. I spent a couple of weeks in one on the Nahanni River and felt that it was made for that kind of river.

For local trips with lots of portages, the seventeen-foot (4.7 m) is heavy and the smaller loads don't justify the larger carrying capacity. But the sixteen-foot (4.5 m) Royalex prospector is available at seventy-six pounds (35 kg). This canoe is easier to portage and has that classic Chestnut prospector feel. I took one on the Dumoine River and found it superbly suited to the smaller rapids and lighter payloads of this four-day trip. Apart from the prospector performance, the best feature of this canoe is the tough Royalex hull. On several rapids we tried new lines that would have been out of the question in a more fragile canoe.

The third new prospector is built out of lightweight Royalex called R 84 and will be available in the prototype stage in 1995. At sixty-six pounds (33 kg) it will be a coin toss as to who has to carry the pack and who gets the canoe.

I competed recently in the Gull River Open Canoe Slalom Race in the men's tandem class. My partner and I, paddling a sixteen-foot (4.5 m) Royalex prospector, placed third against several hot new whitewater playboat designs. We were both surprised that a tripping canoe could be so quick. Of course there are canoes that are faster, some that are quicker turning, and others that are drier, but I don't think any of the new designs do it all as well as the prospector.

— Paul Mason

The toughest canoe

Some of the most durable canoes are made with Royalex, which is a vinyl, ABS, vinyl layup. The shapes usually lack fine lines, but if strength is all you care about, it's the canoe for you. It's become very popular for canoe rentals. You've got to be really awful to demolish a Royalex.

One of my first experiences with the Royalex canoe was on a river in Quebec called the Magnassippi, in the late fall when there was very little water. We knew nothing about the river and couldn't find any information about it. The contour lines on the map indicated either a river with many falls or many rapids or both. We flew in to the headwaters to begin our journey as high up as possible. Wally Schaber was paddling stern in my Kevlar and another couple were paddling his new Mad River canoe made with Royalex. As we began our journey we realized to our disappointment that the water conditions were indeed very low. On a difficult river this would be very hard on the canoes. I began to suspect that I would regret my choice of the Kevlar instead of my beat-up old Grumman. I had opted for lightness rather than strength when I had my Kevlar made. You just can't have both.

I was anxious to see how the Royalex Mad River canoe would do. At the time I knew nothing about it except what I had read. Well, it wasn't long before Wally and I realized that paddling a rough river without much water was more fun for our friends in their Royalex canoe than for us in our Kevlar. It was unbelievable what they got away with. They bent that canoe through the most impossible places. They slipped and slid and oozed their way down that river. The slippery characteristic of the material made it possible for them to literally power over rocks just beneath the surface. If there was enough water in the channel for a drink, they could get through. Their high level of skill was an important factor, but they ran

that canoe through the most impossible places. If they hit, there was no price for failure. The canoe just buckled and sprung right back into shape.

For Wally and me it was a nightmare. Really, the river was not runnable. We should have portaged about eighty percent of it. Of course, neither of us was willing to do that, even to save a $900-canoe. We did our best to get down it with minimal damage, but every time we crunched to a stop it hurt. At first we were very careful but after miles of back-breaking work, lifting and sliding the heavily-loaded canoe over the rocks, we became more and more ruthless. I tried to not wince each time we ran aground but Wally knew I was concerned and it really took the fun out of it. It wouldn't have been quite so bad if it weren't for the two clowns in the other canoe. Their whoops and shouts of joy didn't help at all. Fortunately, most of the time they were so far ahead of us, we couldn't hear them. To appreciate the way Wally was feeling about our lack of progress, you have to understand that nobody is more in love with running a canoe down flowing water than Wally Schaber. If it flows and it's got a rock in it, Schaber will run it!

At first we would run until the river widened out into shallows, then we would jump out just before we hit. As the miles passed, we began staying in the canoe more and more in the hope we could squeeze through. We often couldn't and the canoe would grind to a halt. Sometimes as we were tracking a mean stretch of water with rocks choking the main channel, we could hear the hoots of pleasure of our friends in the Royalex canoe. Wally would order them out of his canoe at the bottom and portage it back up so he and I could run it too. The Royalex canoe might look and feel like a wounded duck in comparison to my Kevlar

but that canoe wouldn't have to step aside for a Sherman tank. Wally and I comforted ourselves with the knowledge that if the river had been higher, the rocks would have been covered. Then the superior shape of my canoe would have been an asset, not to mention its light weight on the long, difficult portages.

The next time we do that river in low water, we'll take Wally's Royalex canoe. In high water, we would take my Kevlar prospector. If I have given the impression that my canoe was badly damaged, keeping in mind it weighed only sixty pounds, it did very well, amazingly well, in fact. It sustained most of the damage wherever there was a reinforcing rib. Because the canoe would not give as readily at these points, the only alternative was for the Kevlar to chafe and become abraded. The shape was relatively unaffected. My Chestnut cedar and canvas prospector would have been a write-off in such conditions or we would have had to portage it for about eighty percent of the river. Remember there was no going back because we were flown in. In shallow-water conditions, it's important to select the right canoe for the job.

The canoes described here are the most familiar ones you will see today. To get some idea of the incredible variety of canoes that have evolved from the log or the bark of a birch tree, I would suggest a trip to the Canadian Canoe Museum. For more information, or to donate an old canoe or money to support the museum, contact Jack Matthews at P.O. Box 1338 Lakefield, Ontario P0M 2N0. The museum houses a truly astounding collection of canoes from around the world. It is the fulfillment of a dream of Kirk Wipper to put together the largest collection of canoes in the world. For the canoe lover, it is a trip to Mecca.

Repairs

Temporary repairs on all types of canoes can be made by applying duct tape on the outside of the rip or hole. Five-minute epoxy also can be used to patch almost any kind of canoe, at least temporarily. I have had patches like these last for a year and one-half before I got around to putting on a permanent one.

Aluminum
First, hammer the rip, tear, or hole flat with two rocks. Then apply liquid solder or five-minute epoxy or both. Next, sand smooth and cover with duct tape. For a permanent repair job, have it welded by a shop that knows how to weld aluminum. Even huge dents can be pounded out by holding the canoe in the water and putting the boots to it. A body shop can restore the canoe to a pretty good semblance of what it should look like.

Fiberglass and Kevlar composite canoes
A temporary repair job can be done by sanding the area around the break, applying five-minute epoxy, pressing fiberglass cloth into the glue, and applying a little more glue on top. Cover until cured with plastic wrap for a smooth finish. It is always preferable to put your patch on the inside. For a permanent repair you will have to purchase resins and materials compatible with your hull.

Royalex, polyethylene, and R 84
You can buy repair kits to permanently repair your hull.

Wood and canvas
To patch a rip or hole, round off the hole and smooth the edges. Cut a patch of Egyptian cotton a little larger than the hole. Make sure the wood and canvas are very dry. Work five-minute epoxy in under the canvas all around the hole. Saturate the patch. Push it in under the canvas with a screwdriver. The patch must be positioned just right or it might leak. Apply more epoxy until the hole is level. Put a piece of wax paper over the patch, smooth with your hand, then place a flat weight over the hole until the epoxy hardens. When it has set, remove the wax paper, sand smooth and paint. The patch will last forever.

Broken planking and ribs can only be replaced properly by removing the canvas skin so the copper nails can be removed and the parts replaced. I would never go to this trouble until the canvas has to be replaced because of rot. I just epoxy the splintered pieces back in place.

When a canoe becomes so badly beat up that it will hardly hang together anymore, I remove the canvas, dry the canoe thoroughly and then fiberglass it with light cloth. The fiberglass welds all the parts together again into a hard rigid hull. If the canoe is really beat up and rot has set in to the ends, I wire brush all the rot out and then apply car-body filler to replace the wood. I then sand the canoe smooth again before fiberglassing. If you have the necessary carpentry skills, it would be better to replace all the wood.

If the hull is in good shape, I would prefer to recanvas rather than fiberglass it. Fiberglassing is the absolute last resort.

Repair kit
My repair kit is almost the same for a long extended trip as it is for a short weekend trip. It contains a lot of necessary items, yet it is very small. I could put a canoe back together if I had to, repair a broken shoulder strap on a pack, or splice a broken paddle. A good repair kit gives you security.

I would suggest the following items for your repair kit: a small axe-file, stitching awl, small needle-nose pliers, five-minute epoxy, fiberglass cloth, assorted screws, nuts, bolts, washers, long seat bolts, needle and thread, safety pins, copper wire, sandpaper, multitip screwdriver, piece of cordura fabric, and duct tape. I've carried some of these things for years and have never needed them but they come in handy when you do need them.

Storing a canoe and paddles

Aluminum canoes are the only canoes I would leave outdoors permanently. I store all my other canoes under cover when not in use. Sun will crack paint and weaken and deteriorate fiberglass, epoxy, Kevlar, and Royalex. Rain and sun will also rot wooden gunwales. A canoe with wood gunwales and decks should not be left lying on the ground for any length of time. The moisture from the earth will rot the wood. Rocks should be placed under the bow, stern, and the gunwale amidships to eliminate contact with the ground.

Some canoes will begin to sag if hung upside down from the bow and stern. The keel line will be hogged. If hung upside down, support the canoe near the bow seat and near the stern thwart. If a canoe is left outside resting on two sawhorses during the winter, the weight of any snow will probably break it in half or severely damage it.

Hardwood paddles should be hung up by the grip end out of the sun and rain. They should never be left on the ground or they will warp. Laminated paddles should be stored the same way; however, they rarely warp.

Renting a canoe

I once took a friend on his first canoe trip. When we arrived home he thanked me profusely. He thanked me because the trip told him what he wanted to know before he invested in any equipment. He didn't like canoeing. If you have never been canoeing and think you would like to learn, I would suggest that you go with friends or rent the necessary equipment the first couple of times.

Many outfitters will rent you a canoe, probably a little worse for wear, so the replacement cost isn't too high if you ding it up a bit or even wreck it. If you own a very good but fragile canoe, it also makes sense to rent an old tough canoe when running rapids, especially for the first time.

First aid

I recommend carrying a first-aid manual and a first-aid kit. Hopefully, by being constantly safety-conscious, you will never need to use either. The most difficult part of first aid is knowing which injuries are serious, can have dangerous side effects, and/or lead to permanent damage if not attended to as soon as possible. When you are three or four days away from the nearest road or help, you need to know what to do.

One solution is to take a wilderness first-aid course. These courses go beyond emergency first aid and deal with what to do when you can't phone for help. Talk to an outfitting or guiding company to see whom they hire to teach their staff. This is what we did in Ottawa and it worked extremely well. Those of us who attended the course of eight three-hour sessions each feel that we would be able to patch up a victim and make a decision whether to continue the trip at a normal pace, speed it up a little, get help to the victim, or get the victim to help just as soon as possible. We also found that many injuries we thought were serious can be treated on the spot.

Standard first-aid kits are often inadequate for wilderness camping. I recommend assembling your own in consultation with a doctor who has a realistic understanding of the problems one might face when not within reach of medical assistance.

Packs

My choice is the large Duluth canvas pack equipped with a tumpline. In spite of all the bright new fancy packs on the market today, I still don't know of any more durable or practical. After thirty years, I am still using the first Woods Duluth pack I ever owned. It's fifty percent patches but still going strong. I have one other pack that I have a personal preference for—my small Woods Nessmuck. It has many exterior pockets for items that I need throughout the day such as sunglasses, sketching materials, map, compass, bug repellent, short bits of rope, extra elastic bands for sealing plastic bags, film, matches, toothbrush, raincoat, tracking lines, etc.

Packs equipped with frames are not suitable for traveling in a canoe. They are hard to get in and out of the canoe and take up valuable space. Unless you are contemplating extensive hiking trips inland, portages generally are not long enough to make the comfort of a pack frame necessary. On a portage, the carrying capacity of a canoe pack is most important. While forty to fifty pounds (18 to 22 kg) is a good load for hiking, eighty to ninety pounds (36 to 40 kg) is not an unreasonable load on a portage. It is the tumpline that makes such loads possible. Voyageurs carried twice that weight. A canoe will hold an amazing amount. I have carried food and equipment for two months. A load like this means a lot of trips over the portages. When the average portage is rarely more than several hundred yards, that's not too great a hardship.

I use plastic liners for each pack so they are completely waterproof. In an upset, the packs will float indefinitely. The alternative to traditional style packs are waterproof plastic barrels. They vary in size from olive jars that you can put in a regular pack to large barrels sporting a padded harness, waist belt, and tumpline. They really are waterproof and virtually indestructible.

Headwaters of the South Nahanni River

12 WILDERNESS Responsibility

The word *wilderness* is a beautiful word. It's fitting that a beautiful word be used to describe a beautiful land. However, the idea of wilderness belongs to the "white man." To the native people, the land was not wild, it was home. It was where they lived, not a hostile environment they had to "tame". It was the "white men" who saw the land as a dangerous place, one that had to be battled; and made to resemble, as much as possible, distant homelands. Today the land, to a great extent, has been "tamed." It's getting harder and harder to find those remote, hidden places where we can enjoy the natural world as God created it. Islands of wilderness still exist, however, if you know where to look and how to get there. The problem is how to keep them that way. There are very few things in life these days that are free. Everything has a price tag, its value estimated in dollars and cents. There are other ways of putting a value on things though. There is the aesthetic value, the spiritual value, the benefits that physical pursuits bring to the body. These values are difficult to measure because our modern society is so used to dealing in dollars and cents. This is why it is not easy to defend the natural world against economic exploitation.

We are all concerned about our vanishing wildlife, and most of us know that one of the major causes of endangering the survival of animals is our destruction of their habitat. The habitat of animals is also the habitat of the wilderness canoeist. But we are only visitors there, and we should behave toward the environment with this fact foremost in our minds. It is their home, not ours. Our presence affects their behavior and their chances of survival.

As one who is somewhat responsible for the popularity of canoeing, I am aware that canoeists and others invade the wilderness home of wild animals, and that it is possible to do great damage to the natural environment.

The problem is how to enjoy these islands of wilderness without changing them by our presence. Even wilderness lovers can destroy the very thing they seek to enjoy. In some areas, such as Yosemite Valley or Algonquin Park, we are loving the wilderness to death. Sometimes I even ask myself what it is that makes me want to make films about the natural world and show others how to get there. Sometimes, when I find a place of exquisite beauty, I can't help asking myself "Why should I tell them?" — "them" being the people who, so far, have had little or no inclination to venture into the wilderness. I often feel this way when I return to a place of rare beauty only to find that it has been desecrated. As I look at the cans and broken bottles, the slashed birch trees, and the pines with broken lower branches, I realize that popularizing wilderness travel has its problems.

On the other hand, having the support of a large segment of society is imperative if these areas, and other areas in the future, are to be protected from economic development. It's a matter of educating or arousing an interest in the value of the wilderness to the people of our modern, technologically oriented society. Our need for wilderness will increase, not diminish. The problem is that there will never be more wilderness than there is today. We will only be able to keep what we've got if enough people are aware of what's out there and will express their concern for it.

When I go through my slides, I often come across pictures of places that are gone forever. I wonder how many people have ever stood beside the seething cauldron of White Dog Rapids on the Winnipeg River and felt the earth shake beneath their feet (*see* photograph 1). When I first saw those rapids, I camped beside them for three days. Sitting in the door of my tent, I studied them day after day. I imagined a thirty-foot (9 m) voyageur canoe attempting to run them. I tried to envision the route the bow

paddler might choose and what would happen if he failed to put the canoe where it had to go. As I sat entranced by the plunging foam, I became that bow paddler. Sometimes I made it through, sometimes I met destruction in the raging maelstrom. Then I would walk upstream to the brink of the rapids and watch the black slick of glassy, calm water as it slowly picked up speed. It raced in a great wide V, narrowing to a fine point just before it exploded into towering

WHITE DOG RAPIDS, WINNIPEG RIVER, ONTARIO

WHITE DOG RAPIDS, DROWNED

Responsibility...

white waves. I imagined how it would feel if one were to be inadvertently lured down that slick. I scared myself half to death just thinking about it.

Then, four years later, equipped with the writings and journals of the early explorers, I returned to relive my fantasies, only to discover that the rapids were no longer there. They lay still and silent beneath fifty feet (15 m) of water (photograph 2). The thick, green forest along the edge of the river was gone. In its place were only tree stumps. In the water itself, the tops of trees showed above the surface. In other places, whole islands had been stripped of trees. The land had been so carelessly surveyed that some places had been cleared needlessly. Completely denuded islands were everywhere. In other places, trees were left standing to become only partly submerged. The trees that had been cut floated in mats that made it impossible to get to shore.

And who was there to protest? Only a handful of people. Now when such abuses take place, people hear about it—people who care! And these people let those responsible for the desolation know they care, and pressure them to consider the alternatives. The fact that people are speaking out shows that more contact with the natural world makes them aware that wilderness is a great natural resource—a resource that makes Canada unique in the world today.

I have always been under the impression that the government had only one purpose. That purpose, I thought, was to pave over the whole country as fast as possible and dam anything that had moving water in it. In recent years, I have been surprised to find that many of the people we elect are just as

avid wilderness enthusiasts as the rest of us. They need our voice and our support to do something about the care and protection of wild places. I enjoy using the medium of film, writing, and painting as a means of soliciting this support. It also gives me an excuse to be "out there," which isn't hard to take. There is no better way to make a living than doing what you enjoy. But this is a selfish reason. I believe that we have a moral obligation to preserve and care for the habitat of animals and plant life because, like us, they were created by God and have a right to exist too.

Conservation organizations

I enjoy sharing what I know about canoeing, and I delight in seeing the enjoyment that people can get from learning to canoe. However, I feel that I am not serving the cause of wilderness preservation if the new canoeists I reach do not become active supporters of the various conservation organizations. As wilderness use increases, it is imperative that these organizations, dedicated to wilderness preservation, survive and even thrive. They need our active and financial support. As in most things that need doing, a very small number of people devote a large part of their time to the task.

No matter where you live in Canada or the United States, there is probably someone in your area who shares your concerns and your interest in canoeing. This general list of organizations should assist you in locating these individuals, as well as other canoeing organizations. Most canoeists are a gregarious bunch who will welcome you. If you are a loner, these organizations are still important to you as a source of information about good canoe routes. They also would be interested in hearing what *you* know about canoe routes. Organizations of this kind are also important to all of us who love the wilderness, because they help us to unite in our efforts to care for and preserve the wilderness.

No-trace camping

The improvement in the cleanliness of wilderness campsites in recent years is remarkable. Things are definitely improving. Most people are aware of and show concern for the welfare of the land. Unfortunately, a small percentage of garbage-strewing people will always be with us. I do believe, however, that the species is on the wane. You get the impression that there are a lot of them out there because of the amount of damage a few can cause. The number of people who are willing to clean up after themselves is on the increase. Whoever came up with the phrase *no-trace camping* deserves a lot of credit because it's an idea that is catching on. Basically it means that when you finish with a campsite, you leave it in such a condition that nobody would know you've been there. In practice, no-trace camping is almost impossible to adhere to completely. On the well-traveled route, there is nothing wrong with leaving a little firewood and maybe some split kindling for the next canoeist. The stones for the fireplace should, of course, be left in good order. I have seen people heave the stones into the lake when they were finished with them because they didn't want to leave behind a trace. This is obviously a dumb idea. If everybody did this, fireplace rocks would become pretty

FIREPLACE

scarce. Some books suggest that you put the rocks back where you found them and scatter the ashes. In seldom-traveled, remote areas, this might be sound advice, but on major waterways it makes sense to just leave the rocks in an orderly manner. It's better that one spot and one spot only be used for building the campfire. The environmental firebox contains your fire, eliminates scars, and is also vastly more efficient than an open fire, thus conserving wood, a concern on well-used routes where firewood is scarce. Once the ashes are doused with water they can be carefully dumped into an existing fire pit or, if you're no-trace camping, buried. To be disposed of safely, the ashes should be cool to the touch. Finding a campsite with a fireplace ready made doesn't upset me, as long as the fireplace is spotlessly clean. Always let your fire burn right down to ashes before you douse it. Judging by the remains in some of the fireplaces I've seen, the group before me must have had a holocaust before they doused it. Leaving unburned paper, plastic, and other garbage in your fireplace is unforgiveable. There's nothing like finding a fireplace full of garbage to kill the mood of a wilderness experience. I find that the dirtiest campsites are usually within walking distance of a road. That's why my policy is to avoid any campsite that is within easy reach of a road.

In many parks, carrying glass and tins is banned. Where they are not banned, the wilderness travelers should carry out what they carry in. It's not hard to burn and flatten the tins and carry them out. Our tins, after a one-month trip down the Nahanni River, weighed only a few pounds. Activities such as cutting tent poles, cutting bough beds, and other things that disturb the fauna are not compatible with the preservation of nature. Toilets should be no less and no

more than eight inches (20 cm) deep. The earth you remove should be replaced when you leave. Toilet paper and all other combustibles should be burned. The easiest way is to bury the poop, place the used toilet paper in a paper bag, and before bedtime or *after* breakfast build up a hot fire with smalls sticks and burn the paper bag. I find that one bag per six people is okay.

Here are some thoughts to keep in mind regarding kitchen waste. The best disposal method for food scraps is to eat them! If that doesn't work, then the leftovers should be burned. Dishwater should be disposed of by pouring it through a small spaghetti strainer into a shallow hole well away from the campsite. The bits of food collected can then be burned. Wash your cans and take them along with any plastic to a recycling depot. There will be different practices in different parts of the country, so do a little research before your trip.

Wilderness undiminished

It is certainly not my intention to convince everybody they should grab a canoe and take to the wilderness. We are all different, and our interests vary. That is how it should be. Some people are content to enjoy the land from the edge of the road or campground. Others are only happy when isolated from the synthetic world by many portages and miles of trackless wilderness. I used to think it was a major tragedy if anyone went through life never having owned a canoe. Now I believe it's only a minor tragedy.

The important thing is for those people who are not wilderness lovers to realize that it's good to have places where modern technology can never intrude — not for the sake of canoeists, but for the sake of the animals that live there. Their well-being should concern us. We wilderness freaks also have to realize, though, that we can't turn the clock back. We can only hope that, at least in certain areas, we can stop the clock. Every day, somewhere, a road is pushed a little farther, penetrating deeper and deeper to provide easy access into wild places. For those who love truly wild places, a road that cuts through a wilderness area diminishes its size by half. For the animal and plant life, the land has diminished that much more.

I would much prefer to paddle, portage, track, and wade up some unnavigable waterway to the base of a spectacular waterfalls, pitch my camp, and sit there drinking in their beauty, than travel there by road. It isn't the same. The falls you have to work to get to are always the biggest, the best, the most spectacular, even if they aren't as high.

Recently I was in Banff, Alberta. I wanted to climb a mountain but had only one free day, and I didn't have any transportation. Therefore, my choices were limited to nearby Sulphur Mountain or Mt. Rundle. Sulphur Mountain has a gondola lift; Mt. Rundle doesn't. I rationalized that if I took the gondola up Sulphur Mountain, I could spend all day in the high country. Then again, if I climbed Mt. Rundle, I suspected it would be a good feeling to look down over the lip from the peak, having got there under my own steam. I chose Mt. Rundle. I got up long before daybreak and set out early to allow lots of time. I made it almost to the peak before the clouds lowered and it began to snow, making it dangerous to continue. But I did make it to the lip and was able to peer down the vertical face of the cliff. I couldn't see a darn thing, of course. All I saw was the cliff dropping away below me into the clouds. But I knew what was there — a six thousand foot (1850 m) drop — and I had gotten there on my own. It *was* a very good feeling — a feeling I never would have had if I had taken the gondola up Sulphur Mountain. As I sat there in the silence, I was very glad there was no easy way up Mt. Rundle. Chairlifts, gondolas, and roads make mountains very small. Why do we always want to make them small? I like them much better big. I can understand the need for chairlifts for downhill skiing. I know the thrill of soaring down the face of a mountain on a pair of skis. But I am always sad when I hear of another mountain that has been diminished or a lake that is no longer as big as it used to be because there is now a road around it. Many times I have been canoeing on a wild, remote river and found a camper truck parked at the water's edge, half way down. All of a sudden the river doesn't feel so endless anymore. It's a totally irrational feeling, I know, but I'm stuck with it.

It might seem like we own the earth, and we certainly act that way, but I don't believe we do. I think this lack of sensitivity toward the natural world is a result of our alienation from it. We don't see, hear, or feel the land anymore. We only see it from the point of view of what we can do with it. We have become so totally committed to changing our environment that we have become oblivious to the fact that the world around us is a creation in itself — God's creation. Some of humanity's greatest masterpieces have been inspired by this same Creator: Handel's "Messiah," The Sistine Chapel, St. Paul's Cathedral, the list is endless. Standing beneath the dome of St. Paul's Cathedral is a moment I will remember for the rest of my life.

I am grateful for men and women who have created great monuments, but when I compare these monuments with the natural world, it's no contest. I could take you along the shore of Lake Superior in my canoe, and we could track, pole, and portage up rapids and falls to a place where heaven itself seems to open up and spill down a cascading torrent of pure white foam and spray. I would ask you to sit and stare at this scene for awhile. Then I would ask you, "Given the choice, what would you pick, the dome of the cathedral or the falls?" As much as I love and appreciate the great works of art, I know what my choice would be. And the thing I like the best about these falls is that you can only get there by canoe — the most beautiful and functional object that humanity has ever created.

Denison Falls, Dog River

Reading List

Since no one book will ever be the definitive source on a subject, here is a list of supplementary books, magazines, periodicals, and videos.

BOOKS

Bechdel, Les, and Slim Ray. *River Rescue*. Boston: Appalachian Mountain Club Books, 1989.

Davidson, James West, and John Rugge. *The Complete Wilderness Paddler*. New York: Alfred A. Knopf, 1975.

Franks, C.E.S. *The Canoe and White Water*. Toronto: University of Toronto Press, 1977.

Glaros, Lou, and Charlie Wilson. *Freestyle Canoeing*. Birmingham, Ala.: Menasha Ridge Press, 1994.

Lessels, Bruce. *AMC Whitewater Handbook Third Edition*. Boston: Appalachian Mountain Club Books, 1994.

Mason, Bill. *Song of the Paddle*. Toronto: Key Porter Books, 1988.

McKown, Doug. *Canoeing Safety and Rescue*. Calgary: Rocky Mountain Books, 1992.

Meyer, Kathleen. *How to Shit in the Woods*. Berkeley: Ten Speed Press, 1989.

Morse, Eric W. *Freshwater Saga*. Toronto: University of Toronto Press, 1987.

———. *Fur Trade Canoe Routes of Canada/ Then and Now*. Ottawa: Information Canada, 1968.

Nickels, Nick. *Canoe Canada*. Toronto: Van Nostrand Reinhold, 1976.

Norman, Dean, ed. *The All-Purpose Guide to Paddling*. Matteson, Ill.: Great Lakes Living Press, 1976.

Olson, Sigrid. *Listening Point*. New York: Alfred A. Knopf, 1958. *Open Horizons*. New York: Alfred A. Knopf, 1969. *Reflections from the North Country*. New York: Alfred A. Knopf, 1976. *Runes of the North*. New York: Alfred A. Knopf, 1963. *The Hidden Forest*. New York: Viking Press, Penguin Books, 1979. *The Lonely Land*. New York: Alfred A. Knopf, 1961. *Wilderness Days*. New York: Alfred A. Knopf, 1972.

Ray, Slim. *The Canoe Handbook*. Harrisburg, Pa.: Stackpole Books, 1992.

Riviere, Bill. *Pole, Paddle, and Portage*. New York: Van Nostrand Reinhold, 1969.

Ruck, Wolf. *Canoeing and Kayaking*. Toronto: McGraw-Hill Ryerson, 1974.

Rutstrum, Calvin. *North American Canoe Country*. New York: Macmillan, 1964.

———. *Paradise Below Zero*. New York: Macmillan, 1968.

———. *The New Way of the Wilderness*. Rev. ed. New York: Macmillan, 1973.

———. *The Wilderness Life*. New York: Macmillan, 1975.

The Mountaineers. *Medicine for Mountaineering and Other Wilderness Activities*. Seattle: 1992.

MAGAZINES AND PERIODICALS

American Whitewater
P.O. Box 85
Phoenicia, New York   12464

Canoe
10526 N.E. Sixty-eighth, Suite 3
Kirkland, Washington

Che-Mun
P.O. Box 548, Station O
Toronto, Ontario   M4A 2P1

Kanawa
1029 Hyde Park Road, Suite 5
Hyde Park, Ontario   N0M 1Z0

Nastawagan Journal
P.O. Box 48022, Davisville Postal Outlet
1881 Yonge Street
Toronto, Ontario   M4S 3C6

Paddler
4061 Oceanside Blvd., Suite M
Oceanside, California   92056

Wooden Canoe
Box 226
Blue Mountain Lake, New York   12812

VIDEOS

Kent Ford
Solo Playboating: Take the Wild Ride
160 Hideaway Road
Durango, Colorado   81301

Bill Mason
Path of the Paddle Series, Song of the Paddle, Waterwalker

Holbourne, P.O. Box 309
Mount Albert, Ontario   L0G 1M0

CONSERVATION ORGANIZATIONS

In Canada:
Canadian Environmental Network
1004-251 Laurier Avenue West
Ottawa, Ontario   K1P 5J6

Canadian Nature Federation
1 Nicholas Street, Suite 520
Ottawa, Ontario   K1N 9Z9

Canadian Parks and Wilderness Society
160 Bloor Street East, Suite 1335
Toronto, Ontario   M4W 1B9

Federation of Ontario Naturalists
355 Lesmill Road
Don Mills, Ontario   M3B 2W8

Friends of the Earth
215 Laurier Avenue West
Ottawa, Ontario   K1P 5J6

Pollution Probe Foundation
12 Madison Avenue
Toronto, Ontario   M5R 9Z9

Sierra Club of Ontario Foundation
517 College Street, Suite 303
Toronto, Ontario   M6G 4A2

World Wildlife Fund
90 Eglinton Avenue East, Suite 504
Toronto, Ontario   M4P 2Z7

In the United States:
The American Whitewater Affiliation
P.O. Box 85
Phoenicia, New York   12464

For other organizations in the United States, consult the *Conservation Directory*, available from:
The National Wildlife Federation
1412 Sixteenth Street N.W.
Washington, D.C.   20036

INDEX